Protestantism and Political Conflict in the Nineteenth-Century Hispanic Caribbean

Protestantism and Political Conflict in the Nineteenth-Century Hispanic Caribbean

Luis Martínez-Fernández

Rutgers University Press

New Brunswick, New Jersey, and London

Library of Congress Cataloging-in-Publication Data
Martínez-Fernández, Luis, 1960–
    Protestantism and political conflict in the nineteenth-century Hispanic Caribbean / Luis
Martínez-Fernández.
        p.   cm.
    Includes bibliographical references and index.
    ISBN 0-8135-2993-X (cloth : alk. paper)—ISBN 0-8135-2994-8 (pbk. : alk. paper)
        1. Christianity and politics—Caribbean Area—History—19th century.
        2. Christianity and politics—Protestant churches—History—19th century.
        3. Caribbean Area—Church history.   I. Title.

BX4835.C27 M37 2001
280′.4′097291—dc21

                                                                                    2001019293

British Cataloging-in-Publication data for this book is available from the British Library.

Manufactured in the United States of America

Dedico este libro a mi querida tía, Mercedes Fernández Cisneros. Por todas las oraciones y resos elevados a Dios y a la Virgen María por su sobrino protestante.

CONTENTS

ILLUSTRATIONS

PREFACE

I began to write this book, not knowing it then, some thirty-four years ago on the deserted playground of the San Marcos Apostol School, which was run by English Catholics in Lima's suburb of Miraflores. Periodically, all my classmates left the campus bound for the splendid church of the Virgen Milagrosa de Miraflores. While the other seven-year-olds were preparing for their coming first communion, as the school's only non-Catholic I did not participate in either the ceremony or its elaborate preparation and rehearsals. In fact, I was excused from Catholic religious instruction altogether. These early experiences made me aware of the differences and potential conflicts between Catholicism and Protestantism that are the heart of this book.

Years after San Marcos and thousands of miles beyond Miraflores, I encountered new situations that continued to spark my interest in the study of religions and their relation to culture. As a Protestant foreigner growing up in predominantly Catholic Puerto Rico, I came to realize that religion involved much more than faith and theological principles. Culture shaped religion as much as religion shaped culture. I confirmed this idea years later, when I moved to the Bible belt of the United States: even though I was a Protestant in the theological sense, I had remained the product of a Catholic culture. The writing of this book has been influenced by these and many other experiences I have confronted as a Protestant in Peru and Puerto Rico and as a Hispanic in the United States.

This book is also the result of extensive archival research on several continents during the past thirteen years, and I am grateful for the assistance and guidance of numerous institutions and individuals. I began my research in 1988–89 while visiting The Johns Hopkins University on a Tinker Foundation Fellowship. Further research and writing were made possible with major support from a Pew Evangelical Scholars Program Fellowship and a Rutgers University Competitive Fellowship leave. I was also aided by a visiting fellowship from the Episcopal Theological Seminary of the Southwest, a Rutgers University Minority Development Grant, a Rutgers University Research Council Grant, and a Rutgers University Board of Trustees Fellowship for Scholarly Excellence. During the summer of 1998 I benefited from participation in a Working Group on Cuba workshop jointly funded by the American Council of Learned Societies and the Social Science Research Council. Of course, this study would have not been possible without the aid of the staffs of the many archives, libraries, and depositories where I have worked, all of which are listed in the bibliography.

I am also grateful to Cambridge University Press for allowing me to reproduce in revised form my article "Crypto-Protestants and Pseudo-Catholics in the Nineteenth-Century Hispanic Caribbean," which appeared in the *Journal of Ecclesiastical History,* and to the editor of the *Journal of Religious History* for allowing me to reproduce parts of my article "Marriage, Protestantism, and Religious Conflict in Nineteenth-Century Puerto Rico." A generous subvention from the Rutgers University Research Council helped support the publication of this book.

At various stages of this project I benefited from the assistance and advice of archivists, fellow scholars, and friends, none of whom bear any responsibility for the final version of this work. At the risk of leaving out many names, I would like to thank Richard Abbott, Leopoldo J. Alard, Jorge Alonso, Carlos Bartolomé, Víctor Burset, Georgette Dorn, Richard Foley, Jean Forbis, F. Garner Ranney, Araceli García Carranza, Blanca Gómez, Filiberto González, Justo L. González, Manuel Hernández González, Pedro Herrera Macías, Dennis Hidalgo, Letitia Hurley, Franklin W. Knight, Valentín Llanes Macate, Félix V. Matos Rodríguez, Juan Ramón de la Paz Cerezo, the late José Prats, Louis A. Pérez, Jr., Jennifer Peters, Robert Rabin Siegal, Patricia Ramírez, Richard Ramos, Reinaldo Sánchez Yanes, Samuel Silva Gotay, Ramón Suárez, Bill Sumners, John J. TePaske, Gladyz Torres, Marta Villaizán, Mark Wasserman, and Oscar Zanetti.

My gratitude is extended to Marlie Wasserman, David Myers, Marilyn Campbell, and the other editors and staff members of Rutgers University Press. I have enjoyed working with them through the various stages of this book's editing and production.

I am also grateful to my wife and two sons in New Jersey and the rest of my family in San Juan and Havana, thanking them all for their love and encouragement. The fact that I continue to work as a comparative historian of the Hispanic Caribbean reflects my desire to mend the separation produced by exile and emigration.

Finally, I thank God for His everlasting love.

*Protestantism and Political Conflict in the
Nineteenth-Century Hispanic Caribbean*

Introduction

❧❀❧

$\mathcal{T}$he origins of Protestantism in Latin America have received relatively little scholarly attention, and what studies exist generally focus on experiences in the larger countries of continental Latin America: Brazil, Mexico, and Argentina. Not only have early Protestant activities in the Hispanic Caribbean received almost no attention, but they do not respond well to the application of models derived from continental Latin American cases. According to Hans-Jürgen Prien and other scholars, the first Protestant communities in Latin America can be categorized as either immigration Protestantism or mission Protestantism. Immigration Protestantism was essentially manifested as elite, self-contained clusters of merchants and other well-to-do foreigners from predominantly Protestant nations such as Great Britain. Although mission Protestantism was also foreign-led, it focused on proselytizing native populations that were either nominally Catholic or practitioners of indigenous religions.[1] For examining the early Protestant communities of Cuba and Puerto Rico, however, this typology is only partially useful. In these cases, immigration and mission Protestantism often coexisted within congregations, with natives carrying out some of the first missionary works. Moreover, in contrast to Protestant immigrants in other countries, many congregants in Cuba and Puerto Rico were neither wealthy nor members of demographic minorities. The simultaneous influence of Spanish colonialism and U.S. neocolonialism, the frantic expansion of the plantation socioeconomic complex, and the region's chronic political instability were just a few of the reasons behind these variations in Cuba and Puerto Rico. Immigration, seasonal migration, exile, return migration, and forced immigration also shaped the unique context of the first Protestant communities in the Hispanic Caribbean.

From its inception, Protestantism in the Hispanic Caribbean was a hybrid phenomenon that drew—and continues to draw—from the cultural foundation of Mediterranean Catholicism, with its hierarchical proclivities, possibilities for negotiation, and emphasis on the organicity of society. It also emerged from a Protestant theology that contained elements of Puritanism, doctrinaire intransigence, and, to some extent, extreme individualism. In other words, Protestantism in the region potentially combined either the best or the worst of two worlds. Furthermore, both Protestantism and Catholicism were influenced by West African religious practices and beliefs. The resulting syncretism varied according to the extent of creolization among the black and mulatto populations. For example, slaves and their descendants who had been Christianized and exposed to Creole culture tended to retain formal African worship styles, while superficially Christianized or African-born slaves and their descendants tended to be theologically African beneath a superficial Christian gloss, perhaps using icons of Catholic saints to stand for West African deities. With these variations in mind, my interpretation of creolized Protestantism challenges the widely espoused notion that the Hispanic Caribbean's Protestant experience was essentially foreign and imperialistic.[2]

The recognition of hybrid, or creolized, religious forms in the region demonstrates that religious phenomena are complex and cannot be fully understood outside their cultural and social contexts. Preexisting cultural patterns shape religious practices and beliefs, which in turn reshape culture. For example, a theological principle that holds that surviving relatives and friends can play a role in the salvation of a dead person's soul has different cultural and social implications from those produced by the belief that salvation is an individual matter determined before the moment of death, perhaps even before birth, and that remains independent of one's works. Similarly, a hierarchical, closed social structure reinforces beliefs in a spiritual hierarchy and the need for spiritual intermediaries more than an egalitarian, fluid social context does. Religious rituals and practices also have social as well as spiritual and theological meanings. The sacrament of baptism, for example, has a spiritual and theological dimension: the welcoming of a soul into the community of believers, a precondition for salvation, and the cleansing of original sin. Socially, baptism can mean several other things, among them a celebration of fertility and procreation, a rite of initiation, and a mechanism to extend family links and reinforce social obligations and solidarities.[3]

Although Cuba and Puerto Rico shared similar laws and historical developments, their early Protestant experiences differed dramatically, to a great extent reflecting the social compositions of their Protestant communities and the political circumstances surrounding their emergence. For example, the particular demographic and social realities of Ponce, Havana, Matanzas, and Vieques (the four jurisdictions in which the region's earliest organized Protestant activities occurred) shaped Protestant emergence in distinctive ways.

My effort to trace the links between Protestantism and politics in the region builds on previous studies of the nineteenth-century Hispanic Caribbean, which see the Catholic church as an important actor in the development of the region's plantation systems and the struggles for the emancipation of the slaves and national independence.[4] This book traces the Catholic church as one of five main actors participating in a complex regional drama. The other four were the laboring masses, the agrarian bourgeoisies, the mercantile bourgeoisies, and the colonial state. Alliances among these actors were precarious and changeable as players became more or less involved in three overlapping struggles. First was the struggle of labor, essentially a struggle between classes, with free and unfree laborers in contraposition to sectors wishing to maintain the socioeconomic order: the planter and mercantile elites, the colonial state, and usually the church. The second major struggle was the struggle for nationhood, which took place between Creoles, mostly of the propertied and professional classes, and those segments of society wishing to maintain the colonial link and trade privileges for the metropolis and its colonial agents: peninsular merchants, colonial administrators, and the church. The third struggle, and the one that has received least attention, was the struggle of religion, in which the church clashed with various anticlerical forces: capitalism, secularism, modern science, and popular religiosity. Clearly, then, dividing the region's actors into two distinct and opposing sets of allies is not easy. Any given sector might find itself in alliance or opposition to any of the other sectors, depending on the focus of the particular struggle. In the late nineteenth century, for example, the church found itself at odds with the state regarding the establishment of civil marriage and control over cemeteries. At the same time, however, church and state shared a common agenda concerning other matters, such as preservation of the colonial link and application of anti-vagrancy laws. To complicate the situation, none of the five sectors was either monolithic or constant in its goals and pursuits.[5]

Protestant presence and the right of Protestants to worship according to their faith were snarled in these struggles. The issue of religious tolerance, a central element of the struggle of religion, became entangled with the struggle of labor and the struggle for nationhood. While the Catholic church (the official church of the state) was increasingly identified with conservative, pro-slavery, and colonialist causes, Protestants and their sympathizers, particularly in Cuba, gravitated toward nationalistic and progressive politics. To be sure, these links were neither haphazard nor accidental; the theological foundations of Protestantism were already more compatible with the tenets of nineteenth-century liberalism. Moreover, at the international level, the United States and Great Britain—both Protestant countries—represented republicanism and abolitionism, respectively, unlike the slave-based, Catholic, monarchic Spanish empire.

One challenge of focusing on a culturally marginal population whose religious activities were illegal is that individuals left few incriminating records. Nevertheless, historians studying other historically marginalized groups have developed methods and sources of social history that I have used to create faces and voices for the region's otherwise anonymous early Protestants. Ironically, the sources that allow us to best reconstruct their experiences, behavior, and values were gathered and kept by contemporaneous individuals and institutions working to silence them.[6] The extant Protestant documentation on the particular congregations of the region varies widely in terms of quantity and quality depending on original record-keeping capabilities and survival of records. In some cases, for example, published sermons have survived; in others, we have access to detailed demographic information from parish books of baptism, marriage, and burial; in yet others, the personal papers of the clergyman are available for consultation.

The Hispanic Caribbean's Protestants exhibited varying degrees of religiosity. Some were nominal Protestants who spent years and even decades separated from the ceremonies and holy services of their faith. Many actually became pseudo-Catholics, partaking publicly of Catholic sacraments and attending holy mass. Others, whom I call crypto-Protestants, struggled to preserve their faith behind closed doors and sought holy ceremonies in a variety of creative ways. The path that Protestants chose was a matter of personal spiritual need and individual decision, depending in some cases on a person's capacity to withstand the loss of social capital associated with the public affirmation of Protestant affiliation. The driving force of unmet spiritual needs in a religious context that offered little beyond ritualism and religious taxation is another important factor to remember.

Among the region's Protestants and other non-Catholics, the moment of death and its immediate aftermath offered clues to their religious practices and values as well as to the reactions of the islands' civil and ecclesiastical authorities. Since the burial rights of non-Catholics were at the epicenter of religious conflict, the struggle to secure or deny those rights sheds much light on the significance of broader religious conflicts and the actors who took sides in them.

Using the Spanish revolutionaries' 1869 declaration of religious tolerance as a watershed, I have divided this book into two parts. Each begins with an introduction (chapters 1 and 4) that establish the broad political and religious context of the period. Chapter 2 discusses the extent of the Catholic church's efforts to retain spiritual control over the populations of Cuba and Puerto Rico during the era of Catholic exclusivism as well as the church's mechanisms for exerting that control. The dearth of studies on the region's Catholic church makes this chapter particularly relevant to our understanding of the context in which Protestants struggled for their faith. Chapter 3 reconstructs and analyzes the experiences of Protestants who settled in the Hispanic Caribbean before the declaration of religious tolerance, explaining why some sought the crypto-Protestant route while others followed the pseudo-Catholic one. Chapter 5 looks at Puerto Rico's first Protestant congregations (the Anglican churches in Ponce and Vieques), while chapter 6 traces the development of Cuba's first—the Episcopal mission of Havana. Finally, chapter 7 examines the region's true first Creole Protestant communities: the Cuban exile congregations of New York City and Key West and the Cuban congregations of Havana and Matanzas.

In the last three chapters I propose an alternative to the models of immigration and mission Protestantism, inspired by the work of the Cuban anthropologist Fernando Ortiz, who six decades ago masterfully counterpointed sugar and tobacco as crops that produced opposing sociocultural results: the hierarchical, authoritarian, and foreign-dominated Cuba of sugar versus the egalitarian, liberal, and nationalistic Cuba of tobacco.[7] Recognizing that the material demands and social reverberations of particular economic activities play a role in shaping culture, and building on Ortiz's *Cuban Counterpoint,* I argue that the early Protestant communities of the Hispanic Caribbean reflected the sociocultural milieus in which they emerged and were profoundly shaped by the economic activities of their congregants. This influence affected not only the congregations' composition but also their theological and political orientation. Ponce's Protestant congregation reflected the sugar plantation in its entirety, while Vieques's Protestant community mirrored only part of it: the laborers' village. Cuba's first Protestant congregations mirrored two different worlds: the unsettled context of Havana's piers and that of the cigar factories of Key West, New York, and Havana.

PART I

The Era of Catholic Exclusivism, 1815–1868

CHAPTER I

Religion and Political Struggle

≈≈ᴈ◉ᴈ≈≈

Conflicts over religious matters, such as the Catholic church's power over people's lives or the rights of Protestants, were intimately tied to the major political and social struggles unfolding in the Hispanic Caribbean during the nineteenth century. Some of the period's most divisive issues—for example, the slave trade, annexation by the United States, and Creole separatism—meshed with the church's efforts to retain power, wealth, and influence as it faced the secularizing forces of agrarian capitalism and an expanding colonial state. Cuba's and Puerto Rico's closening ties with the Protestant north increased religious tension, which became a key component of the interimperial rivalry over Spain's remaining New World colonies. This chapter traces the complex and evolving relations among church, state, and Creole elites in the northern Atlantic region as Spain, Great Britain, and the United States wrestled to maintain or increase their influence in the Caribbean.

Throughout the nineteenth century, Christianity, particularly Catholicism, endured a profound and debilitating crisis. As a result of advances in the natural sciences and increased historical criticism of the Bible and religious dogma, the central principles of Christianity came under attack. Amid these social and intellectual transformations, the Catholic church continued to be identified with the values and objectives of the European monarchies and aristocracies. Thus, the triumphs of science, liberalism, and bourgeois values represented defeats for the church.

Politically, too, the church lost much of its power in Europe. On the Italian peninsula, the once mighty and vast papal states retrenched during the 1860s and early 1870s, retreating into a minute enclave surrounded by the kingdom of Italy.[1] In Spain, where Catholicism and *españolismo* (devotion to Spain) were practically synonymous, the church suffered a marked decline in influence and authority as a result of political developments. Between 1833 and 1840, when Spanish liberals in alliance with the regent María Cristina domi-nated politics, the church suffered from its political association with absolutist monarchical models and its support of the reactionary Carlist faction. At that time a minority within the church reluctantly accepted Isabella as the future queen. During the mid-1830s, the church endured the first suppressions of male religious orders and the secularization of their property. In 1841, under the short-lived regency of Baldomero Espartero, the state extended the seculariza-tions to much of the property belonging to the secular clergy. Pope Gregory XVI's support for the ultraconservative pretender Don Car-los and his refusal to recognize Queen Isabella II's rule further soured relations between church and state. After 1843, the church's standing improved somewhat with the rise to power of more moderate gov-ernments, which with Isabella now joined forces with the clergy to oppose the progressive liberals. The signing of a concordat in 1851 signaled the improved relations between the Spanish crown and the church of Rome. It guaranteed the exclusivity of Catholicism in Spanish territory, secured the church's control over education, and returned or compensated for some of the properties confiscated dur-ing the secularizations of the 1830s and 1840s.[2] Nevertheless, pro-gressive generals led by Leopoldo O'Donnell, formerly Cuba's captain-general, revolted successfully in 1854 and briefly established a government with liberal leanings that implemented yet another round of church property secularizations. A more moderate liberal government, known as the Liberal Union, coalesced in 1856 and ruled until 1868, excluding the progressives. During this period, rela-tions between Spain and the Vatican improved markedly.[3]

In Cuba and Puerto Rico the church's fortunes to some degree mirrored developments in Spain. The mirror was murky, however, since the region's colonial and geopolitical circumstances followed a logic of their own. Both Cuba and Puerto Rico were ruled despotically by Spanish officials; and as the nineteenth century wore on, much of the population became disaffected with colonial rule. Furthermore, because Spain's island colonies were far from the Iberian peninsula, they had developed commercial relations of their own while maintaining rather weak links with the Spanish economy. Meanwhile, two Protestant nations—the United States and Great Britain—were developing stronger economic, political, and cultural links with Spain's last New World possessions. Finally, Cuba and Puerto Rico were slave societies, a circumstance that added to their existing volatility.

At the beginning of the nineteenth century, the Catholic church in Cuba and Puerto Rico was a moderate, even progressive institution attuned to the aspirations and values of the islands' Creole elites. Moreover, it was formed predominantly of native-born clergy. Prelates and clerics such as Puerto Rico's Bishop Juan Alejo de Arizmendi, vicar-general and governor of the Bishopric of San Juan José Gutiérrez del Arroyo, Cuba's Bishop Juan José Díaz de Espada y Landa, Félix Valera, and José de la Luz y Caballero were representative of the region's clerical liberalism during the first decades of the century.[4] In the 1830s, however, the church began to shift to a conservative, pro-Spanish position, which was reflected by the growing peninsular majority within its clergy. Fleeing the newly independent nations of Latin America in the 1810s and 1820s, large numbers of peninsular priests swelled the clerical population of Spain's remaining New World colonies and became willing tools of imperial rule. Particularly in the higher clerical ranks, where peninsulars had rapidly gained in number, the church gravitated away from the reformist or nationalist aspirations of the islands' Creole intelligentsia and bourgeoisie.[5] Even though the Spanish state did not always satisfy the church's demands, church authorities sought to collaborate with colonial officials in part to avoid political independence, the establishment of anticlerical regimes, and the dreaded advent of religious pluralism.[6]

Although the colonial church was somewhat insulated from the extreme, if intermittent, anticlericalism taking place in Spain, other economic, social, and political transformations had eroded the church's standing and reach in Cuba and Puerto Rico and helped break its monopoly over the region's souls. The secularizing demands of agrarian capitalism conflicted with the church's long-held power over lives and secular institutions. In an increasingly materialistic and competitive environment, the industrial noise of the new sugar plantations silenced the prayers echoing from the estates' decaying chapels. The region's sugar barons now placed greater faith in the science of agronomists and engineers than in the supplications of plantation priests. Furthermore, the church's traditional demands concerning sabbath and holiday observance, payment of sacramental and mass fees, and dietary restrictions became increasingly onerous and obnoxious to a planter class struggling to remain competitive in a tight sugar market.[7] Although the Cuban Slave Code of 1842 and similar decrees in Puerto Rico prescribed the spiritual responsibilities of masters for their slaves, the reality was that by the middle of the century priests rarely ministered in plantations. Many slaves either remained unbaptized or "baptized" each other, only a fraction had their conjugal ties solemnized, and many died without the rites of the official church. The heavy flow of slaves, particularly into Cuba, coincided with the church's reduced capabilities, thus influencing the growth of syncretic practices marked by a West African theological core superficially concealed by Catholic forms. Many of Cuba's slaves, for example, worshiped Yoruba deities masked by Catholic icons.[8] Chinese contract laborers, who began to arrive in Cuba in large numbers during the 1850s and 1860s, experienced even greater spiritual neglect and alienation from the sacrament of marriage and adequate funeral services.[9] Catholic influence also diminished among the region's free, white population, particularly in the countryside and the newer urban centers. The general population exhibited an increasing disregard for the prescribed Catholic sacraments.[10]

The church's diminishing human and material resources exemplified the crisis it was undergoing in the Hispanic Caribbean. Following the suppression of most religious orders between 1837 and

1841 and the secularization of the University of Havana in 1842, only 481 men of the cloth remained in Cuba and 120 in Puerto Rico. By 1860, the number of priests in Puerto Rico had fallen to ninety. Most of the few remaining clerics lived and ministered in the capital cities of Havana and San Juan, and many provincial cities and towns had only a token ecclesiastical presence, if any.[11] According to an 1843 report, the clergy in the important Cuban town of Puerto Príncipe, with a population of 51,036 in 1841, was composed of aging and infirm men who possessed little knowledge and practiced unbecoming habits. Reportedly, clergymen were also in short numbers in Matanzas. At midcentury the scandalized archbishop of Santiago, Antonio María Claret y Clará, dramatically described to another prelate the "criminal neglect" to which the Spanish government was subjecting the church and its ministers.[12] New laws in 1858 further aggravated the church's financial standing, placing limitations on its capacity to collect ecclesiastical taxes and sacramental fees.[13]

The expansion of the region's plantation systems strengthened the ties between the Spanish Caribbean and the economies and societies of the northern Atlantic as the islands increased their staple exports and their imports of foreign capital, technology, foodstuffs, manufactured goods, and labor. Ironically, while Spain struggled to maintain colonial domination over Cuba and Puerto Rico on the basis of monarchism and Catholic unity, it was forced by the mid-1810s to open colonial borders, exports, and markets to the United States, Great Britain, and other Protestant commercial powers. As a result, these powers soon displaced Spain as the colonies' principal trading partners, and sizable groups of Protestant immigrants from Great Britain, the United States, Germany, and other West Indian islands established themselves in Cuba and Puerto Rico.[14] Moreover, thousands of transients from predominantly Protestant countries visited the Spanish Caribbean each year for reasons of business, recreation, and health.

As a result of all these pressures, the Catholic church became defensive, seeking a close association with the colonial state and conservative elements on the peninsula as well as in the colonies. For a variety of reasons, ranging from its theological foundations to its association with reactionary elements, the church became allied with colonialist, pro-slavery, and conservative extremists. In spite of having lost much of their wealth and privileges to the secularizing forces of the state, the region's clergy continued to share with secular authorities the desire to curb all anti-Spanish and progressive forces. Though not always in full accord, church and state exhibited a stronger bond in the colonies than on the peninsula. Their symbiotic relationship stemmed from the church's institutional weakness in the Caribbean and the vulnerability of the colonial bond that tied the islands to their metropolis. In both settings the ancient principles and mechanisms of the *patronato real* continued to operate, whereby the Spanish monarchs and their representatives in the New World enjoyed administrative privileges and responsibilities within the structure of the Catholic church. The religious link uniting Spanish subjects on both sides of the Atlantic continued to be a powerful auxiliary to the political connection between colonizers and the colonized. As Puerto Rico's bishop Francisco La Puente explained, "the Christian religion [Catholicism] is the only one that sustains empires with a firm hand and constant support, inspiring in the citizenry the true love of fatherland."[15]

Colonial rulers favored the conservation of religious purity—meaning Catholic exclusivism—as a mean of reinforcing españolismo. Despite growing international pressures, the colonies' clerical and civilian authorities, as well as Spain's metropolitan officials, maintained and defended their exclusivist policies on religion. One argument was that conditions in the colonies, located far from their metropolis and vulnerable to political upheaval and dissension, made these restrictions more necessary than on the peninsula, where some tolerance provisions had been put in place at an earlier date. In an 1850 letter to Captain-General José de la Concha on the topic of non-Catholic places of worship, the Spanish minister of state said that allowing such places to be established could not only destroy Cuba's religious unity but bring with it dangerous political influences.[16] At a time when Spanish statesmen were weaving reconquest ploys throughout the Americas, Captain-General Concha himself significantly suggested that Cuba's Catholicism could be useful in reestablishing political links with the rest of Latin America. Another influential Spanish statesman, Mariano Torrente, advocated the manipulation of religious sentiments to maintain the unity of what was left of the Spanish empire and called for greater state support for the church. "The ecclesiastical arm . . . ," he wrote unabashedly, "shall be not only the defender and diffuser of the doctrine of Christ, but also a powerful auxiliary to secular authority." Torrente's faith in the Catholic link went so far that he believed that the pressures exerted by 3 million Catholics living in the United States would help stop the U.S. filibusterers' plots to free Catholic Cuba from Spanish rule and annex it to the United States.[17]

Nevertheless, progressive voices within the colonial state hierarchy did call for some religious openness, particularly on the smaller island of Puerto Rico, where the political situation was less volatile, foreign aggression from the Protestant north less likely, and, equally important, foreign capital and immigration more desperately needed for the expansion of the agricultural export sector. In the mid-1840s Puerto Rico's Junta de Comercio y Fomento and the island's intendant spearheaded a movement to derogate article 8 of the 1815 immigration law, which required immigrants to be Catholic. This requirement, critics argued, kept needed capital and immigrants from flowing onto the island. Proponents of reform maintained that such restrictions were "vexatious" and that the firmly entrenched Catholic faith could not be shaken. Puerto Rico's intendant argued that the restrictions, as they stood, in fact brought the worst kind of Protestants—those who lied and falsified documents to prove Catholicity—while keeping away the honest ones. Puerto Rico's governor Juan Prim (1847–48) and the top authorities of the island's principal towns supported the relaxation of immigration, a change that was temporarily put into effect by a governor's decree in 1848. A few months later, however, with the threat of U.S. filibuster aggression looming over the Spanish Caribbean, Madrid ordered the reestablishment of the immigration law's religious restrictions. In Cuba, a decade earlier, Captain-General Miguel Tacón, who often clashed with the church hierarchy, had recognized religious intolerance as an obstacle to immigration into the region.[18]

The arrival of numerous foreign Protestants in the Spanish Caribbean and the consequent debates surrounding the issue of religious tolerance coincided with a period of dramatic political transformation in Cuba and Puerto Rico. Particularly in Cuba, the 1830s through the 1850s were decades of growing political polarization in which Creoles and *Peninsulares* became increasingly hostile to each other. Ideological camps formed around such divisive issues as slavery, colonial representation in Madrid, taxation, and freedom of the press and religion. While church and state authorities generally came together under the banner of Catholic exclusivism, Cuba's and Puerto Rico's progressives and anti-Spanish voices tended to favor the establishment of religious tolerance and often sympathized with Protestantism and its theological precepts. In this way the religious struggle became linked with ongoing domestic and international struggles.

The religious struggle also shaped and reinforced the work of Cuba's political actors during the late 1840s and early 1850s, a critical juncture marked by the growth of the Cuban annexationist movement, which sought to turn Cuba into a state of the United States. Although students of Cuban Protestantism have concluded that there was no link whatsoever between annexationism and Protestantism, the historical evidence clearly points to the entanglement of political and religious debates and shows that clear parallels emerged. For example, the Cuban annexationists, a few of whom were Protestants or Protestant sympathizers, called for the end of religious exclusivism. That many of the Cuban annexationists were Freemasons further marked them as anti-Catholics.[19] Gaspar Betancourt Cisneros, Cristóbal F. Madan, Porfirio Valiente, and other annexationists spoke out against what they saw as oppressive Spanish Catholicism and castigated priests as tools of the state. The more aggressive, filibuster brand of annexationism was also marked by anti-Catholicism. Narciso López, although certainly no Protestant, had among his fellow filibusterers many Protestants; and one of his first measures, had his filibuster attempts succeeded, was to be the declaration of religious tolerance in Cuba.[20]

In a speech delivered in New Orleans after he had grown disillusioned with the annexationist route but still remained rabidly anti-

Spanish, Betancourt Cisneros explored the topic of church-state relations, arguing that religious liberty should be one of the foundations of the Cuban revolutionary program: "There can be no independence [and] there can be no civil liberty, where there is not religious independence and freedom." He quoted the scriptures to support the principle of separation of church and state and accused the Catholic clergy of living in concubinage—worse yet, in adultery—with the Spanish colonial state. The priests, he said, had become "fishers of bodies, . . . bailiffs and catchpoles, informers, and inquisitors of men."[21]

At the other end of the polarized Cuban political spectrum stood the anti-annexationists, also known as assimilationists—Europhiles, who wanted to achieve the same political rights as the Spanish provinces and strengthen Cuba's political ties with its metropolis on the basis of Catholicism and monarchism. Proposing to establish an anti-annexationist newspaper, Domingo del Monte stated that the publication should be "monarchical-religious-constitutional; moderate, but bordering on absolutism." Another opponent of annexation, José Antonio Saco, highlighted the differences separating the Cuban people from the "Anglo Saxon race," including origins, language, religion, and common usages and habits. In what may have been the longest contemporary exposition on the subject, Antonio González Ponce de Llorante warned that annexationism would undoubtedly bring a "humiliating" form of religious tolerance that would signify the end of Cuba's domestic unity and restrict Catholic ceremonies to church interiors. In the same pamphlet he referred to Protestants as apostates from the "true church."[22]

Cuba's annexationists rejected the ultra-Catholic attacks of the assimilationists. Cristóbal F. Madan, whose unabashed annexationism earned him the nickname "semi-Yanqui," denied that the movement was anti-Catholic and that annexation would bring about the end of Catholicism. He cited the example of Louisiana, where the French population had maintained its language, culture, and religion after the territory's incorporation into the United States. In a letter to José Antonio Saco, Madan explained that religious tolerance had always existed in the United States and would certainly be extended to Cuba after annexation. Another annexationist, Porfirio Valiente, also wrote about the tolerance that U.S. laws guaranteed to people of all faiths, including Catholics, and denied that religious pluralism meant that Cubans would lose their ancestral religion.[23]

Although Cuba's midcentury annexationists sympathized with the principle of religious tolerance and many had lived in the United States, they did not convert to Protestantism for some of the same reasons that they were not abolitionists—because they belonged to the propertied classes and thus could lose prestige and social capital in an overwhelmingly Catholic society. They also saw Catholicism's hierarchical, organic conception of society as a necessary prop to slave-based Cuba. The theological egalitarianism of Protestantism appeared threatening to the Cuban master class, even to those willing to risk a war with Spain. In other words, the midcentury annexationists were anticlerical not because of ideological conviction (as Latin America's liberals were) but because of anti-Spanish sentiments and international trade considerations.

After the 1855 collapse of the annexationist movements and the state's co-optation of some of the conspirators, Cuban politics entered a relatively quiet period. In the 1860s, however, religious-political discussion reheated. During the incumbencies of captains-general Francisco Serrano and Domingo Dulce—a period known as the *política de atracción* (politics of attraction)—a free press was established, and several newspapers began publication, notably *El Siglo*, which became the organ of Cuba's reform movement, a movement that incidentally absorbed into its ranks several former annexationist conspirators. Significantly, however, the new liberties of the press did not extend to discussions of slavery, political independence, and religious tolerance. Although *El Siglo* described itself as a Roman Catholic newspaper, it exhibited a moderately reformist, anticlerical stance. It applauded, for example, secularizing laws and acts of confiscation against the Mexican church, but its editors did not go so far as to suggest similar actions in Cuba, writing that such matters were the realm of "theologians and scholars," not journalists.[24]

In 1865 Spanish authorities summoned colonial delegates from

Cuba and Puerto Rico to discuss various matters pertaining to the colonies' future. Nevertheless, in the inaugural ceremonies of the Junta de Información held in Madrid, the overseas minister emphatically stated that three matters were not open for debate: the monarchy, the empire's religious unity, and the empire's territorial integrity. These limitations notwithstanding, Cuban delegates asked for the implementation of religious toleration in Cuba, which already existed on the peninsula, to help attract much-coveted white immigration to the island. Puerto Rico's more liberal delegates echoed these demands and incorporated them into a daring proposal for the abolition of slavery.[25]

As politics repolarized, Catholicism became a defining point of contrast between Cuba's pro-Spanish element and the more tolerant reformists of both islands. Revealing links emerged, with pro-Catholic voices also supporting slave trade interests and monarchism. Cuba's conservative delegate Manuel de Armas, for example, voted in a junta session against the abolition of slavery, basing his vote on arguments from Catholic theologians. A conservative delegate from Puerto Rico, Manuel de Jesús Zeno, defended the institution of slavery on biblical and moral grounds. Jerónimo de Usera, the dean of the Cathedral of Havana and appointed conservative delegate to the Junta de Información, voiced his opposition to a measure declaring slave trading an act of piracy. "Blacks," he stated, "are still savages."[26]

As commercial and immigration controls collapsed and Protestants and their publications began appearing in Spain's remaining American colonies, the Catholic clergy and activist laity increased their condemnations from the pulpit and through the press. Inspired by the defensive theology of Jaime Luciano Balmes, contemporary ultramontane postures, and Pope Pius IX's reactionary Syllabus of 1864, Cuba's and Puerto Rico's clerics denounced the spiritual evils of Protestantism and called its manifold social and political repercussions "the work of darkness." Catholic periodicals such as *El Boletín Eclesiástico de Puerto Rico* and Cuba's *La Verdad Católica* were filled with vitriolic attacks against Protestantism's theological principles; Martin Luther and other leaders of the Reformation; as well as Germany, England, Sweden, the United States, and other Protestant nations.[27]

Articles in both periodicals, especially a twelve-part series in *La Verdad Católica* titled "El protestantismo," scathingly attacked the perceived theological foundations of Protestantism. The authors denied any legitimacy to this branch of Christianity, deeming it heretical at best and diabolical at worst. According to one article in *La Verdad Católica,* Protestantism was a political and mercantile doctrine rather than a religious faith. Another claimed that it was devoid of symbols and that its "articles of faith [were] as diverse as the aberrations of the human spirit." Other pieces equated its beliefs with extreme rationalism, deism, pantheism, and even the denial of Christ's divinity. Such writings underscored the Protestant propensity to splinter into denominations and sects, its lack of institutional cohesion, and its theological and institutional disorganization. According to the editors of *El Boletín Eclesiástico de Puerto Rico,* "no one can ignore today that among Protestants there is no truth, there is no unity, and there can be nothing other than exterior struggle and interior disorganization and corruption."[28] Heeding Balmes's ultramontane call for a religion of order and obedience as opposed to Protestantism's reputed libertinism and anarchy, the editors underscored the political implications of Protestant penetration into a region already under precarious colonial rule. Like Balmes, they deemed it a dangerous instigator of dissociation and disloyalty. Articles in *La Verdad Católica* denounced Protestants as revolutionaries from the north and declared that Spanish subjects who embraced the theology committed treason against both God and the fatherland. One of the articles in the series "El protestantismo" even claimed that Protestantism would lead to socialism and communism.[29]

Catholic propagandists were prone to establish comparisons between Protestant countries such as England and Catholic ones such as Ireland and to adjudicate the advantages of Catholic countries using the sole variable of religious affiliation. In one such attempt, *La Verdad Católica* pointed to the problem of street children in London, "the stronghold of heresy," when questioning the reputed humanitarianism and progressiveness of Protestantism. A more extensive pseudo-scientific article in *El Boletín Eclesiástico de Puerto Rico* compared crime statistics in London and Ireland, including murder, bigamy, suicide, theft, and so on. Its author concluded that "morality is the result of religion: in Ireland there is no exterior visible police, but the people listen to the inexorable voice of the law that guides every conscience, and the fear of God is the loyal and mighty constable that stops evil before it arises and arrests injustice before it comes out to light."

Another propaganda tool was the report of Protestant conversions to Catholicism. According to *El Boletín Eclesiástico de Puerto Rico,* in 1859 alone, 1,000 London Protestants became Catholics.[30]

The 1840s and 1850s were marked by sharp international rivalry over Cuba. Although issues pertaining to slavery and other geopolitical considerations were at the heart of this rivalry, religious issues such as the rights of Protestants became involved in the ideological battle for control over the Hispanic Caribbean. Captain-General Miguel Tacón (1834–38) accused the British, who were leading the struggle against the slave trade, of staging a campaign to liberate Cuba's slaves. He persecuted several British Protestants, mostly Methodists, whom he claimed had imported an adulterated version of the Bible. Tacón went to the length of dispatching a spy to the neighboring Cayman Islands, where conspiratorial Methodist activities against Cuba were allegedly brewing. One of his successors, Pedro Téllez y Girón, also denounced British Protestants for their supposed plans to liberate the slaves, even at the expense of the extinction of the island's whites. Slave agitation, which peaked in 1841–42 and the 1844 conspiracy of La Escalera, was also attributed to machinations by British consul-general David Turnbull and Quaker abolitionist missionaries. During the crisis of La Escalera, foreign Protestants, both of color and white, became prime targets of state repression.[31]

The British government and its representatives in the Spanish Caribbean complained repeatedly about abuses against the religious rights of British subjects and called for Spain and its colonial administrators to respect those basic rights. In the early 1840s, Turnbull denounced the horrors of Protestant burials and claimed protection for Britons under the provisions of the Anglo-Spanish treaty of 1667.

Puerto Rico's British consul John Lindegren also repeatedly protested against these undignified burials and suggested that Britain retaliate with punitive trade barriers. Representing the demands of British merchants, high-ranking British officials in the 1850s pushed to end the obnoxious regulations that forced British subjects living in Cuba and Puerto Rico to swear allegiance to the Catholic church and the Spanish monarchy. Not coincidentally, interest in religious matters, particularly the emotionally charged issue of Protestant burial rights, peaked in the early 1850s as the British worked aggressively to abolish the Cuban slave trade.[32]

Meanwhile, U.S. filibustering expansionists included religious arguments in support of their desire to acquire Cuba. The spread of Protestantism was one of the pillars of manifest destiny—the belief in a necessary policy of U.S. expansion—and some of its loudest advocates condemned "the cursing, blighting, and contaminating influence" of Catholicism while calling for Cuba's annexation and consequent Protestantizing. One supporter, George Williams, wrote, "I want to see the American eagle stretching its wings from Canada to Panama to establish religious toleration." Another expansionist declared that with annexation "will come the free Bible, the free Pulpit, and the free Press." According to Spanish officials, the expansionist movement in Texas was composed of people with fanatical political and religious inclinations, and several Protestant ministers were said to be among the movement's leaders.[33]

Interestingly, Cuba's Catholicism was exploited by both opponents and advocates of the island's annexation. U.S. senators Zachariah Chandler, John P. Hale, John Perry, and others highlighted religion among the many differences separating Cuba and the United States that made incorporation into the union difficult if not impossible. On the floor of the Senate, Chandler described Cubans as superstitious, vicious, and bigoted: "They are devout Catholics, the Catholic Church is true to Spain and true to despotism." In the same vein, Senator Hale stated that "a republican government can only be maintained, and successfully maintained, on the principle of Protestant liberty." If annexed, Cuba would have a "deleterious influence." Stephen R. Mallory of Florida, who may have been the only Catholic in the Senate, responded to these attacks by stating that his religion was not adverse to liberty. He favored Cuba's annexation and stated that most Catholics around the world also supported it.[34]

In sum, the religious struggles that peaked during the mid-nineteenth century activated not only the Catholic clergy and the region's anticlericals and few Protestants but many other sectors of society, who took sides in various interconnected social and political struggles. Both directly and indirectly, the rights of Protestants became entwined with other political and religious agendas, thus moving far beyond theological or moral considerations to reflect the complex and increasingly tense relations between church and state, Catholics and non-Catholics, and Spanish subjects and foreigners. On the one hand, the Catholic church sided openly with the forces of colonialism and reaction. On the other, progressives and annexationists, albeit for different reasons, sought to break the church's monopoly over the region's religious life. At the international level, British abolitionist and U.S. expansionist pressures were marked by Protestant religious overtones that contrasted with Spain's Catholic colonialism.

CHAPTER 2

The Roman Catholic Grip

Although they disagreed on various particulars, the Spanish Caribbean's government and church hierarchies shared a general interest in preserving the social and political status quo; and they considered the retention of religious unity to be a primary goal. As the nineteenth century wore on, colonial authorities and the Catholic church became increasingly allied against forces that threatened the colonial bond. Although what the church defined as sin and the state defined as crime were often identical, the church's ideology was more dogmatic and the state's more pragmatic. This chapter examines the attitudes of church and state to religious exclusivism and control over sacraments and burial grounds, considering church dictates as well as colonial legislation on immigration, education, censorship, and the officiation of baptisms, marriages, and burials. The ways in which different social groups responded to church and state in these matters highlights the many class and economic agendas that clashed or coincided with the church's desires.

Catholicism was the official faith of the Spanish empire, meaning that all other religions were illegal. Thus, the region's Protestants were deprived of ministers, houses of worship, and even basic religious rights. It was unlawful to advocate religious tolerance in either writing or speech. Matters worsened during the middle decades of the nineteenth century, when the issue of religious freedom became tangled with increasingly tense political struggles on the islands and in the northern Atlantic region. New legislation after 1848, reflecting Spain's improved relations with the Catholic church, tightened the church's grip in the colonies and prescribed even harsher penalties for those who challenged its longstanding religious exclusivism.[1]

One shared goal of the church and the colonial state was to maintain the colonies' religious purity through immigration control. Since the sixteenth century, immigration to Spain's Caribbean colonies, with few exceptions, was restricted to Spanish subjects, who were presumed to be Catholic, and African slaves, who were considered religionless and therefore convertible to Catholicism. Because *limpieza de sangre* (purity of blood) was a requisite for immigration, Jews, Muslims, Protestants, and new converts were legally barred from the colonies.[2] In the early part of the nineteenth century, however, the labor and capital demands of Cuba's and Puerto Rico's burgeoning plantation economies forced the crown to relax immigration restrictions. Royal decrees (such as the 1815 Cédula de Gracias granted to Puerto Rico and a similar decree for Cuba two years later) not only opened the region to non-Spanish immigration but encouraged and subsidized it with tax exemptions and other privileges. Nevertheless, two basic restrictions remained. First, immigrants had to come from nations friendly to Spain. Second, and equally important, they had to be Roman Catholic.[3]

Clearly, opening the Spanish Caribbean to immigrants and long-term, non-Spanish visitors would ultimately result in the arrival of non-Catholic foreigners and collapse the empire's self-proclaimed religious unity. To stave off this dreaded outcome, Spanish law prescribed that any foreigner staying longer than three months or seeking to own property or practice a profession in Cuba or Puerto Rico must formally seek domiciliation and take an oath of Catholicity. Those staying longer than five years had to be naturalized. As one U.S. consular agent joked, foreigners "were immediately galvanized, electroplated and made a Roman Catholic."[4] Clearly, however, there were many ways of circumventing the domiciliation requirement. In 1830, in the Puerto Rican town of Aguadilla, non-domiciled foreigners on average had spent eight years as transients, thus failing to secure the domiciliation required of those staying longer than three months. Likewise, in 1844, in the province of Matanzas alone, there resided 214 non-domiciled foreigners, a few of whom even owned property.[5] Still, the lax manner in which the domiciliation requirement was enforced did not make it any less injurious to non-Catholics settling in the islands.

In the eyes of church and state, the growing influence of West African religious practices, continually reinforced by waves of imported slaves, appeared to pose less of a threat to the social and political status quo than did the much smaller Protestant presence. To begin with, religious and government authorities believed they could control and perhaps eradicate Yoruba and other West African religious practices through the social-control mechanisms of slavery, Catholic indoctrination, and the legalized and monitored Afro-Cuban societies known as Cabildos de Nación. Moreover, theological and formal affinities between Catholicism and various West African religions allowed convergences that Protestantism did not. Nevertheless, while these similarities allowed slaves to be more successfully evangelized, they also allowed them and their descendants to successfully mask West African religious practices and beliefs behind a superficial facade of Catholicism.[6]

Clerical and secular authorities also strove to maintain religious unity through church control of schools and a ban on non-Catholic religious publications.[7] The law declared that "moral and religious instruction [in schools] must be priorities in all classes," and teachers had to be certified by parish priests and magistrates as having "good moral and religious conduct." Ecclesiastical authorities denounced the circulation of Bibles and Protestant publications, which were banned by the colonial state.[8] Because an individual's ability to read the Bible and use it as a source of divine revelation was a pillar of Protestantism, literacy and access to affordable Bibles were essential components of Protestant life. In 1835, Captain-General Tacón denounced the attempts of English Protestant organizations to introduce Bibles into Cuba that allegedly contained adulterated and inflammatory texts. Two years later, James Thompson of the British and Foreign Bible Society arrived on the island with a cargo of nearly three hundred Bibles. Although he sold a few in Havana, he had little success elsewhere on the island. His tour of Cuba ended abruptly in Santiago, where the archbishop denounced his activities and ordered his cargo to be confiscated. Thompson was jailed briefly and later banished from the island for his allegedly abolitionist activities. In 1855, a year of heightened tensions between Cuba and the United States, colonial authorities passed new, stricter laws against the introduction of Bibles into Cuba. At that time, a person who had overseen the distribution of Bibles in Cuba reported to the Female Bible Society of Philadelphia: "In the present state of affairs there this work is impossible." A few years later, during the U.S. Civil War, English Bibles on their way to the Confederate states passed through Havana, where they were shipped to southern ports by blockade runners. Despite the generally friendly disposition of Spanish officials toward the Confederacy, they did confiscate cargoes of Bibles whose ultimate destinations would have been Matamoros and other Confederate ports.[9]

Beginning in the 1810s, Bibles and Protestant literature began routinely entering Puerto Rico via the Danish Virgin Islands but, as in Cuba, were confiscated and censored. In 1834, three years before visiting Cuba, James Thompson also attempted to distribute Bibles in Puerto Rico, but his efforts were curtailed by local authorities. The following year, the mayor of Coamo banned the entrance and circulation of Bibles published and distributed by British Methodists, claiming that these Bibles had been adulterated to undermine slavery.[10] In 1853, government officials banned the sale and circulation of a children's book because it allegedly expounded "the principles of Protestantism." Church and colonial authorities in Puerto Rico continued to attack the importation of Bibles and Protestant literature throughout the next decade. In 1867, the editors of *El Boletín Eclesiástico de Puerto Rico* denounced the U.S. exportation of nearly 1,000 pamphlets entitled *El protestantismo* and *El retrato de la Virgen María en los cielos*. Three years later they condemned the books *La farsa religiosa* by Emilio Blasco as well as Pierre-Joseph Proudhon's philosophical works on religion. The editors of the islands' Catholic journals called on state authorities to prohibit the sale of these books and warned Catholics that anyone reading, keeping, or selling these "heretical" publications would face excommunication. For their part, government censors banned the publication of any book or article attacking or criticizing the official church of the state.[11]

As the Catholic church's wealth, political influence, and credibility among the general population deteriorated, it became more jealous of its control over the most important milestones in people's lives: birth, marriage, and death. In light of diminishing resources and reduced state support, the church increased the relative shares of baptismal, wedding, and funeral fees within its revenues.[12] Civil birth registers and civil marriages did not exist at the time, and the state's church zealously controlled access to the islands' municipal cemeteries. As James W. Steele, a U.S. official stationed in Havana, eloquently declared, "the Mother Church is the mistress of ceremonies of all kinds. . . . She begins at the beginning, and sends the infant into the world with a ceremony and accompanying documents without which it is impossible at any time thereafter to prove legitimacy. She afterward solemnizes a marriage for him, which no other has the power to do. . . . and without her, you had better not die."[13] Monopolistic control over sacraments, funerals, and burials also became key weapons in the church's struggle against irreligiosity and religious dissidence, particularly the growing influence of Protestantism and Freemasonry.

Of all the sacraments, baptisms were by far the easiest to enforce; and the church sought to baptize as many children as it could reach, irrespective of status or race. Since civil registries of births did not exist, baptismal records were, for legal and statistical purposes, synonymous to birth certificates and were important official documentation of an individual's legitimacy and racial status. Reportedly, slaves actively sought the sacrament of baptism as a sign of higher social status. Canon law stipulated that baptisms should occur within two weeks of birth and specifically in the parish where the birth took place. For imported slaves the grace period was one year.[14] Fees associated with baptismal ceremonies were relatively inexpensive, and provisions existed for indigent parents to have their children christened for nominal fees. Often Asian contract workers were baptized on arrival to Cuba at no cost either to them or their masters. Nevertheless, baptisms could also carry rather large secular expenses associated with the ceremony's celebration.[15]

The church even allowed midwives, relatives, and other baptized Catholics to perform lay emergency baptisms for newborns who faced the risk of dying before being baptized by a priest. Cuba's 1842 Slave Code prescribed that slave owners should baptize their slaves in case of danger of death, for "in such cases anyone is authorized to do so." In the San Juan suburb of Puerto Nuevo, for instance, a slave named Fermín baptized a moribund eight-year-old, the child of English parents.[16] Many Puerto Rican peasants considered lay baptisms to be sufficient and did not seek the sacrament from a priest. Although masters were expected to arrange and pay for the baptism of the slaves they bought or who were born on their property, there were many instances in which slaves were only "baptized" by a fellow slave shortly before death. Incredibly, the slaves belonging to Puerto Rico's priest Nicolás Alonso de Andrade had to baptize one another. Since certificates of baptism also served as proof of property, slave masters were more diligent about arranging for the baptism of newborn slaves than about having adult imported slaves baptized, particularly after the slave trade was abolished.[17]

In addition to obeying church dictates, baptisms had social advantages since they established extended family ties through the institution of *compadrazgo* (godparenthood).[18] Among the propertied classes, the Catholic baptism of children was also necessary for inheritance purposes and for individuals to be able to prove ancestry and limpieza de sangre. Moreover, few parents were willing to gamble with the possibility of having a child die and then be denied proper burial and forced to spend eternity in limbo. The ritual of baptism thus not only marked the cleansing of original sin and the entrance of a soul into communion within the Catholic church but was also a deeply entrenched social dictate that cut across class and caste lines. Few wished to challenge its importance.

While most people were willing to comply with the relatively simple affair of baptism, many challenged the more complicated and expensive practice of marriage. According to Jesuit historian Fernando Picó, "marriage was the most expensive and traumatic of the sacraments." Both church and state had requirements and restrictions concerning the rites of holy matrimony. Among them was the rule that church marriages were reserved for single or widowed people who had been baptized as Catholics and had thereafter kept up with the minimum requirements and responsibilities of their faith. Neither ecclesiastical nor state authorities recognized the right to divorce. Moreover, men under the age of twenty-three and women younger than twenty needed parental permission for marriage.[19]

Even the simplest church marriage required a series of preparatory steps involving numerous and often onerous fees. As prerequisites for marriage, many men and women who had not set foot inside a church since their baptism were forced to confess decades of sins before a priest and do the prescribed penances. Three *amonestaciones* (bans) had to be proclaimed in church on the three Sundays preceding the ceremony. People who had lived in more than one parish had to arrange for amonestaciones to be read at each locality. In Puerto Rico in 1840, the bride's and groom's declarations and amonestaciones cost twenty-one reales. Another expensive ceremony, the *velación* (nuptial benediction), usually preceded but sometimes followed the actual marriage. Married couples could not live together or consummate their unions until they had received this benediction. Finally, the wedding ceremony required the payment of a sacramental fee.[20] Moreover, despite an 1858 law that banned further marriage fees, priests usually charged between ten and sixteen pesos for each ceremony, working around the law by offering free marriages only at inconvenient and socially unacceptable times of the day (e.g., seven o'clock in the morning). Sometimes the bride and groom also had to provide a specified amount of candle wax for the ceremony as well as pay for related secular expenses such as clothing, food, liquor, and entertainment.[21]

Couples with special circumstances endured further restrictions and taxation. In cases of *consanguineidad* (blood and familial ties between the couple), dispensations, except for the most outrageously incestuous combinations, were possible after the payment of large sums of money. These fees ranged from a few pesos for distant familiarity to 1,000 pesos in cases of first degree of affinity (for example, father and daughter-in-law). Among elite families seeking to preserve and expand their wealth and status, consanguineous marriages were widespread; and consanguineous concubinage was common among the working poor who lived in isolated towns of the interior.[22] Certificates of *soltería* (bachelorhood or spinsterhood) were also required of foreigners, *vagos* (people without work or a fixed domicile), widows and widowers, and all those who had left their parishes for more than a year. Many of these certifications were long and costly, involving sworn declarations from multiple witnesses as well as voluminous documentation, which sometimes had to be secured from the groom's or bride's European birthplace. People working for the government or serving in the military needed special licenses before getting married, and an 1860 decree stipulated that Cuba's Chinese contract laborers had to secure their masters' permission before marrying.[23] Depending on the wealth of the contractors, priests had the authority to adjust dispensations and other fees and could be either lenient or unyielding depending on whim or other circumstances.[24]

Occasionally, church authorities tried to standardize and reduce marriage fees to discourage cohabitation. Campaigns to force people to get married, such as those carried out by the bishops of Puerto Rico in 1849–52 and 1861, resulted in thousands of marriages. During a pastoral visit to Cuba's Oriente Province at midcentury, Archbishop Antonio María Claret y Clará solemnized more than 9,000 marriages of people who had been cohabitating. Usually in March and December of each year, the church exempted couples from the velación requirement, at which point the number of marriages increased noticeably. In March 1876, when Bishop Juan Antonio Puig y Monserrat visited Ponce, close to half of the municipality's marriages for that year took place, demonstrating that the inability to pay fees may have been the biggest obstacle to marriage.[25]

People from predominantly Protestant countries faced even more obstacles and requirements, and parish priests were ordered to deny holy matrimony to brides and grooms of doubtful Catholicity.

Satisfactory evidence of religious orthodoxy included certificates of Catholic baptism and sworn statements by reputable witnesses, a process that could cost more than fifty pesos. Known Protestants had to publicly abjure their faith and then be baptized as Catholics before they could be married under the auspices of the church. Nominal Catholics living in concubinage and wishing to solemnize their unions were branded as public sinners and forced to undergo penance and separate from their partners before the church would bless their unions.[26]

As difficult and expensive as the marriage process was, both church and state promoted marriage as the ideal status for the adult population; and they vigorously combated fornication, concubinage, adultery, bigamy, homosexuality, incest, and other practices and lifestyles deemed sinful—for example, separating those living in concubinage from holy communion, confession, serving as godparents, and last rites and a blessed burial in consecrated ground.[27] In addition to theological reasons, church and state also shared social, economic, and demographic motivations in favor of marriage. Stable families were easier targets of social control, less mobile, and more dependable and exploitable in the labor force. Not coincidentally, religious and secular authorities in Puerto Rico recognized vagrancy and concubinage as the twin evils of the island's interior. Equating *amancebamiento* (cohabitation) with *vagancia* (vagrancy), colonial authorities established the Juntas de Vagos y Amancebados in 1838 to ensure that the laboring classes remained as settled as possible to maintain a plentiful and reliable work force for the agrarian bourgeoisie. From a demographic perspective, stable families were also a source of population growth and economic prosperity.[28]

With similar objectives, Cuban authorities reportedly encouraged some slaves to get married by giving each couple a pig, with the hope that their status as married "property owners" would reduce their inclination to flee. The 1842 Slave Code ordered masters to encourage marriages among their slaves and provide married slaves with "the means of living under the same roof." Interestingly, the code also prescribed that marriages between slaves belonging to different masters should be avoided. In most cases, however, masters opposed marriages among their slaves because of the sacramental expense and the problems created when slaves were sold.[29]

Church and state authorities used a variety of coercive mechanisms to force couples to seek holy matrimony. Legally, as well as in the eyes of the church and society, children born outside of church-sanctioned wedlock were stigmatized as illegitimate. Sparing one's children from the opprobrium and difficulties of illegitimacy was a strong incentive for marriage—in some instances, even after the children had already reached adulthood. Such pressure was, of course, most effective among upper- and middle-class families who were influenced by the elites' social mores. Interestingly, many couples who had lived outside of Catholic matrimony for decades sought to solemnize their unions just before, or even after, the death of one of the partners to avoid passing on without the rites of the official church and spare their children the social shame associated with illegitimacy. The lieutenant governor of Yabucoa, for example, married his concubine at his deathbed to protect their three children's legal rights. In another instance, Marciala Saleces of Bayamón sought to have her children legitimized, claiming that she and her late companion had requested a marriage dispensation that had arrived after his death.[30]

There were many reasons why the presumably all-Catholic population of Cuba and Puerto Rico did not fully participate in the sacrament of holy matrimony and instead practiced widespread concubinage. In many jurisdictions the baptism-marriage ratio was nearly ten to one. In 1830, the birth-marriage-death ratio for the entire population of Puerto Rico was 7.1 to 1 to 3.7; and in 1897, it was 7.3 to 1 to 8.7. In Cuba's Occidente Province in 1846, the ratio was 8.2 to 1 to 6.1, while Havana's in 1855 was 7.9 to 1 to 12.2. Marriages were even less frequent in Cuba's Oriente Province, where the baptism-marriage ratio was seventeen to one.[31] These numbers show that more individuals were willing to baptize their natural children than be married by the church. The Catholic books of baptism of the parishes of Ponce and Loíza for the period reflect more illegitimate than legitimate births, a good indication that more couples lived out of wedlock than under church-sanctioned unions. End-of-century statistics reflected only slightly more legitimate than illegitimate births for all of Puerto Rico.[32] On the island of Vieques in 1844, the rate of illegitimacy was considerable, with almost twice as many illegitimate births as legitimate ones. Even Vieques's sixty-year-old governor, Francisco Saínz, cohabitated for many years with a woman named Doña Pepa while both remained married to other people. Doña Pepa finally yielded to mounting pressure and left Vieques with her children to settle on the neighboring island of St. Thomas, where the adulterous relation reportedly continued on a commuter basis.[33] By the mid-1860s, with a stronger church presence in Vieques, the illegitimacy ratio dropped to about one-third of all births.[34]

While some people avoided marriage, others sought it more than once, particularly foreigners who had left their wives behind and wanted to remarry in the Caribbean. Ecclesiastical records show that some labor migrants from the Canary Islands remarried in Cuba while remaining married to spouses left behind. Such was the case of Antonio Hernández, also known as Pitango, who married a second time in Havana while he was still married to a woman named María Pérez de la Rosa from Santa Cruz de la Palma. Cases like his occurred often enough to give rise to the legend of the Canary witches—abandoned married women from the Canary Islands who appeared in the Cuban countryside to terrorize the children that their husbands had fathered with Cuban women. According to a priest's testimony, in Puerto Rico some men had "two wives and live[d] together like Moors."[35]

The propensity to defy the mandate of Catholic matrimony was intimately tied to the variables of color, social class or status, geographic origin, and residence. In Puerto Rico, whites were almost three times as likely to be married than people of color were, and the marriage rate among slaves was a negligible 2.6 percent. In 1845, not one of Vieques's 369 slaves was married. Puerto Rico's illegitimacy rates for 1867 confirm these patterns: while only 21 percent of white children were illegitimate, 41 percent of the free children of color were illegitimate, and 97 percent of children born into slavery were illegitimate. Several years later Father Juan Perpiñá y Pibernat testified that concubinage generally occurred among blacks.[36] In Cuba, whites were about five times more likely than people of color to be married. The ratio of illegitimacy among the general population of Cuba was 46 percent in 1846, but within the population of color it was 76 percent. Records of the Versalles parish of Matanzas for 1876 show that illegitimacy rates among whites stood at less than 12 percent, while among free blacks they were as high as 83 percent. Among the free population of the city of Havana in 1860, 20 percent of whites were married, 15 percent of free mulattos were married, and only 11.5 percent of free blacks were married. Slaves in the larger plantations of Cuba's Occidente, some of which reportedly had all-male work forces, were rarely married. Masters sometimes officiated over "marriage" ceremonies that had no legal or canonical validity. Toward the end of the nineteenth century, the illegitimacy rate among black Cuban children was as high as 50 percent, more than four times higher than the rate among whites.[37] Marriage among Cuba's Chinese contract laborers was virtually nonexistent—in part because the Chinese population was almost exclusively male, in part because masters retained the right of consent.[38] Among all race groups, those living farthest from Havana were far less likely to be married.[39] These statistics point to a clear correlation between race and the rejection of the marriage sacrament: whites complied with church marriage to a much larger extent than did other racial groups. Taken one step further, these statistics show that poorer, more rural, and darker-skinned individuals tended to remain more distant from the Catholic church than did their wealthier, more urban, and lighter-skinned counterparts. Interestingly, early Protestant missionary efforts were more successful among the former group.

Interracial unions were not often solemnized because of the special state licenses required in Cuba and because such marriages represented considerable social loss to the contracting party who "married down." Data for two of San Juan's urban barrios show that 90 to 98 percent of all whites married other whites.[40]

Most of the region's population, particularly people with darker skin, remained unmarried because of their incapacity to support a family and pay for wedding fees, their ineligibility to be married as

Catholics, or their resistance to Catholic control over their lives. Some simply rejected church matrimony either out of principle (that is, they were not Catholic) or because they did not care about it. The less actual and social capital shared by the contracting partners, the less of that capital they had to lose and the more likely they were to reject church-sanctioned matrimony. Inheritance issues were of little concern among the poor, who were also less vulnerable than upper classes to social pressures. This was particularly true among slaves, whose social capital, as measured by the elites, was very low and who ironically were freer than any other group in society (priests excluded) from the pressure to sustain long-term conjugal relations or have them sanctioned by the church. Moreover, the cultural legacy of West African polygamous practices and sequential partnerships coupled with the obstacles to marriage created by slave masters conspired against a higher marriage ratio among slaves and free blacks.[41] Still, the single biggest factor explaining widespread concubinage among all groups appears to have been the incapacity of grooms and brides to afford the church's fees. It is significant that whenever marriage ceremonies were simplified and made cheaper, droves of people "living in sin" came forth to get married.

In addition to baptism and marriage, the church also held firm control over the ceremonies that accompanied the moment of death. Without the approval of parish priests, no one could receive the last rites before death, church funeral services could not be held, and— perhaps most troubling to the moribund and their survivors—no one could be interred in a decent and consecrated burial ground. Authorities had the power to limit all ceremonies and access to cemeteries to members of the Catholic church in full communion. Non-Christians, Protestants, others deemed heretics, suicides, public sinners, the unbaptized, and those rejecting extreme unction were often barred from these rituals and sacred spaces.[42] Unlike baptisms and marriages, however, in which church and state shared a common and harmonious interest in their implementation and registration, control over burials created many tensions between secular and religious authorities. There were no tangible advantages for the state to defend the church's monopoly over burials; in fact, the church's rigid position on the subject of burial rights risked offending public health and order.

Catholic authorities offered a broad range of funeral services to suit the needs and budgets of all social classes, all of which were usually held inside the churches. Because funeral masses, church vigils, priestly accompaniment to the cemetery, and anniversary masses were not specifically required, they were arranged only by those families who could afford them or felt socially compelled to carry them out. Often relatives of the deceased and other mourners held *velorios* (wakes), *rosarios* (funeral prayer gatherings), and other ceremonies before and after the remains of the dead were conveyed to their resting places. Very simple funerals were held for *pobres de solemnidad* (the certifiably poor) whose surviving relatives could not afford to pay.[43]

Always important sources of income, funeral and burial fees became critical in light of dwindling church support from the state and the population. In Puerto Rico, which was less affluent than Cuba, records dating back to 1772 show that double funerals with vigil and chanted mass cost fifty-eight reales, plain funerals eighteen reales. In 1836, a visitor in Ponce reported that rich people's funerals cost the equivalent of three hundred to five hundred dollars.[44] In Cuba an average funeral, not counting parish and interment fees, cost one hundred pesos. Funerals among Cuba's proverbially lavish planter elite could cost tens of thousands of pesos, including many years' worth of funeral masses for the soul of the deceased. Reportedly, at midcentury there were eighteen luxury funeral carriages in Havana, the most lavish sporting magnificent velvet draperies embroidered in silver and gold and pulled by four caparisoned horses crowned with flaring tufts. Even former slaves such as María Josefa Fiera, a Carabalí (that is, a person born in present-day southeastern Nigeria or southwestern Cameroon) who died in Cuba in 1860, had splendid funerals; hers cost 325 pesos and included eight free black lackeys and transportation in a first-class funeral carriage. Funeral extravagances got so out of hand that in 1841 the municipal government of Havana intervened to set limits on costs, and luxury taxes were levied to combat the most ostentatious extremes.[45]

Although priests seldom accompanied corpses to the cemeteries and never held funeral services there, they retained the privilege to exact burial fees, even from non-Catholics if they wished to allow them Catholic burial. In Cuba at midcentury the basic fee was 7.50 pesos for an interment license. Children and blacks were charged slightly less, and fees were reduced in rural areas. In addition, there were expenses for grave digging and other services, all of which added up to at least 25.50 pesos. Because there was no limit to how much could be spent, some families rented or owned elegant niches and mausoleums.[46]

Although the church had some provisions for those who could not afford burial expenses, it insisted that masters pay for their slaves' burials. The law, however, provided certain exemptions—for example, during major epidemics and when the plantations where the slaves died were located more than fifteen miles from the nearest parish church. Isolated plantations had their own makeshift burial grounds, and slaves reportedly took charge of many of the funeral and burial ceremonies. Still, payment of slaves' burial costs remained a source of tension between the master class and the church. In 1855, for example, parish priest Pedro Alboy took Bayamón planter Manuel Fernández to court to make him pay the fifty-one pesos he allegedly owed for the burial of twelve slaves who had died during a recent cholera epidemic.[47] A similar case involved planters Rafael González of Wajay and Juan Bautista de Sanz of Managua, who lost dozens of slaves in epidemics and refused to pay for their interment. The priest of the parish of Nueva Bermeja complained that this behavior was widespread and caused "noticeable injury to the church and the parish priests."[48] While it is hard to document this claim, there were plenty of allegations that slave masters surreptitiously buried their slaves and forced illegally imported slaves or illegally reenslaved *emancipados* (free blacks under forced labor contracts) to take the place and identity of the deceased. There were also widespread instances of trustees who did not baptize the newborns of emancipadas under their custody to hide their birth and keep them as slaves. Reportedly, some priests connived in such frauds, producing false certificates for a fee, or collected sacramental fees from planters in land and slaves rather than cash.[49]

The nineteenth-century burial process had changed since early colonial times, when it had been carried out inside the churches. The wealthier the dead person, the closer to the main altar his or her remains rested. Beginning in the early 1800s, however, public health considerations, the growing power of the state over such matters, and increasing demographic pressures forced burial ceremonies outdoors into municipal cemeteries. Havana's Espada Cemetery was consecrated in 1806, Matanzas's in 1811; San Juan's, Ponce's, and Puerto Príncipe's first cemeteries were built in 1814 and Santiago's in 1825.[50] The new cemeteries were usually segregated by race and status, and access to mausoleums and niches was restricted to whites. The extravagance of many of the mausoleums in Havana's monumental Colón Cemetery, which opened in 1872, testify to a culture that sought to mark class distinctions from cradle to grave. Nevertheless, although the new burial grounds were partially built with subscriptions and public funds, the church claimed great control over what could happen inside them and who could be admitted for burial.[51] Throughout the century, church and state were involved in a jurisdictional tug of war over these matters.

By most accounts, the average burial in Cuba and Puerto Rico was a rather plain affair. Not only did priests avoid performing ceremonies in the cemeteries, but clerical and state authorities sought to limit any sort of public mourning. In Cuba, for example, blacks were forbidden for many years to accompany their dead to the cemetery. Even when they were eventually permitted to participate in burial ceremonies, their actions were rigidly regulated: they could not wear extraordinary clothing or costumes, they had to march in files of two, and their processions could not stop at public establishments to or from the cemetery. On both islands, elegy speeches or compositions of any kind were banned. Regulations prohibiting emotional expressions at the time of burial targeted blacks in particular. An early synod of the Bishopric of Santiago ordered parish priests not to allow loud cries and other expressions of grief. Night burials, prescribed in

FIGURE 1. Funeral in Cuba, circa 1898. From F. Tennyson Neely, *Greater America* (1898).

some African traditions, were out of the question; and bodies could only be transported in church-approved vehicles.[52]

In Cuba, less expensive burials were performed in shallow mass graves, usually under three feet deep. At the cemeteries in Havana, Matanzas, and elsewhere on the island the common practice was to open mass graves and deposit unshrouded, unconfined bodies side by side. Once the length of the ditch was filled, a thin layer of soil was cast over the corpses.[53] In the 1860s, Havana's social reformers and conservatives agreed that Espada's and El Cerro's cemeteries were no longer adequate for a city the size of Havana. In an 1865 editorial, the reformist *El Siglo* scorned the Espada Cemetery as unworthy of "the most miserable village."[54] Thus, beginning in 1868, corpses were buried outside the limits of the new Colón Cemetery, while burials in the old Espada Cemetery continued only in niches and vaults. Once the new cemetery was officially opened in 1872, no more burials were made in the old one after 1878. Although the church was in charge of the new cemetery's construction, state authorities selected its location and retained the authority to establish its regulations and fees. An 1867 regulation called for the end of common graves and prescribed minimum dimensions for future individual graves.[55] Mirroring the changes in Cuba, Ponce's cemetery, which had been built in 1843, was expanded in 1867 when its planners sought improved hygiene and an end to profanations.[56]

Because the space in most cemeteries was insufficient for demand, human remains were eventually removed from the ground after the burials—in some cases, within a few weeks—and placed in bone deposits called ossuaries to make space for new bodies. A host of European and North American travelers have left eyewitness accounts of this gruesome turnover of corpses. One U.S. visitor described Havana's Espada Cemetery: "thousands of bones lie either in heaps or scattered over the burying grounds, exposed to the scorching rays of the sun, or bleaching in the dews of the night, resembling one vast charnel house." A visiting Protestant clergyman wrote: "The whole ground has been so often used that the surface is strewed with fragments of human bones on which you can not avoid treading at every step. . . . there formed are vast piles of human bones of every kind promiscuously heaped up & exposed to the elements and the public gaze. In the side of the open graves sculls and bones may be seen protruding from the tops of the filled graves. Limbs & sculls and [illegible] remains may be seen sticking out. The soil seems to be made of human ashes & bones."[57] Reportedly, some of the bone ashes were recycled for use in the clarification of sugarcane juice—or so believed some terrorized Chinese contract laborers. The region's poorer rural and village cemeteries, which did not have high walls like the city cemeteries did, were looted by roaming dogs, vultures, and other scavengers. This was the case even in the Ponce Cemetery, where animals reportedly entered the grounds with great ease.[58]

The case of the profanation of the remains of a white woman buried in the cemetery of Quemados exemplifies this generalized problem. Only one year after the burial, her remains were exhumed and transported to the graveyard's ossuary to make space for other bodies. According to the medical examiner's report "some [of her] bones were bare but most of the body was still covered with skin and in a state of corruption." Part of an arm was missing, and later a dog was found gnawing it while it was still inside the black sleeve of the tunic in which she had been buried.[59] In this and other cases, payment of higher burial fees would have guaranteed a longer permanence in ground graves, and even higher payments would have opened space in the niches.

To control access to consecrated burial grounds, parish priests retained the privilege to issue or deny interment licenses, without which no remains could be buried in the region's cemeteries. Laws passed in the early 1860s confirmed that priests had exclusive say over which bodies were allowed inside and which were left out.[60] From a theological perspective, church authorities justified this prerogative on the basis that among Catholics death means a passing to another stage in a soul's communion with God; therefore, their mortal remains must not be contaminated by exposure to heretics, suicides, and other non-Catholics. A seventeenth-century order by the bishop of Puerto Rico, Damián López de Haro, mandated that if this kind of contamination took place inadvertently, the remains of the infidel must be exhumed and deposited far enough away so that a person standing there could not hear the nearest church celebrate mass. During the centuries when burials were carried out inside churches, the burial of a known excommunicated person or a pagan was believed to profane the temple. By the same token, the bodies of dead Catholics were deemed sacred and had to be buried in blessed ground to assure their continuing communion within the community of the faithful.[61]

The church's representatives used the threat of burial denial as well as actual denials as coercions against irreligiosity and heterodoxy, as considerable evidence makes clear. In 1835, for example, church authorities in Puerto Rico refused to bury an executed convict in consecrated ground because he had rejected extreme unction and confession. He had to be buried outside the walls of San Juan's Cemetery by the sea. The priest of the parish of Lares, Puerto Rico, later refused to bury Antonio Andújar, a peon, because he had lived in sin with a woman and was a *borrachón* (drunkard).[62]

Even children who were not known to be baptized were denied burial in consecrated ground. Such was the case of an infant girl born to a slave named Francisca in 1858. After the priest of Ceiba Mocha refused to bury her because she had not been baptized, the slave's master, Nicolás Bello, buried the newborn a few feet outside the cemetery. A newborn boy found dead underneath a bridge in suburban Havana was ordered buried in a plot destined for non-Christians. The bodies of Havana's unbaptized slaves of all ages were routinely disposed of in the wooded suburban preserve of El Vedado.[63]

Suicides faced similar fates. Priests refused to bury Manuel Trévalo, who allegedly hanged himself from a tree in Manzanillo in 1862, and a slave named Tomás, who had hanged himself in Bejucal. The bodies of both men had to be buried in unconsecrated soil, Tomás's already decomposing because of the time taken to resolve the matter. Likewise, in Matanzas a few years earlier, a local official ordered that José Carabalí be interred on the coast in a place dubbed Playa de Judíos because he had committed suicide and was unbaptized. Similar fates awaited the slave Diego Lucumí, who hanged himself above a well in the Havana parish of Nuestra Señora de Guadalupe, and another black man, who reportedly committed suicide inside Havana's Tacón Jail.[64] Suicide among slaves was seven times more frequent than among whites, in part reflecting West African beliefs that it was a dignified route for captives of war and that spirits liberated by death returned to Africa to join their ancestors. Between 1839 and 1847, 1,337 suicides were recorded in Cuba, 1,171 of them slaves. The yearly number of slave suicides doubled during the 1850s.[65] Unbaptized Chinese contract laborers, a disturbingly high proportion of whom committed suicide, were also denied interment in consecrated ground. The rate of suicide among the Chinese was one hundred times greater than among whites. Remarkably, out of 346 incidents of suicide recorded in Cuba in 1862, 173 (50 percent) involved Chinese immigrants. Reportedly, many Chinese believed that suicide without mutilation or shedding of blood transported the spirit back to its ancestral home. Their burial conditions were as bad, if not worse, than those of the slaves.[66]

Non-Catholics or those suspected of being non-Catholics were also denied entrance to consecrated burial grounds. One French visitor to Cuba recorded an incident in which the priest of Havana's Monserrate parish allegedly refused to allow the burial of a foreigner simply because he could not translate the dead man's name into Spanish. There was another instance in Cárdenas, a Cuban coastal city with a large foreign population, in which the priest did not permit a man to be buried in the cemetery because he did not know whether the man was Catholic or not. Colonel William Crittenden and several dozen filibusterers under his and Narciso López's command were executed in August 1851 after being captured by Spanish troops; their deaths are recorded in the Catholic parish records of la Iglesia Nuestra Señora del Pilar, but they were denied burial in consecrated ground.[67] Apparently, the rule of thumb was "when in doubt, leave out." The priests' arbitrary power of decision left room for corruption, for it was widely known that some bodies that should have been left out were buried with full ceremony and pomp—and had been paid for.[68]

The church's position regarding access to cemeteries often forced state authorities to intervene to curb public scandal and threats to public health. The lieutenant governor of Cárdenas argued that it was better to have the remains of "infidels" next to the faithful than have the former next to beasts. In the case of Antonio Andújar just discussed, the local authorities of Lares deemed him a "hardworking" man and ordered him buried inside the cemetery. Appeals and discussions went on for several months until a royal order declared that the *alcalde* (mayor) of Lares had erred in his determination and that Andújar's body must be exhumed for interment outside the cemetery. In Manuel Trévalo's case, on the contrary, higher political authorities determined that his remains must be disinterred and buried inside the cemetery of Manzanillo.[69]

Hoping to put an end to leaving corpses out of the cemeteries, Puerto Rico's governor José María Marchesi issued an order in 1866 that local authorities, in accordance with priests, separate spaces within the cemeteries to be destined exclusively "for the burial of those corpses of children dying unbaptized, Protestants, and others to whom the church denies ecclesiastical burials." Cuba's Consejo de Administración raised a similar petition in 1864 to put into practice a law that had been in effect on the peninsula since 1855. State officials had given orders in 1847 that Chinese people of unknown religion be interred at El Cerro's cemetery. An 1856 order established that in Cuba the church could no longer exact burial fees from the Chinese and others who died unbaptized.[70]

Church authorities in Puerto Rico and Cuba resisted what they deemed "acts of desecration" and insisted on separate enclosures with separate entrances. Although in some cases (as in Ponce for some time) areas for Protestants were separated inside the general cemeteries, in others (as in Matanzas and Vieques) a separate enclosure with its own fence was erected next to the main burial ground.[71] In the worst cases (Havana, for example), the remains of those denied entrance to the Catholic burial grounds were conveyed to makeshift graveyards near the coast, where the bodies were exposed to the elements, scavenger animals, and other humans.[72]

Another matter that sparked much civil and ecclesiastical controversy was the granting of certificates of poverty that allowed free burials for the poor. As reflected in the parish records of the Salvador del Mundo church of El Cerro, close to one-quarter of all burials were classified as *de limosna* (charity).[73] In late 1846, the bodily remains of a man named Nicolás Ramos were abandoned at the portals of the Church of La Vereda Nueva in San Antonio because the local priest, Felipe Merlo, insisted on being paid before issuing an interment license. In view of the impasse, the alcalde ordered the decomposing body to be interred. A few months later, in another incident, the priest of Wajay, Ramón del Pino, denied Christian burial to the district captain, Pedro del Pino, whose relatives claimed they could not pay the eleven and a half pesos the priest demanded. The priest remained firm in his position not to bury the captain, a decision for which he was later reprimanded and punished by the bishop of Havana.[74] Recurrent controversies and abuses forced the state to intervene in these matters. At one point in the late 1840s, Cuba's captain-general, Federico Roncali, gave local authorities the right to issue certificates of poverty but instructed his subordinates to grant them only in cases in which the dead were really poor.[75]

These tensions continued even after the prerogative to issue poverty certifications formally went to the civil authorities.[76] On June 29, 1851, shoemaker José Hernández, of the Havana neighborhood of El Prado, lost his six-month-old son. The neighborhood's watchman denied him a poverty certification for the infant's burial on the grounds that he was an employed artisan, not an indigent. The grieving man then went to the district's commissary and the parish priest, both of whom refused to grant the certification. The latter, Hernández testified, threatened that he would let the infant's body rot unless he received seven pesos. Facing such a prospect, Hernández agreed to pay for the burial license in installments: four reales each week. By his own account, he then proceeded to the cemetery, carrying his lifeless child on his shoulders, where he faced even more monetary demands from the cemetery's administrators.[77] A few years later, a similar confrontation occurred in the town of Roque, when the parish priest and the cemetery's chaplain refused to recognize the poverty status of the Asian Ciriaco Souá. The town's mayor had no option but to order the body's interment as a matter of public order. Church authorities claimed that people such as Hernández and the surviving relatives and friends of Captain del Pino and Souá were in a position to pay for the burials and that during the year since civil officials had begun to grant the poverty certifications the church in Cuba had lost revenue amounting to 14,000 pesos.[78]

Death and burial did not necessarily signify that one's body and soul were free from the dictates and financial demands of the church. Priests, mourners, and the larger community of believers could still play a role in the soul's speedy journey through purgatory, and manifold restrictions and fees associated with the corpses' place of repose still remained. Bodies could not be moved or exhumed until a specified period of time had elapsed, unless they had been embalmed at the time of burial, a procedure that cost several hundred pesos. Embalming also required two different death certificates and special permission from the islands' highest government authority. Bodies interred with Catholic rites had to be exhumed with Catholic rites, which mandated the payment of yet more ecclesiastical fees. Sanitary certificates and payment of considerable exhumation fees were also required to authorize disinterment.[79]

In sum, colonial administrators in Cuba and Puerto Rico welcomed and supported the church's enforcement of baptismal and marriage sacraments as mechanisms of social and labor control. With regard to burial rights, however, there emerged serious and recurrent tensions between church and state as government officials sought to protect public health and avoid international controversies that could hurt commerce and affect the islands' political stability. While state authorities worked to gain more power over the sacred spaces of burial, the church insisted on retaining its prerogative. In addition to the theological implications of controlling the cemeteries, the church used this control as a way to force Catholics to comply with the other sacraments and combat religious heterodoxy. Nominal Catholics could postpone their marriages indefinitely in defiance of the church and even postpone or avoid the baptism of their children, but the moment of death possessed an urgency that required all past accounts with the church to be cleared. Many nominal Catholics who had lived adulterous lives, refusing confession, communion, and other church dictates, felt compelled to sanctify their conjugal unions if they fell ill or reached old age. Others who had failed to have their children baptized did so if they became ill in order to secure a decent burial for them. The fear of being denied a church burial was powerful enough to encourage some Protestants and other so-called heretics to abjure their faith, even if insincerely.

CHAPTER 3

Crypto-Protestants and Pseudo-Catholics

⋇⋐❦⋑⋇

$\mathcal{B}$y the first decades of the nineteenth century, immigrants from the Protestant north and the non-Hispanic Caribbean began practicing Protestantism in Cuba and Puerto Rico. Because until 1869 the religion's presence in the region was almost exclusively related to immigration, an understanding of the history of immigration in the Hispanic Caribbean is vital to any study of early Protestant activities there. Struggling in isolation to retain or hide their illegal faith, foreign Protestants were rarely visible as communities but as scattered clusters of individuals.

The varying origins and social status of these immigrants and transients influenced the distinctive characters and orientations of the Protestant clusters that first formed in Ponce, Havana, Matanzas, and Vieques. Class, for example, helps explain Protestants' various responses to official Catholic exclusivism. While some individuals pursued crypto-Protestantism (that is, maintaining a low religious profile while privately adhering to their faith), others responded as pseudo-Catholics: remaining Protestants at heart but publicly participating in the sacraments and other ceremonies of the Catholic church. Moreover, geography and demography affected where Protestants settled and thus limited their individual religious options as well as state and church response to their presence.

Beginning in the 1810s, new immigration and commercial legislation permitted thousands of non-Spanish immigrants and transients to enter the Spanish Caribbean each year, many of whom were Protestants. As discussed in chapter 2, these laws established a number of domiciliation and naturalization requirements for foreigners. Nevertheless, like most matters in the region, these laws were corruptible and applied flexibly and arbitrarily. For example, French settlers and black laborers arriving in Vieques from the British West Indies were exempt from these regulations, just as slaves and Chinese contract laborers were exempt from most immigration requirements.[1]

Through the 1870s, Cuba's and Puerto Rico's Protestant clusters developed within the rigid, tense, and conflict-filled world of Spanish colonialism, which was nonetheless building commercial ties with the rest of the world based on principles of economic liberalism. With its need for imported capital and technology, foreign markets, and foreign labor, the sugar industry was at the heart of this tension between colonial domination under Catholic Spain and economic dependence on the Protestant north. Not coincidentally, the first clusters of Protestants to emerge in the region included foreign investors and merchants associated with the sugar trade, foreign field hands and technicians for the plantations, and foreign sailing crews for import and export—all of them settling or visiting in cities and regions vital to the sugar industry. Havana and Matanzas were hubs of Cuba's nineteenth-century sugar boom. Ponce was Puerto Rico's

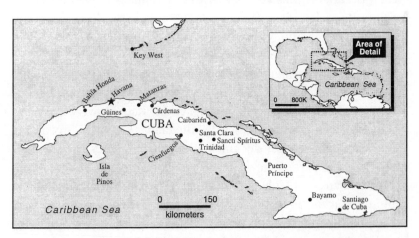

FIGURE 2. Cuba. Map by Michael Siegel, Rutgers Cartography (2000).

biggest and most successful sugar-producing jurisdiction, while Vieques, an island eight miles off the coast of Puerto Rico, experienced a dramatic surge in sugar production during the last third of the century.

Cuba's sugar revolution began in the late eighteenth century, several decades before Puerto Rico's; and by the middle of the nineteenth century, the Havana-Matanzas sugar industry was reaching its peak. Its production and trade transformed the jurisdictions of Havana and Matanzas. Their populations exploded as imported slaves, indentured Asian workers, foreign technicians, and others were incorporated into the frantic world of sugar production. Simultaneous with this population growth was the development of a rigid, hierarchical social system that combined the worst exclusionary aspects of caste and class.[2]

As Cuba's ties with the outside world increased along with the demands of the plantation complex, Protestant immigrants began to arrive in large numbers. Most settled in Havana, the island's capital and mercantile and political center, which had a population of nearly 215,000 at midcentury. A smaller number settled in the exporting coastal cities of Matanzas and Cárdenas, each with total populations of more than 60,000. According to the census of 1846, 1,256 U.S. citizens and 605 British subjects lived on the island. In Havana alone were 463 U.S. citizens and 179 Britons. Estimates in the mid-1870s for the entire island indicate close to 2,000 U.S. residents and about the same number from Germany and Britain, combined.[3]

Few foreigners from the Protestant north managed to gain ownership over Cuba's sugar estates, where Cubans remained dominant for most of the century. Instead, Havana's and Matanzas's British, North American, and German residents gravitated toward commercial, diplomatic, professional, and skilled labor activities. According to domiciliation-request documentation for the 1850s, most immigrants seeking permanent residence in Cuba were skilled or semi-skilled artisans and technical workers: U.S. mechanics, Neapolitan cauldron makers, French carpenters, and the like. Records of non-domiciled foreigners in Matanzas (1844) and U.S. citizens in Cuba (1871) indicate a majority of clerks, machinists, and carpenters but

very few property owners.[4] Another important category included seasonal and semi-permanent mechanics and engineers who served the
sugar industry. By midcentury, between 1,000 and 1,500 mechanics,
mostly from the United States and Great Britain, resided in Cuba,
many of them only during the grinding season. As a group, Havana's
foreign-born residents from the Protestant north never achieved high
rank, visibility, or social and economic power. In fact, many were
wretchedly poor. In the words of U.S. consul Charles Helm, they
were "destitute . . . broken down in health, scarcely able to walk,
without money, and unable to speak the language of the country . . .
crippled, sick, ragged, hungry, weeping."[5] Revealing their social isolation is the fact that many settled in suburban districts such as El
Cerro and El Horcón, where they tended to reside on particular
streets such as Tulipán and Buenos Aires.[6]

Although its population was one-eight the size of Havana's
(28,156 in 1860), Ponce was richer than San Juan, Puerto Rico's capital, and more intimately tied with the trade entrepôts of the Lesser
Antilles, particularly St. Thomas, and later with the ports of the
northern Atlantic.[7] Ponce experienced many of the same transformations that had accompanied the earlier sugar revolutions in Cuba and
elsewhere in the Caribbean—namely, the massive importation
of slaves, the land consolidation required by the plantations, and

FIGURE 3. Puerto Rico and neighboring islands. Map by Michael Siegel, Rutgers Cartography (2000).

growing financial and trade ties with the outside world. Its industry differed, however, because it allowed—arguably, required—the dominance of foreign immigrants.[8]

A sizable number of foreigners from the West Indies, Germany, Great Britain, and the United States immigrated to Ponce and established a solid foothold in commerce and agriculture. According to the 1838 census, 277 immigrants resided in the city; and four decades later there were 811 foreigners among Ponce's 33,514 inhabitants.[9] Foreign-born residents, many from Protestant countries, dominated the city's burgeoning agriculture industry during the first half of the nineteenth century. In 1827, 80 percent of Ponce's planters were immigrants; in 1845, 75 percent. Foreign-born merchants, who were often associated with slave trading, also dominated Ponce's sugar trade with St. Thomas and other regional entrepôts.[10] By 1870, Protestants such as José María Archebald, Thomas Davidson, William Lee, Thomas G. Salomons, James Gilbee, George Weichers, José Henna, Guillermo Oppenheimer, James Gallagher, and John Van Rhyn figured among Ponce's wealthiest planters and businessmen. According to the 1872 census of slaves, Gilbee, Salomons, Archebald, and the successors of Guillermo Oppenheimer were listed among the masters who owned the largest number of slaves.[11]

While Havana, Matanzas, Cárdenas, and other Cuban cities had a considerable proportion of U.S.-born permanent residents, few U.S. citizens lived in Puerto Rico. Compared with the 1871 register of U.S. citizens in Cuba, which includes almost 1,400 of them residing on or visiting the island, a similar register in Puerto Rico for 1870–75 lists only fifty-seven U.S. citizens.[12] Geography explains this difference in part: Cuba was much closer to the United States, only ninety miles from the Florida keys and several days nearer than Puerto Rico by ship. In contrast, Puerto Rico was closer to the Lesser Antilles. In the early 1800s, a sea journey between St. Thomas and Ponce took twenty-four hours or less; it took at least that long to travel overland between San Juan and Ponce. Moreover, Puerto Rico's commercial ties with Europe and the Caribbean's European entrepôts were stronger than its ties with the United States, which became even more evident when the island's economy oriented away from sugar and toward coffee during the last third of the nineteenth century. In 1860, the U.S. consul at San Juan reported that U.S. mercantile presence on the island was very small.[13] Interestingly, the U.S. Department of State encountered enormous difficulties when staffing its consular corps in Puerto Rico.[14]

Ponce's foreign-born elite was intricately interconnected through endogamy, compadrazgo, and business links. Because it also had family and business connections with the city's Spanish-speaking elite, this group was subject to close social scrutiny.[15] In addition to these upper-class foreigners, however, Ponce also attracted large permanent and semi-permanent migrations of black and mulatto skilled and semiskilled workers from the British, Dutch, Danish, and French West Indies. In 1838, 39 percent of Ponce's immigrants, not counting imported slaves, were black or mulatto. As immigrants, they were mostly male and single. Many of the free immigrants of color who settled in Puerto Rico from the neighboring Antilles had been brought there by white West Indian planters and entrepreneurs. Immigrant planters from depressed locations such as St. Kitts and St. Croix also imported West Indian slaves during the early decades of the century, bringing many of them illegally and even kidnapping some of them into slavery.[16]

Unlike recently imported Cuban slaves, most of these immigrants of color were Creoles who had been successfully Christianized on their home islands. While retaining African-derived modes of expression and certain religious attitudes, their Christian theology was primarily derived from Protestantism, which allowed less syncretism than did more iconic Catholicism. Because most of Puerto Rico's general population of blacks and mulattos had been born on the island (recently imported slaves constituted a very small proportion of the population), they, too, were well creolized. These factors help explain why Santería and other syncretic religions were virtually nonexistent in Puerto Rico but prevalent in Cuba, where large numbers of slaves had arrived at a time when the Catholic church was incapable of evangelizing them.

Vieques's sugar boom took off in the 1860s, four decades after Ponce's, precisely when Puerto Rico's industry had entered a prolonged crisis. The small island's historical trajectory was markedly different from those of the larger islands to the west. For centuries, Vieques had remained a frontier over which the European powers had fought for control. Beginning in the 1680s and lasting well into the 1860s, British and Danish forces had repeatedly attempted to wrest Vieques from Spain.[17]

The first successful Spanish-sanctioned effort to settle Vieques took place in 1823, more than three centuries after Columbus first claimed the island for the Spanish crown. In that year French adventurer Theófilo J.J.M. Le Guillou arrived on Vieques with two hundred French citizens and their slaves to keep it from falling into British or Danish control. In 1839, fewer than a thousand people lived and worked on Vieques, and it remained mostly covered by forest.[18]

Although Le Guillou and his fellow adventurers succeeded in settling and protecting the island from foreign encroachment, by the early 1840s Spanish officials were questioning the wisdom of having a foreigner serve as Vieques's highest authority. When Le Guillou died in 1843, colonial authorities transferred power to a Spanish subject, Francisco Saínz.[19] One mechanism used to achieve Hispanization was the establishment of a Catholic presence and infrastructure. In 1841, however, the governor of Puerto Rico reported that one of the obstacles to the effective settlement of Vieques was the lack of a church building and a cemetery: "I heard complaints to the effect that they had to cross the sea with their new born children in order to have them baptized in one of the towns [of Puerto Rico]." The governor added that he had personally heard Puerto Ricans refuse to go to Vieques for fear of being buried on the beach if they died there.[20]

During the two decades following the transfer of power to actual Spanish hands, the island underwent an enormous demographic, social, and economic transformation. While its population as a whole quadrupled between 1846 and 1866, the slave population dropped from a peak of 369 in 1845 to 159 in 1860 to only 36 in 1872 on the eve of Puerto Rico's abolition of slavery. Particularly dramatic was Vieques's growth in agricultural exports, which it achieved through large sugar-producing estates that employed imported contract laborers.[21] The industry brought in most of these contract workers from the neighboring British islands, offering meager but attractive daily salaries of 25 cents for women and 50 to 62.5 cents for men. Nevertheless, debt peonage was widely used to keep workers from freeing themselves once their contracts expired.

Like their counterparts in Ponce, most of the laborers on Vieques were Creoles, and their religious beliefs had been profoundly Europeanized. Employers reportedly preferred workers from the British Antilles to the Puerto Ricans because, as Protestants, they "only required an occasional holiday besides Sunday."[22] By 1871, some 1,175 foreigners of color worked on Vieques. This population was predominantly male and seasonal, with much higher numbers on the island during the sugar harvest than during the rest of the year. Their presence could be volatile: the *Tortoleños,* as these workers were called, staged major uprisings in 1864 and 1874.[23]

Transient foreigners increased the presence of Protestants in Cuba and, to a lesser extent, Puerto Rico. The growing trade, particularly in sugar, between the Spanish islands and the countries of the northern Atlantic meant that each year thousands of crew members, officers, and passengers from U.S., British, and other nations' vessels called in Havana, Ponce, and other Hispanic Caribbean ports. In the mid-1850s a yearly average of 883 U.S. ships with 14,682 passengers visited the port of Havana alone; three decades later the number had reached approximately 32,000. Estimates for Puerto Rico suggest that as many as 8,000 North American sailors visited the island's ports each year. Some crews remained in port for weeks or even months while their vessels were being unloaded and reloaded.[24]

Hundreds of visitors from the United States and other predominantly Protestant countries spent short periods of time in the Hispanic Caribbean each year. In 1857, the U.S. consul at Havana complained: "We have at one season of the year more [illegible] American citizens stopping here than in any other foreign nation." A later consul stated that 6,000 visitors from the United States passed through Havana during the winter and spring of 1860. Many, perhaps most, were invalids from the northern United States, who visited the islands for health reasons.[25] These health pilgrims, most suffering from consumption, were advised to avoid staying in the Caribbean during the sickly summer months and to keep away from the pestilential city of Havana and its environs. Accounts of the period abound in descriptions of these unfortunate visitors, en route to the Caribbean, sitting pale, quiet, and motionless on the decks of passenger ships, overdressed to avoid exposure to wind. Some were so weak that they had to be propped up with pillows or tied to their deck chairs. Their hollow coughs made their condition clear, as did the vanishing hope in their sad faces.[26]

Once on the islands, invalids frequented the famous San Diego baths at La Vuelta Abajo, Cuba, whose warm, sulfurous waters were credited with curing or alleviating "rheumatism, strains of muscles, tumor, syphilis, gout, catharh, bronchitis, leuchorhea, and chronic diahrreah and dysentery." Mineral baths in Coamo, Ponce, and Hato Grande in Puerto Rico were also popular destinations.[27]

Colonial and ecclesiastical authorities insisted on maintaining the fiction of religious purity even as it became clear that Protestants had established a permanent presence in Cuba and Puerto Rico and a majority in Vieques. When British officials asked if Protestants dying in Puerto Rico could have a decent burial and their property rights respected, the island's governor responded that Protestants did not live on the island and that since one had to live in order to die, Protestants could not die there.[28]

As a growing Protestant presence in the region attested, the oath of Catholicity required of all long-term visitors was an obnoxious inconvenience rather than a real obstacle to settlers. According to contemporaries, few foreigners actually took the oath, which was only mildly enforced. Moreover, the oath did not forbid short-term visitors to the Spanish islands. The domiciliation documentation of scores of immigrants from predominantly Protestant countries demonstrates that the process had many holes and no adequate system of verification. British citizen George Booth, for example, arrived in Havana in 1818 with the intention of establishing himself as a carpenter. He claimed to be Catholic but had no documentation to prove his statement. Nevertheless, he received domiciliation status anyway. Although officials accepted his claim, the odds are that he was not in fact Catholic. David Clark, another Briton, declared on his arrival in Cuba that he, too, was Catholic. Although he failed to produce evidence, he found three witnesses who had heard him say that he was Catholic. Their testimony sufficed. In 1841, a Philadelphia merchant surnamed Beylle was certified as Catholic by a witness who claimed to have seen him participating in Catholic religious activities.[29] Yet despite these examples, immigrants continued to produce baptismal certificates and other documents proving Catholicity—perhaps, however, only those who actually could do so.

Some foreigners who took the religious oath in the presence of Spanish officials quibbled by omitting the word "Roman," thus accepting allegiance to a more unspecific and inclusive apostolic Catholic church. (Protestants may view themselves as apostolic and even as universal Catholics but not as Roman Catholics.) Others signed documents swearing adherence to the "C A R church," which could have stood for *Católica, apostólica, y reformada* (Catholic, apostolic, and reformed). George C. Backhouse, a British official stationed in Havana, reported that these kinds of omissions and substitutions were common, satisfying both Spanish officials and "the consciences of Protestant Foreigners who take the oath." Some foreigners circumvented the matter altogether by hiring agents to handle their domiciliation procedures. Still others avoided presenting actual proof of Catholicity by paying a fee or purchasing a certificate either on the islands or abroad.[30] Nevertheless, the requirement remained a source of humiliation for Protestants; and Spanish officials could use it to harass or punish them, forcing many to lie, quibble, or falsify documents. For some foreigners the oath was reason enough to shorten their stay on the islands. One visitor to Cuba wrote that before taking the oath "I shall demand my passport, shake the dust from my feet, and leave this natural Eden to its serpent."[31]

All foreign non-Catholics, even those just passing through the region, were vulnerable to the accusation of heterodoxy. Even when they had proven their Catholicity, visitors from predominantly Protestant nations were viewed as suspect and could become the targets of harassment and discrimination.[32] For instance, George Coggeshall, a U.S. merchant who visited Puerto Rico in 1816–17, was advised to attend Sunday mass so that he could go on with his business during the rest of the week without being ostracized as a heretic. The value of the advice was proven a few days later, when Coggeshall had an argument with a man who was delivering a ship's cargo—"a ferocious, savage-looking mullatto fellow." Foaming at the mouth, the man drew a large knife and pressed it against Coggeshall's chest, threatening that "there was no more harm in killing a vile heretic like [Coggeshall] than in killing a dog."[33] When in 1853 Spanish officials sought to deprive British subject George B. Mathews of his properties in Vieques, they made use of the Catholicity requirement to keep him from returning to the island. Close to the same time, Spanish authorities also expelled several British subjects who were living in Cuba but were not willing to become naturalized Spanish citizens.[34] Although the British government responded by calling for an end to the "obnoxious regulation" of the Catholicity oath, it failed to achieve any changes.[35]

Most Protestants in the Spanish Caribbean, whether long- or short-term visitors, attended the islands' Catholic places of worship during the first days of their stay.[36] In some instances, their church attendance was a strategy to avoid suspicion of non-Catholicity, which could be detrimental to their business interests.[37] They were generally dissatisfied by what they encountered inside the churches, particularly the graven images that lined the interiors. Several visitors commented on the tawdry nature of the ornamentation, remarking that the altars looked more like toy shops than anything else. Some compared mass to a theatrical or operatic performance: "the splendid robes of the officiating priest, changed in the course of the service like the costume of actors in a drama; the music, to Protestant ears operatic and exciting; the clouds of incense scattering their intoxicating perfumes; the chanting in strange tongue, unknown to the majority of the worshipers,—all tend to give the Roman Catholic service a carnival character."[38] In addition to disliking these externalities, Protestants disagreed with several theological principles of the Catholic faith, among them the practice of confession, belief in purgatory and the pope's infallibility, and the sale of indulgences to grant freedom from unpopular church demands.[39]

During the first three-quarters of the nineteenth century, Protestants in Cuba and Puerto Rico were unable to practice their faith openly and, for the most part, remained alienated from Protestant services and holy ceremonies. As travelogues and diaries attest, however, many foreigners held private Sunday services either in their own homes or quietly in hotel rooms.[40] Both English and U.S. prayer books included the offices of matins and evensong, which nonordained individuals could lead in private services. According to the diaries of George C. Backhouse and his wife, Grace Backhouse, the family held one or two services almost every Sunday during their sojourn in Havana in the mid-1850s, which included the reading of scriptures, prayers, and sermons. After exploring other options, their contemporary Julia Woodruff, a Protestant from the United States, concluded that the best choice was "a quiet reading of our own helpful and satisfying Liturgy, in my own room."[41] Episcopalian bishops Milo Mahan of Baltimore and Henry B. Whipple of Minnesota visited Havana on separate occasions (1868 and 1871) and officiated in services on board ships, in hotel rooms, and in consular offices.[42] In Puerto Rico's western municipality of Aguadilla, a group of Protestants gathered for home services and Bible readings in the early 1860s. Eduardo Heiliger, a merchant from St. Thomas who became a planter in Puerto Rico, and José Antonio Badillo, a merchant from Aguadilla, are credited with forming *los Bíblicos,* as this group came to be known.[43] Such Bible reading, in fact, was a practice that characterized Protestants, in contrast with the region's Catholics, who had virtually no direct access to the scriptures.

Occasionally, British naval vessels offered Church of England services or their U.S.counterparts held Episcopalian, Methodist, Baptist, or other Protestant denominations' services. Members of the local foreign population were welcomed to these events and sometimes treated to after-service lunches. Although the ship's captain usually officiated, an ordained chaplain who could perform sacramental ceremonies might also be present.[44] At other times naval chaplains and other visiting clergymen ventured ashore to officiate clandestinely at holy services, baptisms, and marriages, usually at the British, German, or U.S. consulate. Such visits were rare, however, and only benefited those connected to the consular circle; and one Episcopalian bishop who visited Cuba in 1871 reported that many Protestants had not received communion in more than twelve years.[45]

Protestant parents faced enormous difficulties and delays in securing their children's baptism. Those with greater social and actual capital, whose actions were closely monitored by members of the Spanish and Creole elite, tended to have their children baptized in the Catholic church, which was canonically acceptable to Anglicans and other Protestants who recognized Catholic sacraments. By so doing these parents also secured their children's inheritance rights. Many foreign-born Protestants of the Ponce elite and some of Havana's long-term resident foreigners fell into this category. For example, the parish books of Ponce's Catholic church show that the Davidsons, Salomons, Oppenheimers, Van Rhyns, Penders, Lions, Dodds, Finlays, Eckelmans, Weichers, and other Protestant families who passed for Catholics had their newborn children baptized as Roman Catholics.[46] Baptizing their children as Protestant would have been not only illegal but socially unacceptable—scandalous in the eyes of the upper-class Catholics with whom they mingled.

Some adult Protestants were baptized as Catholics after publicly renouncing their faith. This was the case, for example, of the Irishman John Nott, who in 1840 requested Catholic baptism from the bishop of Puerto Rico. Similarly, Londoner Robert McPherson declared that, although he had been a Calvinist since childhood, he had since concluded that the Catholic church "was the only one where man can find eternal happiness." In 1870, Charles Basanta, the son of Ponce's British vice-consul, abjured Protestantism and was baptized as a Catholic as precondition for his Catholic marriage to Hortensia Mirailh. In the 1850s, María Luisa Iraste and Emilia Bloisant were also baptized as Catholics—both of them adult, foreign-born Protestants living in the Havana suburb of El Cerro. And in order to remain in Puerto Rico, the forty-year-old Dutch Jew Diego Pardo renounced his faith and converted to Catholicism.[47]

Protestants with less social capital were less vulnerable to social pressures and thus could wait for a visiting clergyman or refuse to baptize their children at all. Protestants who believed in the practice of adult baptism felt no urgency about the matter at all. This was particularly true among the somewhat socially aloof Protestants of Havana, who seemed to care little about what Catholics thought. When Grace Backhouse asked Fanny Runge, the Lutheran sister of the wife of the British consul-general in Havana, whether she intended to baptize her child, Mrs. Runge replied that she "had not thought about it." A few years later an Episcopalian priest reported that there were many unbaptized children among Havana's Protestants but their parents remained "indifferent about the matter."[48] The parish books of the Iglesia Salvador del Mundo of El Cerro include virtually no entries with names from predominantly Protestant countries, and there were few Catholic baptisms among Protestant West Indian laborers settled in Vieques. Only a handful of Anglo names appears in the baptismal books of the Vieques parish during the 1850s and 1860s.[49]

The other option for crypto-Protestants was to have their children illegally baptized by a Protestant minister passing through the region. Such visits, however, were short and infrequent. Coincidentally, just three days after the birth of George and Grace Backhouse's child in October 1853, the British man-of-war *Vestal* called in the port of Havana with an Anglican chaplain on board. Reverend Henry Parminster came ashore on Sunday, October 30, to conduct a special service at the British consulate-general, where he christened eight children of various ages. He then proceeded to the Backhouse home, where he baptized the five-day-old Backhouse infant following the Book of Common Prayer's prescribed ceremonies for private baptisms. For the birth of their next child, Grace Backhouse went home to England, where she made sure the infant had an adequate and prompt baptism.[50] A few years later, another visiting Protestant clergyman baptized several Havana children and baptized and confirmed a dying Confederate veteran.[51] Occasionally, Ponce residents took their children to St. Thomas to have them baptized with Protestant rites; and at least one family, the Lees, traveled to St. Croix to ensure that their child was born outside of Roman Catholic Puerto Rico. Their three previous children had died unbaptized in Ponce.[52]

As discussed earlier, the sacrament of holy matrimony posed even greater difficulties and challenges. Unlike baptisms, which Catholic priests did not deny to any child, church marriages were reserved exclusively for communicants of the Roman Catholic church. In Puerto Rico, parish priests received strict instructions about brides and grooms from Protestant countries: no marriage could be performed until the bishop or his provisor could first verify their claimed Catholicity. Unlike natives, foreigners were also required to acquire expensive and time-consuming Catholicity and soltería certificates.[53]

As with baptisms, the foreign Protestants of Ponce were more likely than other Protestants to comply with the social and religious mandates of Catholic matrimony. The sons and daughters of several of Ponce's pseudo-Catholic families were married under the auspices of the Roman Catholic church.[54] These Protestants even complied with the required prenuptial confession, which must have been odious to many. A number made false declarations and even falsified documents to prove their Catholicity, finding witnesses (many of them also Protestant) to lie on their behalf. A small group of pseudo-Catholics regularly served as witnesses in most of these cases. In one instance, Protestant groom George F. Weichers claimed that he was Catholic but was unable to prove his statement because he had no baptismal certificate. He said he could not get one because his far-away birthplace, Vienna, had no communications with Puerto Rico. Actually a native of Hamburg, Weichers got by with the testimony of Bernardo Eckelman, himself a pseudo-Catholic. In another case, Charles Basanta apparently could not pretend or document that he was born a Catholic, so he converted publicly to Catholicism before marrying Hortensia Mirailh, a pseudo-Catholic herself.[55] For these upper-class families, neither concubinage nor a public embrace of Protestantism was an option. Their high propensity to marry as Catholics reflected in part the critical importance of marriage as a vehicle to secure upward social mobility, whether with foreign-born women or women of the native elite. In contrast, among Vieques's Protestant laboring poor, there were virtually no Catholic marriages; cohabitation was an acceptable option to the working poor of all races and religions. Nevertheless, even some upper-class Protestants balked at Catholic marriage. Eduardo Heiliger, the white St. Thomas–born planter who organized Aguadilla's Protestants, had several illegitimate children and never married despite his high economic standing. Ironically, he served on the local Junta de Vagos y Amancebados.[56]

In Havana and Matanzas, foreign Protestants generally had less social rank than those in Ponce, were less immersed in local society, and were far less concerned about social appearances. Therefore, they felt less compelled to marry as Catholics. Pseudo-Catholicism was also less prevalent in these cities than in smaller Ponce, where Protestants found it harder to pass unnoticed. Havana's crypto-Protestant couples were more likely to live in concubinage, which was reportedly widespread among the British and the North Americans. Nevertheless, there were a few exceptions to this practice. In El Cerro's Salvador del Mundo parish, Carolina Smith of New York State renounced her Methodist faith and was baptized with Catholic rites in 1862 as a precondition to her Catholic marriage to Francisco Javier Molina y García, a member of a local wealthy family. They had been previously married in New York by a Methodist minister but felt compelled to remarry as Catholics to legitimate their children "as prescribed by the wise laws of the Catholic Spanish government." There is some indication that at one point the British consul-general at Havana solemnized wedding ceremonies, but they were legally as well as socially and canonically worthless in the Spanish colonies.[57] Earlier in the century one Protestant's Catholic marriage had an interesting twist. A Swiss woman named Enriqueta Faber Caven passed for a man so that she could practice medicine in Baracoa, Cuba. Changing her name to Enrique, Dr. Faber converted to Catholicism and was married on August 11, 1819, to one of her patients, Juana de León. The marriage collapsed a few years later, and Juana pressed criminal charges against Dr. Faber. The doctor ended up in jail and was later banished from the island.[58]

Protestants who rejected or were denied Catholic matrimony but still considered it a sin to live together out of wedlock could either wait for a visiting clergyman or travel to the United States or another Caribbean island where marriage vows could be sanctified with fewer complications and expenses. At least four couples from Puerto Rico traveled to St. Thomas in 1855 to be married at the All Saints Anglican church: Anglican British vice-consul Charles Linde-gren and Roman Catholic Rafaela Gautier; planter John Henry Van Rhyn and Grace Louisa Basanta, both Anglicans; Anglican planter Isaac Easton Bedlow and Lucy Dupont Penchoen (religion unknown); and Roman Catholic merchant Manuel Antonio Toro and Anglican Evelina Basanta. Toro and Basanta had married previously with Catholic rites in Puerto Rico. A few years later, the marriage of Evelina's sister, Josephine, to Thomas Edward Lee was solemnized by the Anglican bishop of Antigua during a visit to Ponce. Report-edly, it was "naturally a quiet social event."[59]

Traveling to St. Thomas or New Orleans to be married was also an option for Catholics who faced consanguinity or other obstacles in Cuba or Puerto Rico. According to Cuban jurist José Ignacio Rodríguez, Cubans often went to New Orleans to be married, a prac-tice noted as "frequent" and "natural." Dispensations were reportedly cheaper and granted more expediently in New Orleans and St. Thomas. Among others, Luis Bonafoux and Clemencia Quintero of Guayama and Mr. Valton and Miss Quilmin of the French West Indies but residing in Vieques traveled to St. Thomas to get married. In the latter case, the Vieques parish priest had not been positively convinced that Valton was a widower. The register of marriages of the Dutch Reformed church of Christiansted, St. Croix, includes entries for several weddings between residents of Puerto Rico, some of whom were Catholic.[60] Church and state authorities could, and in some instances did, nullify marriages performed outside the bride's and groom's place of residence, which were considered illegal. Such couples could lose the right to inherit their deceased spouses' prop-erty, and their children could be deemed illegitimate. Later in the cen-tury, parish priests in Cuba were instructed to facilitate dispensations "even in the higher degrees" of consanguinity to avoid the risk that contractors would seek marriage from a non-Catholic minister.[61]

The Caribbean's notoriously unhealthy climate, especially during the summer months, made the issue of funeral and burial rights particularly critical to unacclimated foreigners, many of whom were from predominantly Protestant countries. Foreign visitors and travelers were especially vulnerable to tropical diseases. Dubbed one of the "foulest" ports in the world, Havana saw more than one-quarter of unacclimated foreigners die shortly after their arrival. A contemporary blamed the city's unhealthiness on the fortifications that obstructed the free circulation of air currents, creating "a stagnant cloud of fetid vapour, exhaled from a crowded population and the marshy shores of the harbour." The same observer concluded that no other place in the Caribbean was "so replete with the seeds of mortality as the *Havana*." Puerto Rico's principal ports were somewhat healthier but still a concern to foreigners, many of whom would die there. According to U.S. consul Charles De Ronceray, San Juan had an "unhealthy climate, where a man's life is in danger."[62]

Yellow fever was responsible for the bulk of deaths among unacclimated foreigners in Cuba and Puerto Rico. Records dating to 1857 indicate that almost all seamen dying on board U.S. vessels succumbed to yellow fever, as did most sailors hospitalized in Havana's clinics. Burial records and other sources from Ponce show that among the resident foreign population yellow fever was also a leading cause of death, following close behind heart disease.[63]

Although the death of ailing Protestant immigrants and visitors ended their sufferings, it also marked the beginning of a sad, difficult, and frustrating period for relatives, friends, concerned compatriots, and consular representatives. Their view of the body after death may not have been influenced by Catholic theological principles concerning continued communion of the physical remains as well as the soul, but Protestants nevertheless wanted the remains of their loved ones to receive decent and dignified burial. But survivors of non-Catholics encountered numerous obstacles. As one U.S. official stationed in Havana bluntly advised his compatriots, "don't die in Cuba." In the words of another observer, "all that accompanies death . . . in Cuba is particularly repulsive."[64]

Thus, Protestant visitors and immigrants were extremely concerned about the possibility of dying in the Catholic islands. This was a particular preoccupation of invalids and ill seamen. As U.S. Consul Blythe wrote, "the knowledge on the part of a sick person that his remains will be uncared for is calculated to produce a morbid effect upon the mind unfavorable to his recovery."[65] Some foreigners wrote testaments leaving specific instructions with friends and consuls about actions to be taken in the event of death. One U.S. visitor, after returning from a sobering tour of Havana's Espada Cemetery, told his hotel's attendant that if he were to die on the island, he must be buried at sea. "Anywhere," he added emphatically, "but in a Catholic country." Another visitor, a New Yorker suffering from consumption, was horrified by thought of dying in Cuba. His only wish was that the steamer *Cahawba* would arrive on time so he could die on board rather than on the island.[66] A few years earlier, Francis Harrison, the U.S. consular agent in neighboring Santo Domingo, requested that in the event of his death his corpse be packed in a barrel of rum and shipped to his hometown, Philadelphia, for an appropriate burial.[67]

Protestants wishing to get married or have their children christened within their faith could go on with their lives while they waited for a visiting clergyman or until they traveled abroad. Dead Protestants and their survivors could do neither.[68] The Catholic church held a monopoly over funeral ceremonies and controlled access to the region's cemeteries: "She owns the cemeteries practically, is interested in the sale of coffins and management of hearses, buries the dead, licenses the inhuming and exhuming of all bodies."[69] Often foreign Protestants were denied access to the region's cemeteries unless their surviving friends and relatives could produce evidence of their Catholicity. Not even the most prominent members of the foreign consular corps could claim exemption from these requirements. In Santiago de Cuba the body of British Consul Parsons was barred from the city's consecrated burial grounds because he was not Catholic. The remains of James Gallagher, his U.S. counterpart in Ponce, almost suffered a similar fate, but at the eleventh hour a document was found—or fabricated—attesting to his Catholicity. The reluctant priest then carried out the complete ceremonies: "solemn double services, with chanted vigil and accompaniment to cemetery" of the body of the sixty-year-old Philadelphian.[70]

Crypto-Protestants and nominal Catholics who either avoided Catholic scraments or received Protestant rites were well aware of this situation; and not surprisingly, many were either converted to or returned to the Catholic faith during their last days. In 1803, María Condón, a Lutheran from New York who resided in Puerto Rico, converted to Catholicism just before her death and received absolution from her sins of heresy. Years later Abraham Nicolas Souquin, a Swiss agriculturalist who had settled in Puerto Rico, faced the disturbing prospect of dying outside the communion of the colony's official religion. He then abjured his Protestant faith and converted to Catholicism before dying in San Juan's military hospital.[71] In El Cerro's Salvador del Mundo parish, a dying woman named Enriqueta Winch y Shepherd abjured Unitarianism in 1863 and received Catholic baptism from a Jesuit priest, who immediately administered extreme unction. A few years later, while awaiting execution, the Cuban Protestant revolutionary Luis Ayestarán y Moliner reluctantly reembraced the religion into which he had been born.[72] On her death bed, Tomasa Hernández of Ponce requested absolution for the sin of having been married by an Anglican clergyman. She and her husband, Jaime Roura, attested that they were carrying a "great weight on their consciences and that they felt disturbed." They justified their actions on the grounds that the certificate of soltería required by the Catholic priest was expensive beyond their means.[73] As documented in the Ponce and El Cerro parish records, dozens of Catholics living in concubinage sought to solemnize their vows shortly before their deaths. A Catholic priest later in the century said, "Even the free thinkers themselves, when they are going to die, call for the priest." The prospect of being denied a Catholic burial was certainly at the crux of many of these decisions.[74]

Evidence also suggests that before the 1870s many Protestants died as they had lived—as pseudo-Catholics—and were buried with the rites of the Catholic church. Ponce's Salomons family, for example, who later hosted the island's first public Protestant service, owned a splendid mausoleum in Ponce's Catholic cemetery. The Van Rhyns, Basantas, Mirailhs, and most other Ponce Protestant families buried their dead as Catholics in the Catholic burial ground. According to an 1849 report by the capitán pedáneo of the jurisdiction of Havana's Espada Cemetery, most Protestants were buried in Catholic grounds "under the false assurance of Catholicity." Known Protestants had funeral ceremonies at home or sometimes at their consulates, where extraterritoriality allowed for some violation of Catholic exclusivism.[75]

Most Protestants dying in Cuba and Puerto Rico who could not pass for Catholics were buried in desolate potter's fields.[76] One was located close to the shore, not far from the Espada Cemetery. Established in the early 1810s, it came under the charge of a British hotel-keeper named Francis Nichols in the mid-1820s. Reportedly, he charged between ten and fifty pesos for a burial. After Nichols's death, James Tomson (or Thompson) took charge of the graveyard; but after his death it soon fell into disrepair, the gate keys were lost, and part of the walls collapsed. Scavenger animals roamed the ruined "Americans'" graveyard, where they feasted on rotting human remains. During the early 1840s, a yearly average of forty corpses, including foreign Protestants, suicides, and the unbaptized, were buried in Havana's so-called American or English cemetery.[77] In the 1840s, Dr. Charles Belot, who served mostly sailors and foreigners, established a burial ground in Regla not far from his clinic.[78]

Several contemporaries produced revolting accounts of these potter's fields. The British consul-general David Turnbull raised a cry of outrage in the early 1840s concerning the state of Protestant burial sites. He wrote a passionate letter to Cuba's captain-general underscoring "the horrors which prevail at the place known at the Havana by the name of 'the American burial ground,' where dead bodies are left exposed in the face of day, and where the vulture contends with the worm for his share of the human spoil."[79] Other reports confirmed the decaying state of Havana's Protestant graveyard and the fact that vultures and other beasts profaned the bodies. A later traveler described "the ground strewn with the bleaching relics of mortality, and in some corner is a heap, mostly of skulls, several yards high."[80] There was another Protestants' burial ground in Matanzas and also within the city's jurisdiction a burial ground for non-Catholics in the area known as Playa de Judíos. An 1841 report described it as being in a state of abandonment, with a broken gate and its dead "barely buried."[81]

Neighboring Puerto Rico, which had fewer foreign Protestants, many of whom passed for Catholics, possessed no Protestants' burial ground as such but used locations close to the coast or off shore, where the bodies of Protestants and other non-Catholics were cast without ceremony or mark. According to the U.S. consul at San Juan, "the burying place is often profaned by filthy animals roaming there in the night or in the second case left exposed to the open air and often washed away by the beating of the sea." Some foreign Protestants were not even allowed burial on the island. In January 1817, two foreign Protestants, James Coggeshall and his ship's mate, died of fever. According to James's surviving brother, Charles, ecclesiastical burial was out of the question, so he had to take care of the entire matter:

> We accordingly had a coffin made on board, and on the following day in the afternoon, with our own crew took the body to a small uninhabited island, about two miles from the main land of Porto Rico [probably Cayo Cardona], and interred the remains of this worthy, brave and ingenuous young man. To prevent them from being disturbed or desecrated, I left no trace of a grave, but levelled the ground so that the spot where his remains repose, should not attract the idle curiosity of those who should hereafter visit this lonely island; AND HERE MAY HIS ASHES REST IN PEACE.[82]

More than half a century later, Wilbert M. Clifford, a twenty-nine-year-old North Carolinian, died of yellow fever in Ponce during the summer of 1871. Local ecclesiastic and civil authorities would not allow his remains to be buried anywhere on the island but ordered them to be interred on the neighboring islet of Cardona, which had housed a lepers' colony since 1836.[83]

In sharp contrast, in Vieques as early as 1845, Protestants from the Lesser Antilles were granted funeral rights by the island's governor. Because foreign labor immigration was deemed essential to the population and development of the frontier island, its civil authorities exhibited greater religious tolerance than did the larger islands of Cuba and Puerto Rico.[84]

For some Protestants, particularly but not exclusively seamen, burial at sea was a more dignified option than burial anywhere on shore. On his arrival in Havana, Consul-General Turnbull stated that rather than send the remains of a loved one to a potter's field, he would prefer to "consign them to the bosom of the deep." According to a U.S. woman who witnessed a sea burial off Cuba's shore, the cadaver was wrapped in tarred sailcloth and dropped overboard to the words, "We commit this body to the deep."[85]

Another option was embalming the dead for shipment and burial abroad. Both church and state, however, threw multiple obstacles in the way of this practice. Ecclesiastical authorities demanded that special exhumation ceremonies be carried out, and the state required the issuing of special licenses from the islands' highest civil authorities. It was also an expensive option. In Cuba in 1828, the remains of Lieutenant Allen were exhumed at a cost of six ounces (one hundred U.S. dollars) for shipment to the United States. Four decades later the U.S. consul at San Juan reported that it would cost nearly eighty dollars to disinter the remains of Dr. Henry Bryant of the Smithsonian Institution, who died in Arecibo. Embalming could cost as much as five hundred pesos.[86]

In sum, much to the chagrin of the region's state and church authorities, Protestants found their way into Cuba and Puerto Rico by the first decades of the nineteenth century. Unable to worship freely, they lived as either crypto-Protestants or pseudo-Catholics. In either case, opportunities for living and dying as practicing Protestants were almost nonexistent. Demography, geographic setting, and social structure and class had much to do with religious behavior and the extent to which society and church and state authorities could enforce religious orthodoxy. In Ponce, where white, foreign Protestants had assumed economic power, the group as a whole felt compelled to live as pseudo-Catholics. A strong and vigilant Catholic church presence and other social pressures further discouraged Ponce's Protestants from openly declaring their faith. The opposite was true in Vieques, a frontier island where both church and state were relatively weak. Foreign laborers of color from neighboring British islands arrived in large numbers, and no great fuss was raised about their Protestant affiliation and activities. The experiences of Havana's and Matanzas's foreign Protestants stood somewhere in between: these Protestants were neither as rich and visible as their counterparts in Ponce nor as poor and marginal as Vieques's. The larger, more urban context of Havana made their presence less threatening than in Ponce and therefore less of a target to church and state.

Five and a half decades lay between the opening of the Spanish colonies to foreign, non-Spanish immigration and the 1869 declaration of religious tolerance. These years exposed the inherent tensions of a colonial system in transition, one seeking to hold on to old exclusivist restrictions while opening the islands to trade with the Protestant north. Yet despite the fact that their presence was illegal, the early Protestant populations of Ponce, Havana, Matanzas, and Vieques laid the foundations for the types of congregations that would eventually form in the 1870s and 1880s.

PART II

The Revolutionary Cycle, 1868–1898

CHAPTER 4

War and Religion

In the autumn of 1868, three sepa-
rate revolutionary upheavals erupted within the Spanish empire: one
on the peninsula, one in Cuba, and one in Puerto Rico. In Spain, progressive elements led by Juan Prim, Francisco Serrano, Domingo
Dulce, and other statesmen knowledgeable about and sympathetic to
the colonies brought down Isabella II's degenerating Bourbon monarchy, which had been characterized by ineptness, corruption, and
growing conservatism. The result was a temporary cooling of state
relations with the Vatican and the Spanish clergy, relations that had
become closer and more cooperative during the 1850s and 1860s.

Within days of the uprising in Spain, patriots in Lares, Puerto
Rico, and Yara, Cuba, rose in arms against the colonial authorities.
Although Spanish forces immediately crushed Puerto Rico's insurgents, the rebellion in Cuba expanded into a bloody conflict known
as the Ten Years' War that forced thousands of exiled Cubans into
emigré enclaves in Key West, Tampa, New York, Philadelphia,
Jamaica, and the Dominican Republic, among other places. In 1895,
after a period of peace, Cuban patriots again revolted against Spanish colonialism; and again tens of thousands of Cubans sought exile
abroad. During the thirty-year cycle of separatist war, the struggle for
religious tolerance intensified, becoming enmeshed with broader
political struggles as well as the growing influence of Protestantism
both in the region and among Cuban exiles in the United States.

Meanwhile, as a result of war, exile, and ill-conceived peace, new political and religious alliances formed and dissolved throughout the period.

During the provisional Spanish revolutionary government (1868–70), the constitutional monarchy of King Amadeo I (1871–73), and the first Spanish republic (1873–74), Spain's progressives enacted many religious tolerance and anticlerical decrees as well as numerous measures limiting or eliminating the traditional powers and prerogatives of the Catholic church. For example, the new governments revoked several articles of the Concordat of 1851. Religious organizations were disbanded, some churches and convents demolished, and the clergy's stipends slashed in half. The church also lost considerable power over education, marriages, and cemeteries. Beginning in 1870, not only were civil marriages established on the peninsula, but the state declared church-only matrimonies invalid and the children born of these unions illegitimate. The clergy responded by declaring that civil-only matrimonies were equivalent to concubinage.[1]

According to title 1, article 21, of the short-lived revolutionary constitution of 1869, Catholicism continued as the state church, but freedom of public and private non-Catholic worship was guaranteed to all foreigners and Spaniards residing in Spain. This was a radical departure from the constitutions of 1812 and 1837, which had not touched the religious monopoly of the church. Under these new protections, several dozen Protestant congregations formed on the peninsula.[2] Although the new constitution did not apply automatically to the colonies, subsequent legislation extended some of these provisions to all inhabitants of Spain and its overseas empire.[3] In 1870, more moderate revolutionaries seeking to stabilize the government established a constitutional monarchy, recruiting the Italian prince Amadeo of Savoy. His reign, however, was short-lived. Immediately after his abdication in February 1873, the Spanish Cortes established a republican government under the more radical leaders who by June 1872 had gained control in the legislature. But this government also collapsed, yielding less than two years later to the Bourbon Alfonso XII, Isabella II's son—and godson of the pope himself.

Not surprisingly, the bulk of the Spanish clergy applauded the return of the Bourbons; only about 2,000 of Spain's nearly 40,000 clerics had favored the revolutionary governments of 1868–74. The restoration legislation and the new conservative constitution of 1876 reversed most of the anticlerical measures of those governments and placed many limitations on the religious toleration measures enacted by the progressives. During the first years of the restoration, properties as well as powers were returned to the Catholic church. A royal decree dated February 9, 1875, terminated the option of civil matrimony. Non-Catholic worship and ceremonies were now restricted to the interior of consulates and private homes and to other buildings without posters or exterior signs. Protestants could not hold any public activities outdoors, and bell ringing in non-Catholic churches was outlawed.[4]

Nevertheless, the situation in the Spanish colonies of the Caribbean cannot be judged on the basis of what took place on the peninsula. By this time, the islands had developed political lives of their own; and laws passed in Spain were not always applicable to or enacted in the Caribbean, where distance, special legislation, and tradition gave colonial rulers a large extent of discretionary power. Although the intentions of the Spanish revolutionaries were clear regarding religious tolerance and other reforms, the colonial situation remained uncertain and unpredictable, particularly in Cuba, where patriots were staging a full-scale armed struggle against colonialism. Thus, while the revolution on the peninsula did reverberate in the territories, it was delayed and misdirected by colonialism, slavery, and the proximity of the powerful, expansionist United States.

In both Cuba and Puerto Rico, authorities rejected the radical changes taking place in Spain. Francisco Lersundi, who governed Cuba at the outbreak of the Ten Years' War, refused to recognize the revolutionaries, remaining loyal to the deposed queen until he was finally recalled in January 1869. Likewise, Puerto Rico's governor José Laureano Sanz was unenthusiastic about reforms and slow in implementing them.[5] When liberals finally arrived in the colonies with orders to enact reforms, they faced not only a large-scale insurrection in Cuba but virulent opposition from ultra-conservative, pro-Spanish forces, who resisted even slight social or political reform. The liberal Domingo Dulce, who governed Cuba briefly in 1869, faced the daunting task of dealing with both factions—a challenge he could not meet. Blocking his reforms, radical pro-Spanish elements forced him to leave the island within a few months of his arrival. In Puerto Rico, governors Gabriel Baldrich and Simón de la Torre faced similar opposition from conservatives, who blocked the extension of the 1869 constitution to the island.[6] Cuba's patriots also rejected the reforms as too little, too late and continued fighting to end Spanish rule. By the end of 1874, restoration governors ruled over Cuba and Puerto Rico, pandering to conservatives but failing to curb the terrorism of loyal extremists. As a result, recalcitrant colonialists were pitted against intransigent revolutionaries. Predictably, the Catholic church gravitated to the pro-Spanish conservatives, while most anticlericals and Protestants sympathized—or openly sided—with the Cuban cause.

Amid the confusions of 1868–74, reforms and laws guaranteeing religious tolerance and freedom of worship faced an uncertain future in the colonies. In Cuba, even progressive rulers such as Dulce were unable to implement Madrid's radical reforms; and his successors, Antonio Caballero de Rodas and the Count of Valmaseda, refused to act on them at all because of the ongoing revolt. In quieter Puerto Rico, colonial authorities also postponed the publication and implementation of abolitionist and other reform measures that conservatives opposed. Officials could not even adequately answer a U.S. consul's question about whether or not civil marriage had been extended to the island.[7]

On October 19, 1869, Puerto Rico's Governor Sanz reluctantly published in *La Gaceta de Puerto Rico* the revolutionary decree of September 23, 1869, which established in its first article that "all the inhabitants of the Spanish Antilles are guaranteed the public and private exercise of religious worship without any other restriction than the universal rules prescribed by morality and law."[8] In 1873, the new progressive governor, Rafael Primo de Rivera, put the 1869 constitution, including its religious tolerance decrees, into effect. When

Sanz returned to power in 1874, however, he almost immediately revoked those orders and severely restricted non-Catholic religious activities, claiming that the people's lack of education and their racial diversity left them unprepared for such freedoms.[9] The 1874 appointment of archconservative Juan Antonio Puig y Monserrat to head Puerto Rico's bishopric dealt yet another blow to religious tolerance on the island.

In Cuba, where the political circumstances were much graver, the tolerance decrees faced much the same fate as decrees concerning partial abolition of slavery: they were either not published or not implemented. When in 1871 the U.S. consul at Havana asked state officials about the possibility of establishing a Protestant place of worship, authorities said that Madrid had not sent any instructions about religious tolerance, although in fact a decree dated October 23, 1869, had established freedom of worship in Cuba.[10] Nevertheless, despite confusions and delays, the new provisions for religious tolerance permitted the first legal, organized Protestant communities to emerge in Ponce, Havana, Matanzas, and Vieques in the late 1860s and early 1870s. As we will discuss in more detail in subsequent chapters, each congregation varied in time of formation, social origins of members, and connections with political struggles and emigré communities.

In response to the legalization of Protestant presence and public worship, anti-Protestantism, particularly among Spanish-born clerics, became even more energetic and vociferous by the late 1860s. In Puerto Rico, Ponce parish priest José Balbino David and Bishop Puig y Monserrat tried to obstruct the organization of the island's first Protestant congregation and then limit the extent of its activities. The colonies' three highest prelates—the bishops of Havana, Santiago, and Puerto Rico—wrote a joint letter to King Alfonso XII in 1876 demanding the restoration of religious unity in both the colonies and Spain to avoid the spread of heresies and the "venom of error." Havana's bishop denounced Protestant churches as "sinful sects." A few years later the archbishop of Santiago issued a pastoral letter in which he condemned Protestantism as one of the three major threats to the true faith, the others being Freemasonry and spiritualism.[11]

FIGURE 4. Spanish soldiers attending Roman Catholic mass during the Cuban War of Independence. From F. Tennyson Neely, *Greater America* (1898).

The behavior of the Spanish-born conservative clergy during these years also revealed a shift toward extreme españolismo as well as ultraconservative stances on slavery and other social matters. Most clerics rejected all social and political reforms and supported the continuation of slavery, the region's militarization, and the so-called three unities: territorial unity, unity under the monarchy, and religious unity. In Cuba, prelates and parish priests such as José Obrerá y Carrión and

Ciriaco Sancha Hervás became so intensely involved in the political struggle that the liberal-minded Captain-General Dulce was forced to arrest them. Others were banished for similar reasons. During the Ten Years' War, certain priests used large chunks of church revenue to support the armed struggle to preserve the island under Spanish rule.[12]

Not all of Cuba's priests, however, sympathized with Spain. For example, José Francisco Esquembre y Guzmán, a young priest from

Las Villas, blessed the Cuban flag and harangued a troop of patriot soldiers. He was later tried and executed for treason. Braulio Odio also followed his flock to the battlefields. Four other Cuban-born Catholic priests were deported for sympathizing with the Cuban cause: Manuel de Hoyos y Barrutia, Rafael Sal y Luna, Cándido Valdés, and Cecilio Santa Cruz.[13]

Joining the church in the anti-liberal, anti-Protestant struggles of the 1870s was the increasingly powerful and militant Volunteer Corps of Cuba. These well-armed, well-organized battalions and their less militant counterparts in Puerto Rico mobilized to achieve virtual control of the colonial governments, much to the chagrin of the islands' reform-oriented governors. Instrumental in repealing the constitution of 1869 and exiling reformist governors Dulce and de la Torre, the Volunteers later brought captains-general Joaquín Jovellar and Valmaseda and most of their successors to heel as well. Aligning themselves militarily with the Volunteers and politically with the exclusive peninsular club El Casino Español and the periodical *La Voz de Cuba*, the island's Spanish-born conservatives fought not only against Cuba's independence but against any reform leading to the abolition of slavery, religious toleration, or the liberalization of the educational system. Armed royalists were also responsible for hundreds of acts of terror against liberals and their property in both Cuba and Puerto Rico.[14]

There was no doubt that the Volunteers were conservatives first and Catholics second; whenever moderate clergymen threatened their conservative agenda, they attacked them mercilessly. They clashed, for example, with Jacinto María Martínez, a moderate bishop appointed by Spain's revolutionary authorities, scorning him as an "unfortunate priest blinded by demons of ambition." Distributing and posting propaganda to defame the prelate, they plotted to block his return to Havana in 1871 and later to have him banished. The Volunteers were much pleased to see the conservative clerics Obrerá and Sancha elevated to the island's two episcopal seats later in the decade.[15]

On the pages of Cuba's *La Verdad Católica, La Juventud Católica,* and *La Voz de Cuba* and Puerto Rico's *El Boletín Eclesiás-*

tico and *El Boletín Mercantil,* the region's lay and clerical conservatives attacked anything that threatened the monarchy, slavery, mercantilism, and Catholicism. These periodicals were filled with articles denouncing Protestantism, Freemasonry, and even freedom of thought—"nothing other than the pretended right to deny God's revelations." Articles lambasted republican and abolitionist ideals and criticized liberal reforms such as civil marriages and tolerance for Protestants, "that infernal sect, which has caused so much harm."[16]

Created in 1871 by Cuba's conservative lay Catholics, the biweekly *La Juventud Católica* aimed "to combat energetically the errors that the enemies of Catholicism seek to diffuse; to promote intelligence with historical and scientific dissertations and apologetic speeches; to defend the Catholic religion, and to cultivate good literary taste." Although the editors openly declared that politics lay outside the scope of their publication, their writings condemned Cuba's freedom fighters, applauded Volunteer victories, and maintained that "the Virgin Mary has always protected the Spanish flag."[17]

One area that deeply concerned the conservative clergy and laity was the preservation of religious control over education, and many blamed the colonies' social ills and revolutionary agitation on secularism and the increasingly liberal education system. Judge Nicasio Navascués, who ruled over the proceedings against participants in the Grito de Lares revolt, called for Puerto Rico's schools to be placed exclusively in peninsular hands. Governor Sanz closed the Instituto Civil de Segunda Enseñanza and fired many of Puerto Rico's liberal schoolteachers. The island's loudest conservative mouthpiece, José Pérez Moris, proposed that religious and civil education be the realm of "parish priests and good Spanish teachers."[18] Writing in *La Voz de Cuba,* Cuban counterparts proposed far-reaching changes to achieve political loyalty through control of the education system, focusing their attacks on a "gangrened" professorate and Havana's liberal university. The editors proposed the expansion of primary instruction, cuts in the university's budget and reach, and the establishment of a board to examine and certify teachers, who, argued *La Voz de Cuba,* should only be appointed with the recommendation of the police and local priests. In 1871, the preamble of a conservative educational reform package blamed the previous system for igniting the Cuban insurrection and said that the new goals must be "to educate and Hispanicize." The proposal included a comparison of crime statistics from Catholic and Protestant countries and a demand that all public and private instruction come under "the care and vigilance of the Catholic clergy."[19]

While the region's conservatives (pious or not) gravitated to Catholicism, many liberals and progressives, some of whom were not religious at all, gravitated toward anti-Catholicism or even favored Protestantism. Some were both Freemasons and active Protestants who believed that the anti-Spanish struggle promised to guarantee them more religious freedom and reduce the power of the official church. Still others saw religious pluralism, Freemasonry, and Protestantism as ways to debilitate the church of the colonial state. To be sure, not all separatists were Protestant or even anti-Catholic, and not all Protestants participated in the struggle against Spain.[20] Still, most Protestants tended to be separatist progressives favoring religious tolerance and pluralism and the separation of church and state.

A few key figures of the Cuban struggle for independence were either Protestant by conviction or sympathized with Protestantism for political or strategic reasons. Many more were viscerally anti-Catholic. Among those known to be Protestants were Colonel Fernando Figueredo Socarrás, Mayor-General Alejandro Rodríguez, Frederic Fernández Cavada, Alberto J. Díaz, Pedro Duarte y Domínguez, Manuel Deulofeu, Emilio de Santos Fuentes Betancourt, Agustín Santa Rosa, and Luis Ayestarán y Moliner.[21] Santa Rosa, an Episcopalian conspirator, was among Narciso López's supporters in the early 1850s and was later executed for his participation in the separatist *Virginius* expedition of 1873. While exiled in New York, he helped organize a congregation of Cuban Protestants. Ayestarán y Moliner, who was captured in 1870, reportedly refused Catholic last rites before his execution, although his family members later convinced him to receive them. Fernández Cavada died facing a firing squad without receiving those rites because he was Protestant; nevertheless, civil authorities buried him in consecrated ground even though a parish priest had initially threatened to refuse his body. Both

Figueredo Socarrás and Rodríguez were instrumental in the formation of an Episcopalian exile congregation in Key West. Díaz, Duarte,
and Deulofeu, who were all active conspirators against Spanish colonialism, served as Protestant ministers in Cuba during the 1880s and
1890s.[22]

Interestingly, the separatists' most important leader, Carlos
Manuel de Céspedes, was not anti-Catholic. Although his govern-
ment-in-arms did recognize secular marriages (in part because there
were few priests in the territories controlled by his soldiers), he made
no attempt to establish a lay state. Céspedes's opponents within the
ranks, particularly the abolitionist-annexationist Camagüeyanos,
accused him of being too pro-Catholic. In the Camagüey-dominated
constitution of Guáimaro (1869), freedom of religion was guaranteed,
and the Catholic church had no advantage over other faiths. Reportedly, most of the document's signers were Freemasons. Moreover,
despite Céspedes's reluctance to promote anti-Catholicism, Cuban
patriots executed at least two priests.[23]

One result of the Ten Years' War was a massive Cuban exodus.
By the mid-1870s, an estimated 4,500 Cubans lived in New York City,
5,000 in Key West, and 5,500 in other parts of the United States. Hundreds of other Cubans settled throughout the Caribbean, where some
of them formed Protestant congregations.[24] A considerable number of
exiles gravitated to Protestant churches for reasons ranging from previous affiliation, to educational opportunities, to sincere spiritual
desire, to plain anti-Spanish sentiment. While there were probably
Cuban Protestants in all the emigré communities, the largest number
belonged to an Episcopalian congregation in New York City, two
Episcopalian congregations and a Methodist congregation in Key
West, and an Episcopalian congregation in Philadelphia.

The Episcopalian priest Joaquín de Palma and several of his
parishioners at New York's Santiago Church were active conspirators
for the Cuban cause. The separatist editors of the New York–based *La
Revolución* printed ads for Protestant services and articles favorable
to Protestantism and religious tolerance and on April 17, 1869,
included a special thanks to J. P. Newman, Methodist Episcopal
chaplain of the U.S. Senate, for his unyielding support of the Cuban

cause and for having "elevated prayers to the Almighty in the very floor of the Senate, pleading for the success of the Cuban struggle for independence."[25] Another nucleus of Protestant conspirators lived in Key West, including Carlos Manuel de Céspedes y Céspedes (son of the separatist leader), Teodoro Pérez, and Alejandro Ortiz. In an 1870 pamphlet, a Cuban exile in Key West compared the nations of the north, which established their faith with the guidance of freedom and intelligent reason, with those of the south, who followed "with blind obedience . . . the doctrines of Rome." In the latter nations, according to the pamphlet, "fanatical serfdom and stupid idolatrous adoration of the Pope [had taken] deep hold."[26]

Puerto Rico was not engaged in a war, withstanding only a small, unsuccessful revolt in Lares on September 23, 1868. Nevertheless, as in Cuba, conservatives and liberals were polarized over religious tolerance and the official church. Ramón Emeterio Betances, Román Baldorioty de Castro, Eugenio María de Hostos, and other anti-Spanish patriots were intensely anticlerical, favoring religious freedom and pluralism. In Betances's "Ten Commandments of Freedom," religious freedom was listed third. In his short-lived newspaper, *El Eco del Pueblo*, separatist leader Juan Francisco Terreforte of Mayagüez mentioned the Ponce Protestant church and the Ponce Masonic lodge as two signs that the municipality had progressed beyond Mayagüez. Similarly, Ramón Marín referred to the Protestant church as "yet another element of Ponce's progress." In the liberal *La Razón,* Bonocio Tió Segarra published articles that were highly critical of the Catholic church and the pope.[27] And according to the Liberal-Reformist party's 1886 declaration of principles, religious freedom was fundamental to its platform. During a speech in Ponce, the party's leader, Baldorioty de Castro, heard the bells toll from the nearby Catholic church. Interrupting his speech, he remarked: "Behold the last breathing of an idea that is about to die."[28]

Although Ponce's Protestants tended to be far more conservative than their Cuban counterparts (in part because, as mostly foreigners, they were not nationalists), many saw Spanish colonialism and the Catholic church as obstacles to the exercise of their faith. Some even sympathized with liberalism and the struggle against

Spanish colonialism. Significantly, at least four known Protestants were implicated or arrested in connection with the Lares rebellion: John Van Rhyn, José Julio Henna, Alejandro Badillo y Cordero, and Eduardo Heileger. Moreover, the home of Scottish citizen Robert Graham, a founder of the Ponce Protestant congregation, was reportedly a nest of anti-Spanish conspiracy.[29]

The Puerto Rican exile community was relatively small, and those who left the island tended to go to European centers such as Paris or Madrid. Abolitionist Julio Vizcarrondo was among the few in the United States. While a student there, he married a North American woman and converted to Protestantism; and in the 1860s, he tried unsuccessfully to establish a Protestant congregation in Spain.[30]

The Ten Years' War ended in 1878, and the so-called Guerra Chiquita that followed it ended in 1879. Although Cuba's patriots had failed to achieve independence, they did secure peace and the promise of long-awaited reforms. After the wars, colonial rule became relatively relaxed, and extremes of oppression were reduced. Political amnesty was declared and the ground prepared for the gradual abolition of slavery, the implementation of religious tolerance, and other reforms. At this time thousands of exiles were able to return to Cuba.

In the 1880s, tensions between church and state began resurfacing. State authorities had moved resolutely toward secularization, seeking to reduce or eliminate the church's traditional hold over birth registrations, marriages, and burials. In 1885, the church lost its monopoly over the registration of births when civil registers were instituted in both Cuba and Puerto Rico. An 1884 law provisionally extended civil marriages to both colonies, and such marriages were fully established by law in 1886.[31] Although technically the church retained ownership over cemeteries, central and municipal government officials expanded the state's ability to regulate burial practices. In retaliation, the clergy devised mechanisms to combat civil marriages and the burial of non-Catholics in consecrated ground. Priests routinely refused to give certificates of baptism to those seeking civil matrimony until a royal decree in 1893 finally made it illegal for them to deny anyone a baptismal certificate.[32] Although the state had established provisions for the burial of non-Catholics, church authorities fought to keep them out of Catholic cemeteries and continued to use church control over cemetery access as a weapon against Protestantism, Freemasonry, and irreligiosity.

In 1895, Cuban patriots once again rose up in arms against colonial oppression. Culminating with U.S. intervention in 1898, this war of independence wreaked considerably more death and destruction than the previous wars had. Spanish soldiers corralled a large portion of Cuba's rural population into concentration camps to keep civilians from helping the liberation army, and close to 300,000 of these *reconcentrados* perished during the conflagration. Another several thousand Cubans lost their lives on the battlefields. In many towns the death rate among reconcentrados was as high as 80 percent. The death toll in the province of Matanzas, for example, was 98,000 out of a population of 253,000. In Havana, the death rate in 1898 reached ninety-one per thousand, nearly three times the rate of the prewar years.[33] Those who could escaped into temporary exile: some 100,000 Cubans went to Florida, Louisiana, New York, and other U.S. states. As a result of the war, Cuba's agriculture industry was wiped out; and a later study by the U.S. government estimated that two-thirds of the island's wealth had disappeared during that period.[34]

Meanwhile, the religious struggle had been reignited. The Vatican openly sided with Spain and even helped it finance the war effort.[35] On the island, the Spanish-born clergy also supported the Spanish troops, calling for a holy war against the rebels. In 1896, the archbishop of Santiago de Compostela advised departing Spanish troops: "You will . . . fight a religious war because the rebels destroy churches, impede divine services and stand for all that is contrary to our Catholic Spain."[36] Although Catholic authorities denounced what they claimed were insurgents' widespread burning and profanation of churches and religious objects, Bishop Manuel Santander himself authorized the use of Catholic churches as fortifications in the defense against rebel attacks. On July 16, 1896, he declared that the Lord of Hosts was on the side of the Spanish troops in this just war.[37]

Several Protestant ministers became active in the renewed war effort against Spain, among them Duarte, Díaz, Deulofeu, Enrique B.

Someillán, Isidoro E. Barredo, Emilio Planas, and José R. O'Halloran.[38] When Spanish soldiers killed rebel general Antonio Maceo,
Havana's Baptists pleaded with the U.S. government to intervene:
"The triumph of Spain is the triumph of Roman Catholicism and all
that is opposed to our mission work. . . . the hope of Cuba, morally
and religiously as well as politically is now in the balance."[39]
Although many Protestant leaders had to flee Cuba shortly after the
war began, some continued to conspire for the Cuban cause as well as
offer needed relief for the thousands of exiles arriving in the United
States.[40]

Jose Martí, the independence movement's ideological leader,
was profoundly anticlerical and anti-Catholic and often expressed his
admiration for Protestants and their faith.[41] He believed that "Christianity [had] died at the hands of Catholicism."[42] Opposing the
exploitations of organized religion, he denounced the oppressive role
of priests in daily life: "And he charges for pouring water over your
child's head, for saying that you are your wife's husband, which you
already know because you love her and she loves you; he charges for
your birth, for your anointment, for marrying you, for praying for
your soul, for dying; he denies you even the right to a burial if you do
not pay, thus he will never want you to know that all of that was
unnecessary because that day he will stop getting paid for it."[43]
Although he was not a Protestant, Martí welcomed religious pluralism and the modernizing influence of Protestantism. Thanking Reverend Joaquín de Palma for his ministry among New York's Cuban
exiles, he said that "every free man should hang on his walls the por-
trait of the redeeming Luther" and praised the Methodist church for
its work among "the ranks of the less fortunate" and its ability to
"adapt . . . itself to modern times."[44] Martí aspired to a lay Cuban state
with a secular educational system as well as reduced powers for the
Catholic church, claiming that "when . . . that society has been
crushed and another, new society has been created . . . Catholicism
must perish."[45]

His Puerto Rican counterpart, educator-patriot Eugenio María
de Hostos, was also a critic of colonial Catholicism who deemed
Protestantism "more advanced in the religious evolution than

Catholicism." "Protestant societies," he wrote, "are undoubtedly superior in public and private morality, in political dignity, in civilization to those countries that did not partake in the Protestant reformation." Hostos also believed Protestantism to be more congenial to the development of personality. Instrumental in the secularization of public education in the Dominican Republic, Hostos was married to a Protestant, Belinda O. de Ayala, and both were friends of Reverend Palma.[46]

In sum, during the last third of the nineteenth century, political tensions in the Hispanic Caribbean escalated to the point of war as Cuba's patriots embarked on the Ten Years' War, the Guerra Chiquita, and the War of Independence. Religious conflicts also intensified and were played out triangularly among progressive Creoles, the church, and the colonial state. It became increasingly evident that church and state, despite secularizing trends, shared a primary interest in the preservation of colonial rule over Cuba and Puerto Rico, with the clerical ranks recognizing that continued colonialism would preserve many of the church's privileges. In the meantime, however, the region's separatist Creoles responded with heightened anticlericalism and, in some instances, by openly embracing the Protestant faith.

CHAPTER 5

Puerto Rico's First Protestant Congregations, 1869–1898

The first Protestant congregations in colonial Puerto Rico emerged in Ponce and Vieques. Both were Anglican and part of the bishopric of Antigua, and both were profoundly influenced by plantation culture. Although both congregations, primarily because of their immigrant membership, remained disconnected from the broader political struggles of the period, each had a different and distinct social and racial composition. In Ponce, the congregation mirrored the socioeconomics of the sugar industry in which a foreign-born, white minority precariously dominated over a multiracial laboring mass. In Vieques, however, the congregation mirrored only the laborers' world. Thus, its black parishioners were able to establish a community that remained relatively independent from the regimentation and cultural influence of the planter class.

Ponce

On October 19, 1869, Puerto Rico's governor José Laureano Sanz reluctantly published the Madrid-issued religious tolerance decree. On that same day, a group composed for the most part of wealthy, foreign Protestants gathered to celebrate the news and plan for the establishment of a Protestant church. Attending the meeting were planters William E. Lee and Thomas G. Salomons; engineer Thomas A. Dodd; physician Joseph Henna; dentist Charles E. Daly;

merchants George F. Weichers, John Finlay, and F. J. Finlay; Sweden's and Norway's vice-consul T. Bronsted; and U.S. consular agent Peter J. Minvielle.[1] Encouraged by the subscriptions that began to circulate, these men formed a committee and proceeded to work toward hiring a resident clergyman and erecting a place of worship. By November 2, Minvielle was reporting to his colleague in San Juan that "some of the leading and influential Foreigners have subscribed liberally." Reportedly, Protestants from all classes where joining in support of the church.[2]

On November 20, the organizing committee crafted a document titled "Appeal to Protestants" in which members welcomed the recent tolerance decrees and announced their plans.[3] The committee also invited Reverend W. D. Allan of the Dutch Reformed church of St. Thomas to hold the city's first public Protestant service. Nearly two hundred people attended this historic event, which took place on November 28, 1869, at the house of St. Thomas–born planter Thomas G. Salomons. According to F. J. Finlay, the service went well, the prayers were beautiful, and the sermon was appropriate; even the "singing, and performance on the harmonium was of a superior order."[4]

In these early efforts, Ponce's Protestants counted on the active participation and support of the island's consular corps, in part because Spanish law exempted consular representatives from the Catholicity oath, meaning they could play a visible role without risking legal consequences. Three of the original committee members were either consuls or vice-consuls, and several other consular agents participated actively in Ponce's Protestant congregation. U.S. Agent Minvielle took pride in the fact that Ponce was "the first villa in Porto Rico to have a Foreign Church." His colleague in San Juan, Edward Conroy, also supported the church and used his position to help secure the religious rights of Protestants. Daniel Basanta, the British vice-consul at Ponce, was one of the congregation's principal leaders; he was in charge of the parish books for some time and presided over a few ceremonies, including two funerals.[5]

Although it had been organized by members of the white, mostly affluent, foreign elite, the Ponce congregation soon attracted numerous West Indians of color who resided in the city and neighboring towns. Over the years, these West Indians became an increasingly important component of the congregation. As discussed previously, scores had migrated to the region early in the nineteenth century as either free laborers or slaves. After the 1873 abolition of slavery, however, new waves entered Ponce to work on plantations and as skilled and semiskilled workers.[6] Apparently, blacks and whites worshiped together and participated communally in various ceremonies, not as equals but mirroring the social hierarchy. Yet from the beginning, their worship styles probably clashed; and the congregation's white leaders were pressured to muffle the distinctive rhythms and harmonies of African-Caribbean worship.[7]

The congregation's relations with the native Catholic population were complex and controversial. Although the new Spanish legislation guaranteed freedom of worship, in practice such freedom was not always tolerated. Therefore, Ponce's foreign Protestants were careful to avoid enraging church and state authorities or give any impression of direct proselytizing among the natives. "It is not our intention to make converts" explained Minvielle, "nor interfere in any way with the State Religion." He did clarify, however, that the church was open to "those who [chose] to attend of their own free will."[8] Significantly, four months after the congregation was organized, committee secretary Charles H. Daly ordered Spanish translations of Episcopalian prayer books and requested that the U.S. Foreign Missions Society send a clergyman who could preach in both English and Spanish. Daly also reported that a Catholic-born native Puerto Rican had joined the congregation and wished to pursue seminary studies.[9]

Thus, assurances to the contrary notwithstanding, the new Protestant congregation did not exclusively serve foreigners. For numerous reasons, many nominal Catholics found aspects of Protestant worship appealing. Some had been excommunicated and forbidden to receive the sacraments. Some may have thought that affiliation with the new church would be a socially positive move, especially after influential families such as the Lees, Basantas, Weichers, Salomons, Hennas, Oppenheimers, and others had publicly returned to Protestantism. Moreover, some Catholics had grown disillusioned with the official church's demands, rituals, and corruption.

According to F. J. Finlay, Protestant activities created great alarm among the local Catholic clergy: "Sermons are being preached of a most violent character, condemning Protestantism in all its details." In a letter to a high-ranking municipal official, the parish priest also claimed that Protestant organizers were behaving disrespectfully toward Roman Catholics. Finlay concluded, however, that these attacks had done more good than harm; and he regretted not having yet received the "translated Prayer Books and Bibles as enquiries for them are frequent, all being anxious to read these condemned works."[10]

Although Ponce's Protestants represented numerous denominations (many were Dutch Reformed or Scottish Presbyterian), they agreed early on to form an Anglican-Episcopalian congregation in the city. Not only were many already linked to this communion, but it was theologically and aesthetically closer to Catholicism and therefore might be less objectionable to the Catholic church, the colonial state, and the general population.[11] Anglican communion also recognized the Catholic sacraments of baptism and marriage and avoided missionary work among Christianized populations. Moreover, knowing that Methodist, Baptist, and Moravian missions had mobilized the black masses in other areas of the Caribbean, Ponce's wealthy Protestants desired to avoid encouraging such results in Puerto Rico.[12]

Ponce's Protestants were willing to raise 1,000 dollars each year for a presbyter's salary (generous compensation considering prevailing salaries on the island) plus another 1,000 dollars toward church upkeep. Nevertheless, the U.S. Episcopal church refused to grant missionary status to churches in Christianized territories and thus would not dispatch an Episcopalian minister to Ponce. Although U.S. church officials suggested that the congregation elevate a member to the position of lay reader, the Ponce committee rejected that alternative, arguing that Puerto Ricans were used to priests as figures of religious authority.[13] Clearly, the region's Protestantism was being shaped by the underlying Catholic culture.

Still in search of a clergyman, committee members decided to look in the West Indies, where many had business contacts and several had been born.[14] In March 1872, they offered a monthly salary of one hundred dollars to an Anglican cleric from Barbados, but for some reason negotiations fell through.[15] During this search period, the congregation was visited by Anglican ministers from the Danish islands of St. Thomas and St. Croix as well as by Bishop William W. Jackson of Antigua, their closest Anglican bishop. All told, Bishop Jackson, John C. Du Bois (rector of St. Paul's of St. Croix), and C. J. Branch (rector of St. John's of St. Croix) visited nearly ten times between January 1872 and the spring of 1874, when the first permanent rector began his duties in Ponce.[16] During these visits, they led public and private services in different homes (the church had not yet been built) and performed sacramental ceremonies, including ten marriages and nine baptisms. On June 4, 1872, the congregation officially entered the Anglican bishopric of Antigua and assumed the name of the Ever Blessed Holy Trinity. Du Bois was named interim rector.[17]

At their first organizational meeting, committee members had discussed the need to build an adequate place of worship, which would be the first Protestant church built in the Spanish Caribbean. George F. Weichers, a German merchant and warehouse owner and one of Ponce's wealthiest men, donated the lot on which the church was eventually built. Located in Calle Sur (today Calle Marina), it stood at the place where a newer church stands today.[18] By March 1872, the committee had collected enough funds to order a prefabricated building from Liverpool, England, probably the first such building to be raised in the region. Possibly local architects and builders would not agree to build a Protestant church for fear that it would hurt their business. (Similarly, a few years later, when construction of a Protestant cemetery was opened for bids, no one came forward.) On the afternoon of January 24, 1873, Holy Trinity's first stone was set.[19]

Thus, the Protestant church arrived like its congregation: from abroad and in segments. Reportedly, Britain's Queen Victoria took a

FIGURE 5. Holy Trinity Church, Ponce. From *Puerto Rico Ilustrado* (June 7, 1941): 20.

personal interest in its erection and donated some construction materials. By August 1873, the building was ready for use. A sober, imposing, Gothic structure of galvanized iron and gray wood, it contrasted markedly with the lush tropical vegetation and Ponce's bright blue sky. Large enough for 350 worshipers, the church had a circular stained-glass window above its main entrance and a bell tower with a small cross on top. It had cost 13,500 dollars to erect, a sum paid in full by 1874, notwithstanding the fact that six hundred donated dollars were lost in a bank failure. Bishop Jackson consecrated the church on July 23, 1874.[20]

Although after the fall of 1869 clerical visits became more regular and frequent, the city's pseudo-Catholics were slow to openly acknowledge themselves as Protestants: many continued to receive Catholic sacraments during 1869, 1870, and 1871. Even some families connected to the church committee continued to live and die as Catholics. In 1870, for example, Charles Basanta was baptized as a Catholic and married another pseudo-Catholic, Hortensia Mirailh, with Catholic rites; and Carlos Oppenheimer and his wife, Ana María Van Rhyn, baptized their newborn child, Carlos Gustavo, with Catholic rites in 1871.[21]

Beginning in January 1872, Holy Trinity Church kept parish records indicating adherents' professions, status, race, age, place of birth, gender, compadrazgo ties, and marriage patterns, which reveal much about the behavior and attitudes of this otherwise silent population. Between January 1872 and April 1874, nine baptisms, eleven marriages, and only two burials took place—an unusual 0.8 to 1 to 0.2 ratio that contrasts sharply with the roughly 10 to 1 to 10 ratio of the city's Catholic baptisms, marriages, and funerals.[22]

The first recorded baptism was that of an illegitimate girl named Ángela, daughter of Ángel Fernández Durand and Dolores Ayot. The ceremony took place on March 10, 1872, with C. J. Rector Branch officiating during a visit from St. Croix. Over the next two years, Rector Branch, Bishop Jackson, and Rector Du Bois baptized eight more children, two of them illegitimate with no reported father, another the son of a Puerto Rican carpenter from the neighboring town of Salinas. In accordance with Anglican doctrine, the church did not require second baptisms of those already baptized as Catholics, nor were any adults baptized.[23]

Although having a child baptized into a particular church is not an absolute sign of the parents' affiliation, baptismal records nevertheless indicate the early composition of the Ponce congregation. The first nine baptisms show the predominance of foreign elite families (Lion, Lee, Basanta, Mirailh, Finlay, and Dodd) but also represent the native and black West Indian laboring classes. From the very beginning, then, some Spanish-speaking parents (presumably nominal Catholics) respected the Protestant church enough to have their children baptized under its auspices.[24] Moreover, in contrast with most denominations in the southern United States, which by now had separate white and black churches, Ponce's Anglican church followed the West Indian model of multiracial worship within internally segregated churches.

Marriage records also shed light on the congregation's composition and the attitudes of its early adherents. Interim Rector Du Bois, Bishop Jackson, and a passing British chaplain solemnized a total of eleven marriages between January 8, 1872, and March 30, 1874.[25] Noteworthy is the large number of marriages relative to burials and baptisms. This may have been partly due to the fact that some couples, particularly poorer ones, postponed their marriages until a Protestant minister became available. In addition, however, Protestant ceremonies were simpler and cheaper than Catholic ones. According to the records, marriage charges were known as "offerings" rather than fees and fluctuated with contractors' ability to pay. Most offerings were four pesos, with some as low as two. Otherwise, the records do not show any other requirements or fees—nothing beyond a simple verbal declaration of being Christian and single.[26]

The first recorded Protestant marriage took place between John Peter Nielson and Christina Cramer on January 8, 1872. Among the next ten marriages were Lee-Basanta, Finlay-Basanta, Marstrand-Dalmain, and Schroeder-Henna unions. A couple with non-Spanish surnames (Rodeck and Fadema) traveled from Mayagüez, on the western coast of Puerto Rico, to be married in Ponce. Two Spanish-surnamed couples were also married during this time: merchant Juan Monserrate Borrelí to Edelmire Rivas y Ortiz and laborer Marco Rodríguez to María Feliciana Rivera. There is no way to know if any of these four contractors were Protestants, sympathized with Protestantism, or were simply looking for a cheaper and more expedient way to solemnize their unions. None of their names reappears in the Protestant parish books thereafter as either baptizing children or being buried. Finally, during this early period, two marriages seem to have been culturally mixed: one contracting partner had a Spanish surname, the other a non-Spanish one. Both couples belonged to Ponce's working classes.[27]

Records before the arrival of a permanent rector mention only two Protestant burials: four-month-old María Rebekah Dodd, who died on December 26, 1872; and John Gunther, a Scottish mechanic who died on February 2, 1873. Neither death coincided with a visit from Reverend Du Bois or another Protestant clergyman. Both bodies were buried in the Catholic cemetery as Protestants, with Britain's vice-consul Basanta officiating.[28] Although the exact number of Protestants who died in Ponce and its environs during the organizational phase of the congregation will never be known, it is highly unlikely that a population with at least eleven marriages and nine baptisms had only two deaths. This imbalance suggests that few Protestants were willing to risk non-Catholic funeral and burial. It was one thing to be branded a sinful concubine or be told that one's child would spend eternity in limbo if he or she died unbaptized, but it was quite another to argue with the local Catholic priest while one's father or wife lay decomposing in the living room. In the case of María Rebekah Dodd, her parents may have not had the option of burying her with Catholic rites because she had been publicly baptized as a Protestant in 1872.[29] Since the Catholic church did not recognize that baptism, the girl would have been deemed unbaptized and therefore outside the communion of the church. Records do show that a known Protestant, consular agent Peter J. Minvielle, died on September 10, 1873, but was not buried as a Protestant. Since his name does not appear in the Catholic book of burials either, his survivors may have had his body illegally shipped for burial to his birthplace in Barbados. Ironically, a few months before his death, Minvielle reported to his colleague in San Juan that Protestant baptisms and marriages had already taken place, joking, "We only need now a dead Englishman or Yankee to top off the ceremonies."[30]

The first permanent rector of Holy Trinity Church, Alfred L. Giolma, arrived in Ponce in the early part of 1874. A married Englishman who spoke Spanish and had ministered in Tobago, he encountered numerous obstacles during his brief tenure, both from the Catholic clergy and from pillars of his own congregation. The Bourbon restoration of 1875 had renewed many restrictions on

Protestant worship, encouraging the island's Catholic hierarchy to interfere with the Protestants' gains of 1869–74. In fact, local authorities had temporarily closed Holy Trinity Church, silenced its bell, and forbidden it to exhibit exterior signs indefinitely.[31]

Moreover, within two months, Giolma clashed with several church leaders, ostensibly over his refusal to have the church consecrated until its 3,000-dollar debt was cleared. Unhappy about Giolma's decision, four influential leaders—Lee, Basanta, Dodd, and James McCormick—handed him a letter of dismissal and denounced him to Ponce's mayor for preaching against the Roman Catholic church and the pope.[32] The mayor also received reports of Giolma's "arrogant or irascible character," his condemnation of the Corpus Christi procession, and his having married Catholics in the church. The mayor took the church keys from Giolma at once. Nevertheless, counting on the support of many members of the congregation, the rector claimed that he was the target of calumnies and threatened to go to court to have the church reopened.[33] In the meantime, twenty-six church members, including Eckelman, Salomons, Lion, Schroeder, and several West Indians of color, wrote directly to Governor Sanz demanding that the church be reopened in accordance with the new religious tolerance legislation. Sanz ordered the keys returned immediately but asked the mayor to remain alert for criticisms against the Catholic church.[34]

In an attempt at mediation, Bishop Jackson met on July 18 with Giolma; his supporters Lion and Salomons; and his detractors Basanta, Lee, and McCormick. On July 23, 1874, the bishop finally consecrated the church; and soon a new pro-Giolma church board was organized that included Salomons, Weichers, and Augustus Ganslandt. Animosities lingered, however; and Giolma felt that Bishop Jackson had not been supportive enough. He resigned on June 26, 1875, little more than a year after his arrival in Ponce. He was reportedly given a purse of gold before leaving.[35] Probably other factors had contributed to the congregational split, perhaps pertaining to Giolma's preaching style or his theological orientation. There is also some indication that his critics, most of them scions of old Anglican families, considered him to be too antipapist.

In April 1876, Zachariah Vall Spinosa took the post of rector. A Catalan by birth, the Cambridge-educated pastor served the church for more than eight years, leaving in January 1885. Shortly after his arrival, he married Carolina Armstrong, daughter of one of Ponce's most prominent families. Described as a "short man with flowing black whiskers," Vall Spinosa, like his predecessor, preached in both Spanish and English; and some of his services were exclusively in Spanish.[36] He held two services each Sunday—one in the morning, the other in the evening. At this time, the church had nearly four hundred members, with more than one hundred people attending each service. During 1876–78, an average of seventeen people took communion when it was offered. In addition to regular Sunday services, special midweek services were held during Lent. During Vall Spinosa's vacations, B. Noel Branch of St. Kitts (brother of C. J. Branch) served as acting rector. According to some, he was better liked and more revivalist than Vall Spinosa was.[37]

The children's Sunday school and the rector's school for boys were important aspects of Holy Trinity's work among the community's young people. According to a contemporary Episcopalian bishop, investing in the young had many advantages: "we can accomplish more in attending to the younger part of the population than by preaching to the elder, who, with Spanish pride, are indisposed to listen to the preaching of foreigners." Vall Spinosa's school for boys was first located in Luna Street but later moved to his own house in Calle Sur.[38]

The parish books between April 1874 and January 1885 illuminate the congregation's evolving composition and its relations with different groups in the community. During that decade, English speakers who were white and foreign-born or first-generation Puerto Ricans dominated. Pew rental information for 1879 mentions the Oppenheimers, Brandsteds, Lees, Salomons, Eckelmans, Dodds, and Basantas, among others from that group.[39] Nevertheless, black and mulatto West Indian laborers were becoming more important in the congregation, among them the Roebuck, Westerband, and Van Brackle families. Two Spanish surnames, Mota and Tirado, also appear in the pew rental records. Significantly, these rental lists and corroborating information confirm the church's racial segregation. According to Albert Edward Lee, "the pews were distributed by having the center ones facing the altar and those on the sides, separated from the center pews by aisles, facing each other. By common consent the side pews on the North were used by the colored folks while those on the South were occupied by white families. As the congregation grew, the same division was established in the center pews, the races having each an aisle to themselves." Most likely, as was customary among Anglicans in the British West Indies, black and white worshipers approached the communion table at different times.[40] Puerto Rican and Spanish families, mostly laborers, also participated in the ceremonies; but their membership remained small.

Although the baptismal books also reflect the changing racial patterns of the congregation, for several reasons they may not reveal the congregation's actual composition. To begin with, many (maybe most) parents who baptized their children as Protestants were not members of the church and were probably not even familiar with the basic theological principles of Protestantism. Spanish-speaking parents in particular may never have set foot in the church again, and many couples did not bother getting married either before or after the christening. Moreover, the baptismal records underrepresent the core group of older foreign-born planters and established merchants, many of whom were beyond childbearing age.

During the early 1870s, baptisms of white children predominated; but by the second half of the decade, more children of color were being baptized. Forty children were baptized as Protestants in 1877 and 1878. Of them, twenty-nine were classified as either black or of color and only eleven as white. Of forty baptisms, nineteen were children with Spanish-surnamed mothers, eighteen with Spanish-surnamed fathers.[41] Baptismal records also provide information about fathers' occupations, showing a diverse range of occupations—from merchants and engineers to coachmen and servants.[42]

The records provide numerous insights about marriage patterns and relations among the congregation's different groups. Close to one-fifth of all marriages during this period appear to have been culturally mixed and presumably religiously mixed. For example, the fact that most West Indian immigrants were male and single meant that they needed to marry outside their group. Not surprisingly, most mixed marriages occurred among poorer brides and grooms; such cross-racial liaisons were not acceptable among the elite. Ponce's general population also followed this pattern. In Barrio Sabanetas, for instance, most married, white, day laborers had a black or mulatto wife. In contrast, Ponce's wealthy whites, whether Catholic or Protestant, native- or foreign-born, commercial or agricultural, continued to marry whites.[43]

Information about godparents also reveals social links and attitudes. Children of the foreign Protestant elite were sponsored by other members of the city's tightly knit, white elite, following the model that Sidney W. Mintz and Eric R. Wolf call horizontal compadrazgo.[44] Consider the following case, in which William Edward Lee, son of Thomas Edward Lee and Josephine A. Basanta, was sponsored by William Van Rhyn, Henry Basanta, Adele de Basanta, and Louisa Lee.[45] As in similar examples, the sponsors included one or more close relatives as well as unrelated members of the local elite. This pattern suggests that, as in Catholic baptisms, Protestant baptisms strengthened existing familial ties and established new links with other powerful families. In some instances, members of the elite sponsored children of the working classes—what is called vertical compadrazgo. Moreover, according to the parish books, a few sponsors with Spanish surnames who were apparently not affiliated with the church came forward as sponsors for foreign elite children. Apparently, some Catholics of the native elite were willing to risk their own social capital and publicly lend credibility to "the heresy of Protestantism" by partaking in such ceremonies. Spanish-surnamed sponsors were also common among working-class baptisms.[46]

Protestant baptismal records for 1876–80 show a legitimate-illegitimate ratio of 1 to 0.68, which contrasts markedly with the much higher 1 to 1.07 ratio among the city's Catholic baptisms. This variation was partially due to the large number of high-status foreigners in the Protestant congregation, who tended to reject concubinage as both socially and morally unacceptable. If one examines the subgroup of Protestant baptisms in which the fathers had Spanish surnames, however, the legitimate-illegitimate ratio rises higher than the ratio for all Catholic baptisms. These numbers suggest that legitimacy and illegitimacy were more intimately tied to status and class than to ethnicity or religious preference.[47] Nevertheless, illegitimacy could have been seen as more inexcusable among parents baptizing their children as Protestants because Protestant marriage posed fewer obstacles and was less expensive than Catholic marriages were. Interestingly, not one couple who baptized illegitimate children as Protestants during 1874–79 went on to marry as Protestants within the following five years. Thus, for these families, christening their children at Holy Trinity Church was not a first step in a process of Protestant integration.[48]

Marriage entries corroborate many of the conclusions derived from the baptismal records. There is a disproportionately high number of marriages in the books kept during the rectorships of Giolma and Vall Spinosa: nine in 1874 (after April), five in 1875, twelve in 1876, eight in 1877, seventeen in 1878, fourteen in 1879, and twenty-three in 1880. Entries show that the foreign elite continued to marry within its group, much as it had when members were pseudo-Catholics. Such marriages, however, were only a small portion of Protestant marriages solemnized between April 1874 and December 1880.[49] Although government authorities did not actively guarantee the right to civil marriage and church authorities continued to combat it vigorously, many former pseudo-Catholics and nominal or excommunicated Catholics made use of the Protestant option. Furthermore, Protestant ministers seemed to use marriage as not only a way to combat the sin of cohabitation but a proselytizing tool. Significantly, they were less rigorous about marriage requirements than were their counterparts in the predominantly Protestant British West Indies.

The occupations of the contracting partners demonstrate a growing diversity among those who approached the Protestant church. A closer look at the twenty-three marriages solemnized in 1880 shows a variety of professions and a growing working-class and nonwhite composition. The grooms included coachmen, clerks, carpenters, tailors, tobacconists, and wharf workers. Only three (Fernando M. Toro, Benjamin Adams, and Maximilian Eisenlohe) were merchants. These three were married to three of the four brides classified as "gentlewomen" (Jane E. Lee, Victoria Longueville, and Amelia Gumbels). Significantly, eighteen of the brides were manual laborers—seventeen seamstresses and one unspecified. Marriage data for the year also show growing Hispanic affiliation with (or recourse to) Protestantism, particularly among working-class brides and grooms. Sixteen unions involved contractors with Spanish surnames, five involved contractors with Anglo or other foreign names, but only two were mixed Anglo and Spanish.[50]

Closer attention to two cases reveals prevailing attitudes among nominal Catholics about Protestant marriages. First cousins Bernardo Avenau and Herminia Ibeson married as Protestants on January 9, 1875, admittedly "for no other reason than to avoid the cost of the dispensation because he was so poor at the time that he could face no expense whatsoever." Several years later, the widowed Avenau, wishing to remarry, begged church authorities for forgiveness and requested permission to remarry with Catholic rites. Because the documents do not reveal the whole story, it is not clear if he had reluctantly married as a Protestant the first time or if on both occasions he was looking for an easy way out.[51]

Another case concerns Jaime Roura, a Catalan, who soon after his arrival in Ponce sought to marry Tomasa Hernández. He was a twenty-five-year-old carpenter, she a thirty-one-year-old seamstress. Both were illiterate and signed their marriage certificate with an *X.* According to Roura's testimony, because the required soltería certificate was so expensive, he had "the bad idea of approaching the Protestant Church to get married." No documents were required of him there, and the entire proceeding reportedly cost only ten pesos.[52] A year into their marriage, Tomasa fell ill with tuberculosis and nearly died, and the two felt compelled to clear their consciences and settle their accounts with the Catholic church. In their plea to the church hierarchy, they revealed "a heavy burden on their consciences and remain preoccupied by the fault they have committed and assure that neither before nor after the marriage ceremony have they set foot in a Protestant church and much less have they participated in ceremony, [or] worship . . . and they detest such beliefs and confess that if they committed this fault it was, besides for the reasons exposed, to demonstrate publicly that they were married but they recognize that in this regard they have been badly tricked and they are repentant." Following public confession, their excommunication was lifted, and the bishop authorized them to marry as Catholics.[53] Thus, in at least some instances in which Spanish speakers sought marriage in the Protestant church, their motivation was to unite expediently and inexpensively. Significantly, such contractors did not pursue further links with the Protestant community, and eventually many tried to reconcile with the Catholic church.

Burial records may provide another approximation of actual religious affiliation and congregational composition. While Protestant marriage and baptism were in many instances more convenient than Catholic rites, Catholics had no reason to choose Protestant burial. Strikingly, Holy Trinity's burial records show a very small number of Protestant burials during the first few years of religious tolerance. Between Giolma's arrival and May 15, 1876, when a separate cemetery was made available for Protestant burials, only four persons were buried with Protestant rites. These numbers contrast markedly with the much larger numbers of baptisms and marriages during the same period. Those burials included three members of the congregation's founding families: Basanta's son Charles, who four years earlier had publicly abjured Protestantism but was now being buried as a Protestant; Augustus Lion; and James Gilbee, one of the city's wealthiest planters. The other was the infant María Belén, who had not been baptized as a Catholic and therefore risked being denied a Catholic burial.[54] Thus, even though part of the municipal cemetery had been ceded to Protestants in June 1872, many Protestants during this period still had reservations about non-Catholic burial.[55] As discussed, the Ponce community was deeply rooted in Catholic culture and its attitudes toward death and the afterlife, beliefs that clashed with Protestant theology. In addition, the simpler Protestant ceremonies clashed with the ostentatious funerary culture of Ponce's Catholic elite. Furthermore, the Catholic church zealously retained control of its sacred spaces. Although priests could do little to prevent people from visiting the Protestant church, getting married there, or christening their children as Protestants, they held a powerful card in the final hand.

Control over cemeteries had manifold theological, legal, diplomatic, and public health ramifications. Although the colonial state tried to mediate among the sides, frequent government transitions in Spain and Puerto Rico complicated matters. A royal order dated July 1871 established that spaces be separated inside cemeteries for the burial of non-Catholics. As mentioned, by June 1872, an unfenced lot measuring 130 by 7.5 feet in the cemetery's northeast corner had been reserved for the burial of Protestants and other non-Catholics. Some Protestant families even purchased plots in the section.[56] An 1875 order established that Ponce's Protestants were responsible for the costs of erecting a fence to separate their part of the cemetery. Although they agreed to pay, there is no evidence that the fence was ever raised. Soon after, under pressure from the Catholic church, authorities issued a new order prescribing that non-Catholics had to be buried outside municipal cemeteries unless a section had already been designated inside.[57]

Tension and confusion about burial spaces peaked in the spring of 1876. Encouraged by the new regulations against outdoors Protestant activities, local church authorities fought to reclaim some of the exclusive powers they had lost during anticlerical rule in Spain. Viewing Protestant burials as offensive outdoors activities with proselytizing potential, they sought to end them. With this object, Puerto Rico's Bishop Puig y Monserrat issued strict orders on April 4, 1876, to the Ponce parish priest: "in no case and no matter what reasons are expounded, will you permit the burial in the Catholic cemetery of the corpse of anyone dying outside of Our Holy Religion, because proprietary rights do not carry the right to burial."[58]

The test case was the burial of Captain James Alexander Gavin, a forty-five-year-old Protestant and British subject from Nova Scotia, who died of a heart attack on board a vessel bound for Puerto Rico. The captain, who died on May 16, 1876, had no links to the Ponce congregation and probably had never been to the city. As customary, and because Catholic and state authorities would not attend to the body, Reverend Vall Spinosa took charge of the corpse and ordered a grave to be dug in the Protestant part of the municipal cemetery. On May 17, when the hearse attempted to enter the cemetery, local police barred it and the mourners from the premises. With no other option, they dug a grave outside the cemetery against the enclosure's eastern wall, a location recommended by the mayor in accordance with Father David, the parish priest.[59]

The British consul at San Juan denounced this abuse of his "unfortunate fellow countryman." He deemed the place of burial utterly inadequate and the whole affair "inconsiderate toward the sentiments of those who although [they] may have a different faith are at least human and not beasts." He demanded that Gavin's corpse be exhumed and buried inside the cemetery's walls where Protestants had been buried before. In response, Ponce's mayor argued that the fence erected around Gavin's grave provided ample protection and stated that the consul's accusations were unfair and exaggerated.[60]

News of the Gavin affair soon appeared on the desks of the island's highest authorities and eventually of officials in Madrid. In the meantime, Ponce's Protestants continued to die and require burial, and civilian officials requested instructions about how to proceed. On June 24, for example, the mayor of Ponce inquired about what to do if the ailing wife of Thomas G. Salomons died, given that the Salomons owned a mausoleum in the Catholic part of the cemetery.[61] Then on June 29, 1876, another known non-Catholic died—sixty-two-year-old French physician John Colleman. The mayor immediately telegraphed the governor to ask if he should have Colleman buried next to Gavin. The governor's council voted unanimously to recommend that Colleman be buried inside the cemetery, Gavin's remains also be moved inside, and a fence raised to separate the Catholics from the non-Catholics.[62] Bishop Puig y Monserrat raised a furious protest, demanding that Colleman's body be exhumed and the area for Protestant burials be separated from the Catholic area and have its own entrance. The burial of Protestants alongside Catholics, he argued, "is a sad spectacle that makes it impossible for that place to continue being the final resting place for Catholics." In protest, Father David refused to sign any more burial licenses.[63]

Seeking to end the crisis in a way that would satisfy both Protestants and Catholics, the island's central government ordered the construction of a new cemetery for non-Catholics, the first to be built on the island. Almost immediately, plans were drafted by the city's architect, Juan Bertoli, with a projected cost of almost 2,000 pesos. The new cemetery would be built around the grave of Captain Gavin using the older cemetery's eastern wall as one of its own walls and erecting an independent entrance. It would measure 105 feet by 79 feet, about one-tenth the size of the Catholic burial ground.[64] In the still-standing (but no longer in use) cemetery, recently renamed Panteón Nacional, one can see its peculiar upside-down *L* shape: a main rectangle with a smaller rectangle attached to its northeast corner. The original fence that separated both grounds is no longer standing, but there is still an access entrance leading from what today is called Calle de los Protestantes to the Protestant burial ground. The cemetery was completed in March 1877 and by the following year several of Ponce's Protestants began to purchase plots, among them Henry Schroeder, William Lee, Thomas G. Salomons, James Francis Finlay, and Ignacio Basedas.[65]

The new cemetery meant that many more dying Protestants and their survivors now felt comfortable about seeking burial as Protestants. There were ten Protestant burials in 1876, eight in 1877, fifteen in 1878, seventeen in 1879, twenty-seven in 1880, twenty-seven in 1881, twenty in 1882, twenty-five in 1883, and twenty-five in 1884. Still, natives remained reluctant about burying their loved ones as Protestants, even when they had publicly converted. Among a total of thirty-two people buried with Protestant rites between the death of Captain Gavin and the end of 1878, only eight had Spanish surnames. Seven of these were infants who had probably not been baptized as Catholics and therefore risked being denied Catholic burials. In 1882, Heraclio Tirado, who had baptized his natural son as a Protestant and a year later buried him the same way, himself died at age forty-seven and was buried as a Catholic.[66] Why? Perhaps some new Protestants did not express their last wishes to relatives, their wishes were not complied with, or their commitment to Protestantism was a matter of convenience.

Beginning in the mid-1880s, Ponce's Anglican congregation entered a crisis. As baptismal records attest, the congregation reached its maximum size during the first half of the 1880s, when a yearly average of thirty-six individuals was baptized. By the early 1890s, however, that average had dropped to only twelve.[67] The reasons behind the crisis were manifold. First, during the last three decades of the nineteenth century, the sugar industry in Puerto Rico was also in crisis; and many of the church's benefactors were planters, merchants, or warehouse owners. The Lees, Van Rhyns, and others endured severe economic losses during this time.[68] Second, in response to the troubles of the sugar industry, immigration came to a virtual halt. Third, many of the sons and daughters of the church founders seem to have lost interest in sustaining the church's work. Finally, many of the congregation's white founders and their children may have resented the dominance of West Indians of color and thus withdrawn their support from Holy Trinity.[69] Increased official repression in Puerto Rico's southern and western regions during the late 1880s and 1890s may also explain the reticence of Puerto Ricans to establish links with the Protestant church.

After leading Ponce's Protestants for slightly more than eight years, Reverend Vall Spinosa left his post in January 1885, apparently not on very good terms with the congregation. His explanation in the Clergyman's Record exhibits some jealousy toward his substitute, B. Noel Branch: "In view of the great disunion & discord created in the congregation during my leave of absence, I have rendered my resignation." A subsequent note by Coadjutor Bishop C. J. Branch, dated February 21, 1885, contradicts Vall Spinosa's: "Having read the above, I feel bound to express my disapproval of and my dissent from the statement made therein. The Rev. B. Noel Branch, the clergyman left by the Rector never created any disunion or discord whatever. The Rev. Z. Vall Spinosa, the Rector, resigned after being requested by me to do so. I urged his resignation because I believed that his ministry was not acceptable to the great majority of the congregation, and that therefore his resignation was the well being of the Church." Vall Spinosa remained in Ponce temporarily, making a living teaching English.[70] In the meantime, B. Noel Branch organized a boy's choir and a coeducational school and continued as rector of Holy Trinity Church until 1893. A former student of both rectors later said that Vall Spinosa was inclined to punish his students physically; and when Branch took over the parish school, "flogging became a thing of the past."[71] In 1893, after Joseph Emory served briefly as acting rector, H. M. Skinner took the post of parish rector. He left in 1895, and his last entry in the Clergyman's Record is dated July 7, 1895. At that point the rectorship remained vacant until after the occupation of U.S. forces in the summer of 1898 during the Spanish-Cuban-American War.[72] During those three years, the church remained under the care of a vestryman, a black man named Alexander Horton. It remained closed for two years until the bishop of Antigua, Herbert Mather, visited in April 1898, when close to two hundred Protestants gathered for worship. During the entire period after Vall Spinosa's departure, the bishop continued to make sporadic visits to both Ponce and San Juan.[73]

Vieques

The second organized Protestant community to form in Puerto Rico was on the island of Vieques. Thanks to its peculiar history and proximity to the British and Danish Virgin Islands, the island attracted a large population of French Roman Catholics during the 1820s, 1830s, and 1840s, with Protestant black contract laborers arriving from the British West Indies during the last four decades of the century. Although a Protestant population may have existed on the island since the 1840s and there is some sign of organized Protestant activity by the late 1860s, a formal community did not emerge until 1880.[74]

During the cycle of Spanish revolution, there were several attempts to secure the religious rights of Protestants in Vieques. In 1868, Johanes Waldemar Zaccheus, a carpenter and layman from St. Croix, officiated over the island's first public Protestant service under the Spanish flag. In 1870, he secured permission from colonial authorities to establish a Protestant church and school. Although he tried to have a church built in 1874, he did not succeed. Zaccheus expanded his ministry to Puerto Rico's eastern coast, where he organized Protestant meetings in Naguabo, Humacao, and Fajardo; but in 1874, Jesuit priests had him arrested for proselytizing.[75] Possibly, the poverty and migratory nature of Vieques's Protestant community did not allow such work to thrive. Nevertheless, Protestant laborers continued to live and die in Vieques; and by 1845, the island had a Protestant burial ground, which was located next to the Catholic cemetery. Although the graveyards were separated by a fence, one had to pass through the Catholic one to reach the Protestant section. An 1880 document referred to the cemetery as "Cementerio Católico y Protestante del Pueblo." The parish priest of Vieques, the island's sole representative of the church of Rome, was not completely satisfied with the arrangement, however, and demanded a separate entrance for the Protestant burial ground.[76]

Vieques's sizable Protestant population did not have an organized religious community until late 1880, when Joseph N. Bean, a black lay Anglican from Bermuda, formerly a revenue officer in the British colonial service, arrived to establish and lead a congregation. With the help of the British consul, Bean received permission to proceed from Puerto Rico's governor.[77] The emerging Anglican congregation of Vieques, like the one already operating in Ponce, came under the jurisdiction of the bishop of Antigua. Significantly, however, the Vieques work received far less attention and support from the bishopric. Perhaps Anglican authorities felt that the members of the Vieques congregation already had their own congregations on their respective islands. Or perhaps they made a conscious effort not to facilitate the emigration of black laborers away from the labor-hungry British islands. Although Christian doctrine valued all souls as equals, regardless of color and status, in practice the Anglican bishop of Antigua demonstrated a clear preference for the affluent white Protestants of Ponce over the poor black congregants in Vieques. Whatever the case, when Bean requested support from Antigua, he received none but was charged three reales for the congregation's first prayer book. He also bought the church's Bible and himself made the candle stands and other church ornaments. With great sacrifice the congregation raised twenty pesos to purchase a horse, which died shortly afterward.[78]

For several years, the community that eventually became All Saints Church gathered for services at Bean's house. It later moved to an old sugar warehouse on what is today the corner of San José and Muñoz Rivera streets.[79] Bean led the services but was not permitted to marry or baptize anyone since he was not ordained; he did, however, lead burial ceremonies, which were carried out at the island's Protestant cemetery. Vieques's black Protestants, unlike their brethren in Ponce, remained independent from the religious supervision of the master class and were thus able to preserve an African-Caribbean religious culture with fewer restrictions on expressive, communal, and participatory forms of worship.

The congregation depended on sporadic visits of Anglican clergymen from neighboring islands. In 1881, Reverend H. Semper of Tortola twice visited Vieques to officiate at communion services and administer the sacraments. In 1883, he returned to Vieques and baptized the infant son of Nathaniel and Lucinda Bean. In 1883 and again in 1885, Archdeacon Eyre Hutson of St. Thomas visited the congregation. In February 1885, Bishop C. J. Branch visited Vieques for the first time, returning in November 1886 with other clergymen and confirming twenty believers—the first recorded Anglican confirmations on the island. In 1885, the visiting bishop did not deem it proper to license Bean as a catechist but verbally approved his work as a lay reader.[80]

Recalling the 1886 episcopal visit, Bean wrote: "It was agreed by the Bishop that I should seek preparation if I could but he told me he had no means to assist."[81] Therefore, in 1887, the recently widowed Bean left Vieques to enroll at St. Augustine College in Raleigh, North Carolina, where he was ordained as a deacon in 1889. In 1890, he returned to Vieques, where he purchased a house for 1,000 pesos to be used for church services. At this time, the congregation was still composed of seasonal workers from the British Lesser Antilles, as attested by the membership rolls and records of offerings. Significantly, however, there was enough support from the congregation to raise 530 pesos toward payment on the house. Later in the year Bean went back to the United States, where he raised another 270 dollars.[82] In 1893, a bell (a gift from a ship's captain) was installed in the church. Although the Catholic priest complained about the bell ringing, the island's civil authorities declared that the ringing was legal. Bean was finally ordained as a presbyter on February 25, 1893, in a ceremony held at St. John's Church in St. Croix, thirteen years after he took up his work in Vieques. Later that year, the bishop of Antigua visited Vieques once again, consecrated Bean's church (which officially became All Saints Church), and confirmed four parishioners.[83]

Thus, on the eve of U.S. military intervention, after three decades of relative religious tolerance and organized Protestant activity, Puerto Rico had only two Protestant congregations. Their existence was precarious: the dwindling Ponce flock had been pastorless since 1895, and Vieques's newly ordained and aging minister led an impoverished, unsettled congregation of black contract laborers.[84] In a broad sense, both congregations could be seen as examples of immigration Protestantism since they were almost exclusively composed of immigrants and their descendants. Both, however, differed markedly from typical nineteenth-century Latin American experiences in Rio de Janeiro, Buenos Aires, and Mexico City. For one thing, in the rest of Latin America, independence and republican legislation reduced the traditional privileges of the Catholic church. For another, Protestant immigrants in the major cities of Latin America remained minority presences with marginal economic power.

Puerto Rico's Protestantism was marked by the sugar culture and its resulting socioeconomic order. In Ponce, plantation culture was reflected in church structure and the ways in which members of the multiracial congregation interacted. Clearly, the congregation's white elite "owned" the church. They had acquired the land on which it was built, imported the building from Britain (as the planters had imported British-made steam mills), and hired and fired pastors as they would overseers. Like the plantation, the congregation brought together a planter class, a large working class, and an intermediary class of skilled workers. It was an uneasy coexistence marked by segregation and the subordination of the working classes. As on the plantation, endogamy and horizontal compadrazgo helped solidify the position of the elites, while vertical compadrazgo reflected their paternalistic attitudes toward the laboring masses.[85] When the free black and mulatto population became a majority and threatened to impose its own worship style and religious values, the congregation's whites retrenched and withdrew their economic support. So as the end of the century approached, Holy Trinity's nave stood silent, like the factory of an abandoned sugar estate, showing little sign of life.

Vieques's All Saints reflected only part of the plantation world from which it emerged. Far from the plantation's big house, the island's Protestant congregation emerged as a self-contained migrant community struggling with poverty and seasonal flux. Because the church was relatively independent from outside interference, the congregation was able to develop its own culture and worship style, which had strong African-Caribbean roots. Participatory, call-and-response worship styles and communal values were layered onto an European theological foundation.

CHAPTER 6

Cuba's First Protestant Congregations, 1871–1883

◆

*I*n contrast with Puerto Rico's first Protestant congregation, which was organized by wealthy foreigners in Ponce, Cuba's first congregation grew out of U.S. missionary work. As discussed in chapter 3, Havana and Ponce had developed markedly different social structures and thus foreign populations varying in demographics, class, and degree of permanence. Furthermore, the Ten Years' War inhibited the formation of a stable Protestant community in Cuba. Although Havana's first congregation was also composed predominantly of foreigners, it was considerably poorer and less permanent than Ponce's and swelled during the winter when large numbers of sailors and visitors arrived on the island. In other words, while Ponce's first Protestant congregation reflected the plantation, Havana's reflected the piers.

Although favorable demographic conditions had existed in Cuba for many years, one particular event finally prompted the emergence of a Protestant congregation. In February 1871, Henry B. Whipple, the Episcopal bishop of Minnesota (whose work among native North Americans had earned him the nickname "Apostle of the Indians"), embarked on a trip to Haiti commissioned by the foreign committee of the church's board of missions. Unable to find a ship traveling directly to the island, he headed to Cuba in hopes of finding a vessel there. Once in Havana, however, he saw firsthand the wretched conditions of Protestants in the city: their spiritual neglect, the lack of a minister and a place of worship, unbaptized Protestants of all ages, and the hundreds of Protestants dying without care or ministration. During his visit, he led services on board the U.S. ship *Swatara* and at the British and German consulates, where he found numerous opportunities to speak with consuls, foreign merchants, and others about the need for a resident Protestant minister. Although he had intended to hold services at the U.S. consulate, he was dissuaded by existing tensions between the Spanish and U.S. governments.[1]

Several prominent members of the Havana Protestant community encouraged Whipple and pledged economic support, including the British, U.S., and German consuls and merchants such as Carlos E. Beck and Benjamin E. Lawton. During Whipple's sojourn in the city, he collected a total of 3,100 dollars in subscriptions. Then he returned directly to the United States instead of proceeding to Haiti.[2] Immediately, he began working toward the establishment of an Episcopalian clergyman in Havana. Presenting the matter during the annual meeting of the House of Bishops, he instituted a search for a minister to assume the position. From that time on, the home missions subcommittee of the House of Bishops took responsiblity for the support of missionary activities in Cuba.

In response to Whipple's call, Reverend William R. Whittingham, bishop of the diocese of Maryland, brought forward Edward Kenney, a recently ordained Episcopalian deacon from St. Alban's Church in Baltimore.[3] The Philadelphia-born Kenney seemed to be the perfect choice to lead the work in Cuba. Twenty-three years old and energetic, he had an "earnest devotion of soul to the Lord's work." In addition, he was a graduate of the high church seminary in Nashotah, Wisconsin, an institution known for its "Romish tendencies." This, added to the fact that Kenney was single, made him an acceptable candidate for the task of single-handedly establishing a Protestant mission in Roman Catholic Cuba. Kenney enthusiastically accepted the commission and received his orders to leave for the island in early November 1871.[4]

Although some diplomatic arrangements were still pending, Kenney finally departed on November 23, arriving in the port of

Havana four days later. His timing could not have been worse. The city was in turmoil: on that day Spanish soldiers had executed eight young medical students for their alleged profanation of the tomb of publicist Gonzálo Castañón, a Spanish loyalist. In Kenney's words, "I found nothing but excitement and confusion growing out of the trouble occasioned by the volunteers." As a result of the politically charged situation, he began his work faced by even more obstacles than expected.[5]

According to Kenney, one difficulty was U.S. secretary of state Hamilton Fish's lack of support. Reportedly, Fish advised Kenney to abandon the Cuba work because it was an "extremely hazardous undertaking." Even though he himself was from an old Episcopalian family, Fish believed that the United States should establish better relations with Spain before pressing for change. Thus, he opposed exerting any pressure for religious tolerance. Kenney was also discouraged by the reactions of the U.S. consul in Cuba, who advised him to return to the United States because nothing could be achieved on the island at present.[6]

In truth, despite laws supporting religious tolerance, non-Catholic religious work faced obstacles from many quarters. Thus, Kenney proceeded with caution. Deeming it imprudent to push for the immediate establishment of an on-land mission, he set up his headquarters on board the *Terror*, a U.S. warship stationed in the Bay of Havana. The ship's captain welcomed his presence, going to the length of building a vestry on board. Every Sunday, large crowds converged there for holy communion, including fifty to sixty worshipers affiliated with the Episcopal church; and services included a choir and instruments. Gradually, Kenney extended his ministry onto shore, beginning quiet pastoral work in Havana and officiating at private, daily litany services during Lent. By the time the *Terror* was ordered to Key West, Kenney's amphibious ministry had established a foothold on the island.[7]

His next base of operations was the U.S. consulate in Havana. Under cover of extraterritoriality laws, he set up a temporary Protestant chapel there in May 1872. Given the political climate and the ongoing insurrection, it did not seem prudent to establish a chapel anywhere else at that time. Kenney held services at the consulate for about six months until the island's authorities permitted him to move to a more spacious room at the Hotel San Carlos—still without postings and press advertisements, however.[8] About one year after his arrival, Kenney managed to establish a chapel in the hotel: a "large and handsome saloon" with an organ. In November 1873, he reported that the "chapel was crowded with worshipers and at times we had as many as fifty or sixty to partake of the Holy Communion." He rented the hotel space for 10.80 Spanish paper pesos per Sunday.[9]

Shortly after Kenney began his ministry in Havana, he extended his work to neighboring Matanzas and Cárdenas, port cities with large immigrant populations and strong commercial links with the northern Atlantic. In 1873, he traveled every Sunday by train to Matanzas, where he officiated at evening services.[10] Most likely, he spent Sunday nights in Matanzas before returning to Havana on Monday mornings. Nevertheless, the long trips drained his energy and his finances, and he soon reduced his trips to every other week. By 1877, he reported that he was no longer ministering in Matanzas, "owing, in part, to failing health and the wretched condition of our treasury." Later, however, he was able to reestablish his work there: the *Cuba Guild* mentions Protestant services "at Matanzas and Cárdenas, when possible, and at other parts of the Island, as opportunity offers."[11]

Kenney's Protestant flock had spent decades alienated from contact with organized religion of any kind. Scores of unmarried Protestant couples from Europe and the United States had spent lifetimes together, and their children had remained unbaptized for years. Many died with either Catholic rites or no religious support at all. "This state of things," reported Kenney, "has existed so long that the majority of our own people have lost all faith in Christianity, and their children are growing up in the same path of unbelief and infidelity." He saw his work in Cuba "as almost a mission" because long separation from Protestant ministry had made the people callous to and skeptical about religion. He worked among "the scattered and the burdened, the poor and the forsaken in a long neglected land." In

Kenney's eyes, Havana was a place "where indifference, and unbelief and corruption, the very worst, prevail and where Satan seems to reign supreme."[12]

Seasonal transience and poverty were further obstacles to the establishment of a successful, stable, and self-sustaining Protestant congregation. Although some wealthy and influential Protestants did live in and around Havana, most were skilled or semiskilled laborers who saw Cuba as a temporary place of employment. According to Kenney, his flock was "composed of people in moderate circumstances—many of them are poor." Nearly 1,500 mechanics, most of them from North America, arrived on the island each year to work on the sugar estates, returning home after the harvest. Many were American, British, or German carpenters, rope makers and the like who were too poor to contribute much to the sustenance of a Protestant church. Kenney also provided chaplaincy services to a large and transient population of sailors, who contributed little money to the support of Protestant work.[13]

After five years of regular Episcopal services at the Hotel San Carlos (where Kenney also lived), the hotel's owner decided to divide the room in which the services were held. In his 1877 report, Kenney wrote: "It is not advisable for us to hold our services here any longer, if we can possibly avoid it, for reasons which I cannot explain in this report." Although the facts of the matter remain unknown, Catholic priests may have pressured the owner. Thus, in 1878, Kenney moved the chapel to a room in the south wing of the Hotel Pasaje, an elegant, three-story edifice centrally located by Isabella Park. Renting the room cost twenty-seven gold pesos per month.[14]

Nevertheless, the lack of a church building did not keep the enterprising Kenney from holding regular and special services and establishing a children's Sunday school. In 1874, the Sunday school had twenty-two registered students. Easter services were the yearly high point of Havana's Protestant work and included elaborate floral decorations and egg hunts for the children.[15] The holiday's festive and joyous tone contrasted sharply with the gloomy Catholic observances during Holy Week, which emphasized Christ's martyrdom and death rather than His resurrection.[16] After Easter, Protestant activities began

Figure 6. Hotel Pasaje, Havana, circa 1906. Courtesy of the Library of Congress, Prints and Photographs Division, Detroit Publishing Collection.

to wind down: many seasonal residents returned to the United States and Europe to avoid the unhealthy Cuban summer, and maritime activity also decreased. According to Kenney, the congregation "becomes smaller after Easter until as we approach this season, it becomes very small." Services were often canceled or scheduled at night because of the oppressive summer heat. Sometimes Kenney took the opportunity to travel on fund-raising trips to the United States; but when he stayed in Havana during the summer, he avoided spending nights in the lower elevations near the bay.[17]

Given the poverty of his flock, Kenney depended on outside sources of funding for his mission. Significantly, much lay support for the Protestant mission came from mercantile sectors interested in strengthening trade links between Cuba and the United States. From the beginning, S. and William Welsh of the Philadelphia-based Welsh and Company contributed generously toward the establishment of

Kenney's mission. Later the Welshes became trustees of the mission's funds and contributed a sizable portion of Kenney's salary. At one point, a Havana-based merchant offered a room in one of his warehouses to be used as the church's reading room.[18] Interestingly, several of these benefactors did not personally participate in the congregation's activities. As Kenney reported in 1877, "the subscriptions to our work at Havana amount to 578 pesos in Spanish gold for the current year mostly from persons who do not attend church."[19] Perhaps these individuals, while refusing to congregate with lower-status believers, still recognized the benefits of having a Protestant church in Havana.

Despite the support of these wealthy foreigners, the Protestant mission remained dependent on funding from the U.S. Episcopal church. Since neither the board of missions nor the church's foreign committee had officially assumed responsibility for the work in Cuba, lay and clerical organizations were created to ensure the survival of the mission. Early on, Kenney's mentor and supporter, Bishop Whittingham, chaired a committee of lay and clerical members that supported the work. In 1878, a group of mostly New York–based businessmen, many of whom had business interests in Cuba, formed the Cuba Church Missionary Guild with the object of supporting the church's work on the island. The guild's board included George E. Sibley, a New York lawyer; Britton Richardson, a New York businessman with ties to Cuba; William P. Clyde, former president of a steamer company that served Havana; and George W. Kirke, an executive of New York's East River Coal Company. The Episcopal church's presiding bishop led the group, and its clerical officers included William Tatlock of Connecticut as well as R. E. Hoffman and John Coleman.[20]

The mission's records show that, even though the fixed congregation of Havana was smaller than Ponce's, Kenney had responsibility for a larger population of Protestants at large and assorted non-Catholics. On one occasion he arranged and paid for transportation to the United States of a man stranded in Havana "barely [without] clothes to cover him." On another occasion, with the help of the U.S. consul, he saved a four-year-old boy from an abusive circus family, which allegedly had kidnapped the child in the United States. Kenney fought to gain custody over the child, baptized him as Charlie Kenney and adopted him, and then sent him to a home for boys in Cooperstown, New York.[21]

A good portion of Kenney's time and energy went to ministering to the thousands of foreign sailors who called in the port of Havana each year. Although the sailors were not formal members of his congregation, Kenney viewed his chaplaincy work as an important part of his mission: "They who go down to the sea in ships deserve our love, our ministrations and our care." Every year during the winter, he held a series of special services in the harbor especially for sailors, and they "are always well attended and are marked by such enthusiasm as would put to the blush a congregation of easygoing Christians in some of our Northern cities."[22] A particularly vulnerable segment of Havana's transient Protestant population, this group had many needs but little or no financial means to contribute toward Kenney's work.

As in Ponce, the issue of extending Protestant work to Spanish-speaking natives and Spaniards remained a controversial matter. Although the Episcopal church officially avoided competing with established Christian churches, circumstances in Cuba were unusual. Here, the Catholic church had little influence over people's lives; although most Cubans were socially and culturally Catholic, they were mostly adverse to official Catholicism. The church's loyalist leanings during the Ten Years' War had further distanced them, pushing many nominal Catholics to open anti-Catholicism. Facing this situation, Kenney and supporters of his mission were torn between the Episcopal church's official stance and the enormous possibilities for proselytizing among 1.5 million Cubans.[23]

From the beginning, Kenney's work had attracted Cuban and Spanish Catholics. During his first winter in Cuba, Kenney had buried a person from "the house of a prominent Romanist." He later reported that several "liberal minded romanists" were supporting his work and that "at times [services were attended] by many Cubans and Spaniards who have been loud in their approval and seemingly anxious for our success."[24] On another occasion, he expressed his hope "that the Cubans and Spaniards may learn that there is Christianity outside Romanism for we are accounted here by the majority as *free thinkers* and Jews." Kenney reported widespread ignorance of and misinformation about Protestantism, a result of centuries of propaganda. In fact, when two Spanish Catholic merchants visited one of his services, they were surprised to learn that Protestants worshiped God and Christ.[25]

Kenney distributed scores of Spanish-language Bibles and prayer books to natives requesting them. In 1878, the Cuba Church Missionary Guild also sent Spanish books to the island, recognizing "a field of Gospel labor, only second to permission and power to preach the Gospel as St. Paul preached it."[26] Two of the first Spanish-speakers to join Kenney became active in the ministry. The Santiago-born Juan Bautista Mancebo took up seminary studies in New York and North Carolina with the goal of eventually establishing an Episcopal mission in his hometown. The Spaniard Manuel Ferri López began theological studies under Kenney with an eye toward expanding the mission's work among Chinese contract laborers and slaves.[27]

In 1878, the Ten Years' War ended, and Kenney reported: "Our many Cubans-American citizens have returned here since the declaration of peace—a few of them were in Church last Sunday. I trust in time that we shall be able to do much with this element." Now that political tensions had decreased, Kenney was able to begin advertising his mission, which his counterparts in more peaceful Puerto Rico had been doing for more than a decade.[28] Yet he was still concerned about neglected opportunities for proselytizing, as a letter to Reverend William Tatlock makes clear: "There is no effort being made to make proselytes, none whatsoever, and it always seemed to me that the object of the Bishops was to place a pure branch of the Church Catholic here among our own people . . . and that the people of the Island might have a chance to look at something at least pure and true."[29]

According to Episcopalian missionary principles, work among Chinese contract workers and black slaves was less controversial than proselytizing among Spanish-speaking Catholics. It was also more acceptable to colonial authorities, who saw Protestant efforts as steps toward civilizing the population and a potential antidote to suicide, opium use, religious syncretism, homosexuality, and other behaviors deemed antisocial. The Cuba Church Missionary Guild, which did not formally promote proselytizing among Cubans and Spaniards, openly advocated work among "all Coolies and Chinese residents on the Island" and "Negroes unbaptized and uncared for."[30]

As discussed in previous chapters, close to 125,000 Chinese workers, almost all of them male, came to Cuba as contract laborers between 1847 and 1873. Only a few managed to return to China when their labor terms expired, with the rest either dying or remaining in Cuba. By 1875, almost 50,000 Chinese workers lived on the island, nearly three-fourths of them working on large plantations in the Havana-Matanzas sugar belt. Others had joined the ongoing insurrection. Although colonial legislation stipulated that Chinese workers should receive Catholic instruction, they seldom did.[31]

Kenney was particularly interested in the spiritual welfare of this population, which toiled under slavelike conditions. According to his official report, the Chinese were intelligent and voracious consumers of religious publications. To satisfy their need, he managed to acquire and distribute hundreds of Christian books written in Mandarin as well as translated Bibles and religious tracts. Recent Cuban convert Ferri López spent much time ministering among them, as did Professor Charles Hasselbrink, a layman who offered religious instruction in Mandarin. In September 1876, thirty-two Chinese converts were preparing for baptism and confirmation. Three years later, Kenney was seriously considering establishing a school for Chinese children, although no work toward that end was ever finalized.[32]

Protestant work among blacks and mulattos was a more delicate matter since centuries of creolization had to some extent Hispanicized and Christianized both the free and slave populations. Referring to urban blacks, most of whom were presumably free and Christianized, Kenney reported in 1880: "they have applied to us for books, and every application has been met with a liberal supply. They have asked for advice, and it has been given. Much quiet work has been done amongst them in the city, but further than this, we have not thought it prudent to go for the present."[33] He was less reserved about proselytizing among slaves in the countryside: "[they] are strangers—Africans. The Church of Rome does not instruct them— does not care for them. If they ask us for help, it seems, to me that we must give it to them."[34] In 1876, Kenney took under his temporary spiritual care six hundred slaves on the Occitanía plantation of Mr. Himeley. It is unclear if Himeley was motivated by compassion and a true desire to share the gospel with his slaves or was searching for ways to ease the impending transition from slavery to free labor. Nor is there documentation shedding light on the level of Kenney's success with the group.[35]

As in Ponce, congregational data from Havana offer information about the community, its composition, and its values. Nevertheless, since the original church records are missing, the available data are less detailed than Ponce's; only summaries of sacramental activities have been found. In 1877, six years into the mission, Kenney reported thirty-one communicants in Havana and one in Matanzas; however, many more noncommunicants attended services in both cities.[36] The congregation seems to have been mostly male—a large, unaffiliated, transient group that received services from Kenney but did not contribute financially to his work. There were few baptisms, fewer marriages, and a disproportionately large number of burials. Even though there must have been many unbaptized children, Kenney christened only twenty-five in 1873 and thirty-nine between October 1874 and October 1877—very low numbers compared with Ponce's congregation.[37] Moreover, while the bishop of Antigua regularly visited Ponce, Episcopalian bishops rarely visited Havana. Although Whipple returned in 1875, no other bishop appeared on the island until 1884.[38] Marriages were also rare. Even though Kenney fought to reduce the rate of concubinage among Havana's Protestants, once offering to marry "all parties that may be living in such sin, for nothing," he failed to accomplish much, officiating at only twelve marriages between October 1874 and October 1877.[39]

Apparently, few Spanish speakers participated in Protestant ceremonies. In Havana, affiliation with the Protestants had more social and political costs than it did in Ponce; it was also a politically subversive act. Moreover, in contrast with Ponce, the various populations served by the Havana mission did not join for multiracial worship but received separate ministries.

The peculiar nature of the Cuban mission is best revealed in the data pertaining to deaths and burials. Between 1874 and 1877, Kenney recorded 271 burials—seven times more burials than baptisms.[40] This disproportionately large number testifies both to the Protestant population's instability and vulnerability and to Kenney's Herculean efforts among the dead and dying. From the beginning, he spent much time working as a chaplain, ministering to foreign sailors and visitors who had fallen victim to yellow fever and other illnesses. About a year and a half after he arrived on the island, he received special permission from the captain-general to minister at one of Havana's oldest hospitals, where he set up a chapel. According to Kenney, the hospital had the "ablest physicians" and good nursing care. He described his work with the sick and the dying as "a main feature of our work" and reported that local authorities gave him ample freedom to pursue this ministry. During the summer of 1873 alone, he made 1,300 visits to the sick. That work continued to expand, reaching an average of 2,500 visits each year. In an 1879 letter, he reported having made forty-three such visits in one day.[41]

Despite the love and compassion evident in Kenney's ministry, his labor among the dead and dying was lonely, draining, and often dangerous. When promoting support for his mission, he recounted tales of his chaplaincy—for example, the story of a sea captain who "had been dying for three days . . . [who] held my hand as he was dying, and thanked me over and over again as he was passing away." He wrote about a dying man who had to be restrained in a straight-jacket in his final moments and about a twelve-year-old Scottish boy "who called piteously for his father and mother" as he died in pain in a strange land. He described the burial of a captain: "decomposition had set in long before he breathed his last; and at the burial his body [was] in a terrible state beyond any description. Only by the constant application of camphor could I get through the service. It made me sick."[42] During the unhealthy summer of 1873, Kenney read the burial office five times a day. In 1876, the worst summer since 1858, Kenney buried 125 corpses. Between 1875 and 1877, he buried 258 others, "nearly all [dead] from yellow fever." In 1879, yellow fever again created havoc in Havana, and Kenney buried hundreds of corpses.[43]

In need of a burial ground, Kenney established a Protestant potter's field, an "irregularly shaped piece of land, inclosed by a board fence." Although he was not completely satisfied with the graveyard, he found it decent enough, recognizing that other work in Cuba was more pressing.[44] In 1875, part of the splendid new Colón Cemetery was opened provisionally to non-Catholic burials. It is not clear, however, if Kenny continued to bury Protestants in the potter's field or began to bury them at Colón.[45]

Kenny's ministry to the dead became one of the most effective means of promoting support for his mission, particularly when donors considered the state of Protestant burials before he took over the Cuba work in 1871. In an 1874 report, he alluded to those days, when Protestants were buried "like beasts—without coffin, and frequently naked, their clothing been stolen from their bodies. Without a word of sympathy or prayer, our dead were consigned to a pit or trench." Reverend W. A. Leonard described Kenney's compassionate work: "He prepares the dying for death; decently shrouds and coffins the body; and, with the offices of the Church, buries the poor unfortunate in a proper grave."[46] Nevertheless, the dutiful but lonely Kenney wished that "some of our church people at home could witness just one such scene" so that they "would never forget it, and might find it in their hearts to endow such a work as this. The trouble is, no one witnesses these scenes but myself; even the friends of the dying and dead keep aloof. Yesterday I said the office for the dead in a deserted chapel, only a few coffin-bearers being outside the door."[47]

Kenney's work eventually took a toll on his own health. He became ill during the summer of 1876 and again in 1879 and 1880, apparently at one point coming close to death. Finally, in 1880, he was forced to leave Havana, ending his decade-long, single-handed battle to sustain a Protestant mission in Cuba. He was only thirty-two years old when he left the island, never to return. Kenney moved to New York, where he took up the rectorship of St. Peter's Church in Port Chester. He later served as rector of the Church of the Nativity and other churches in New York City. He was married in 1888 and died in 1899 at the age of fifty-one. Without doubt, his years in Havana had shortened his life.

After Kenney's departure, Reverend Edward A. Egerton of the diocese of Long Island replaced him in May 1881. He was unable to withstand Havana's extraordinary challenges, however, and left the island in 1883. During his short stay in Cuba, Egerton contracted yellow fever and was the victim of several violent, bigoted attacks, including an incident in Cárdenas when he was shot at.[48]

In sum, although the Ponce and the Havana ministries developed in the same region at roughly the same time, each possessed distinct characteristics reflecting its population and political climate. Moreover, different links to the outside world shaped their congregations. Not surprisingly, since Cuba's economy was intimately tied to the United States, a U.S. mission backed by U.S. businessmen was essential to Protestant work on the island. In contrast, Puerto Rico's economy was oriented toward European markets and the Caribbean's European entrepôts, which helps explain the link between the Ponce congregation and the Anglican bishopric of Antigua.

Havana's first congregation proved to be far more complex and economically dependent than Ponce's, which resembled a traditional parish serving a settled and self-sustaining population. Strictly speaking, Kenney's work could not be categorized as either immigration Protestantism or missionary Protestantism, although it shared elements of both. While he led parish work among Havana's foreign residents (most of whom were poor and seasonal), he also led a chaplaincy serving a much larger transient population of foreign sailors and visitors. In addition, he attempted to reach three distinct but neglected populations: sympathetic Spanish speakers, Chinese contract workers, and black laborers, including an entire plantation of slaves. Despite its diversity, the Havana mission never became a multicultural community of worshipers; the various groups remained separate and were led by lay workers under Kenney's supervision. This approach reflected in part the segregation patterns prevailing in the U.S. churches.

CHAPTER 7

Revolution, Exile, and Cuban Protestantism, 1868–1898

The early Protestant congregations in Havana and Matanzas were formed primarily of foreigners, but the first native Cuban Protestant congregations emerged in New York City and Key West among exiles escaping the Ten Years' War. The political circumstances under which these congregations formed not only shaped their orientation and composition but eventually influenced the march of Protestantism in Cuba. Both emigré communities included many cigar makers; and both were affected by tobacco factory culture, which included racially diverse labor unions, mutualistic benevolent organizations, and the practice of having individuals read out loud while workers made cigars. Depending on the labor market situation in Havana and Key West, tobacco workers moved back and forth across the Florida strait, carrying with them cultural norms and practices—including Protestantism.[1] This chapter examines the emergence and development of Cuban Protestant congregations in the United States and how they influenced the Protestant churches established on the island during the 1880s and 1890s.

New York City

The Santiago Episcopal Church of New York City served the oldest Cuban Protestant congregation in the United States. Organized in 1866 by twelve men under the leadership of a Reverend

Hawks, Santiago was the world's first Spanish-speaking Episcopalian congregation. Its first rector was a Spaniard named Ángel de Mora, replaced in May 1867 by Reverend Henry Chancey Riley, who served until 1869, when he was elevated to the bishopric of Mexico. Following his ordination, Reverend Joaquín de Palma, a Cuban, assumed the rectorship of Santiago in September 1869.[2]

The Santiago congregation began meeting at 273 West Fourth Avenue in Manhattan. Admitted to communion during the Episcopal convention of 1867, the church then moved to 30 West Twenty-second Street, between Fifth and Sixth avenues. Some of Santiago's special services were held at the Church of the Annunciation on Fourteenth Street. Palma officiated at two Spanish-language services each Sunday and at evening services during the week. For a time, he led Wednesday-night Bible studies in Brooklyn, where another cluster of Hispanic Protestants had gathered. Despite inadequate funding, Palma managed to keep the church going in rented buildings, not even drawing a salary for himself until 1872.[3]

Palma worked hard at outreach and evangelizing. A former personal secretary to the Cuban patriot Carlos Manuel de Céspedes and an active member of the Cuban revolutionary junta, he advertised the church in the patriotic *La Revolución*, simply stating, however, that his services were held in Spanish and the church was named Santiago. The advertisements never mentioned that it was a Protestant church, and some also promoted study sessions. To attract Cubans and other Spanish speakers to Santiago, Palma offered free English classes there. G. Alexy, a student at the Union Theological Seminary, taught them using the Bible and religious tracts as texts. Palma also translated the Book of Common Prayer into Spanish as well as several hymns.[4] His outreach included visits to the homes of Hispanic and Cuban emigrés, where he distributed Bibles and tracts and invited families to services. In his 1873 church report, Palma stated that all members of the church had been converted from "Romanism," which had been "slow and difficult work."[5]

As a result of Palma's aggressive outreach and New York's growing population of Cuban emigrés, Santiago's congregation swelled. The church's first report to the Episcopalian general convention (in 1869) mentioned twenty families and 260 individuals. By the following year, it included thirty families and three hundred individuals. Between 1871 and 1878, the number of families grew steadily, reaching fifty-five in 1873 and fifty-nine in 1878. The number of individual members and adherents peaked in 1873 (with 350), averaging 297 for 1871–78.[6] By 1879, a total of 115 children and adults had been baptized, 68 people confirmed, and 113 marriages solemnized. In that year's report, Palma calculated that, since the beginning of Santiago's work, "about 600 persons of the Spanish race have been converted through the ministrations of the Church of Santiago."[7]

Although the church was composed overwhelmingly of Cuban exiles (both white and black and many of them cigar workers), Santiago also attracted Mexicans, Venezuelans, Colombians, and Dominicans. Palma firmly believed that his New York–based work was having an enormous influence in Cuba and the rest of Latin America. In 1878, he reported receiving constant requests for Spanish-language tracts, Bibles, and prayer books from people throughout the Americas: "The influence of the Church of Santiago reaches all these Spanish countries in America, because, in almost all of them there are some persons who are members of our Church, or have been present at our services during their visits to this country."[8] When the financially strapped church was forced to move its services to the Church of the Annunciation, located next to a large hotel, Palma saw the move as an opportunity to reach the large number of Latin American Catholics who roomed there. Viewing his ministry as a mission rather than a parish, he had great hopes that the seeds planted in Santiago would germinate in Cuba and beyond "to convert the Latin race of America, to emancipate her from the shackles of Romanism." In his eyes, Santiago's Sunday school was "the nursery of the Protestant faith for the Hispano-American countries."[9]

A disciple of the liberal Catholic theologian and early Cuban nationalist José de la Luz y Caballero, Palma was a politically charged preacher.[10] José Martí called him a great patriot. Attracted by Palma's anti-Spanish messages, the exiles filling the pews at Santiago also proved to be open to Protestant theology. Thus, Palma was able to effectively combine his love of God with his love for Cuba: "Will there be anyone who can teach in the name of the Gospel that Christians do not have a fatherland and that we should leave our patriotism at the portals of our temple, that our religion should be vague and mystic, and that corrupting the principles of the Gospel shall destroy in our souls the love of country and family?" He believed that "we can be Christians, and at the same time lovers of our fatherland." Under his rectorship, Santiago occasionally held special patriotic services, which he advertised in *La Revolución*.[11]

At least two of his religious-political sermons were published and widely distributed. In a Thanksgiving Day sermon coinciding with the first anniversary of the execution of eight Cuban medical students, Palma inquired: "And you . . .you come here today . . . what for? to give thanks for your assailed countryside, for your burnt homes, for your scattered families, for your sons who have been murdered in the battlefields or gallows, for the death threats that hang over the heads of your loved ones?" He then alluded to the first book of Peter, chapter 4, verses 12 and 13, where believers were encouraged to rejoice in their trials. In a sermon commemorating the sixth anniversary of the start of the Cuban war, Palma reconciled Cuban patriotism with the tenets of Christianity.[12]

The end of the war in 1878 and the ensuing return of thousands of exiles to Cuba affected both attendance and finances at Santiago. Its number of families dropped from fifty-nine in 1878 to fifty in 1879, while individuals fell from 280 to 230. The number of families leveled at fifty through 1883. By 1880, church income had dropped so much that the congregation could no longer afford to rent space for services. Then in 1884, Palma died at age sixty-one, after fifteen years of pastoral leadership. The congregation struggled on for another decade until disbanding in 1894 on the eve of the Cuban War of Independence.[13] In 1892, a Congregationalist church composed primarily of Cuban worshipers was organized in New York, with fifty-five members under the pastorship of Reverend J. M. López-Guillén.[14]

Key West

The other important Cuban exile community to crystallize in the United States during the Ten Years' War formed in Key West. Located only ninety miles—six hours away—from war-torn Cuba, the small city was taken by storm when thousands of Cubans began arriving in 1868. Great numbers of black Bahamians and West Indians also flocked to Key West during the 1870s and 1880s.[15] While the 1860 census showed a total population of 2,913, ten years later Key West's population had swelled to 5,657, growing to 9,890 in 1880 and 18,080 in 1890. An estimated 5,000 Cubans lived in Key West in 1876, making up more than half of the key's population.[16]

The key's economy also underwent a dramatic transformation; dozens of cigar factories sprang up employing Cuban cigar makers working with Cuban tobacco leaves. By 1876, twenty-nine cigar factories employed more than 2,100 people. Ten years later cigar manufacturing reached its peak in Key West, with almost two hundred factories and 3,000 laborers. Many of these factories, however, were destroyed during the massive fire of 1886.[17]

The experiences of Cuban exiles in Key West were notably different from the lives of Cubans in New York City. Although the communities were roughly the same size, Cubans in New York were a small, marginal segment within one of the world's largest cities. In Key West, however, they were a visible and politically influential population that for a time achieved majority status. When their electoral power allowed them to temporarily dominate local politics, Cubans elected Carlos Manuel de Céspedes y Céspedes, son of the Cuban patriot, as mayor of Key West along with four representatives to the Florida legislature and five justices of the peace.[18] As a result of that strength, combined with the key's strategic military location, the Cuban community was more active politically than New York's and more rabidly anti-Spanish—which became apparent to everyone in 1871, when an angry mob of exiles murdered Spanish conservative publicist Gonzalo Castañón.[19]

There were other important differences as well. The key's proximity to Cuba permitted a degree of circular migration, producing a

less stable population than New York's. Another important variation
was the racial climate. Key West was part of a southern state, and
Cubans arrived there during the Reconstruction era. Thus, racial segregation affected them in ways not so apparent in New York or
Havana. Although biracial (albeit segregated) worship had been the
norm in the antebellum south, both blacks and whites sought formal
church separation during and especially after the Civil War.[20]

Perhaps because of the political fervor in Key West and stronger
anti-Spanish sentiment, most Cubans there rejected Catholicism.
Compared with New York, the Catholic church on the key was a relatively weak newcomer: not until 1846 did a Havana priest officiate
at a Catholic mass there.[21] Cubans in Key West rarely either married
or baptized their children as Catholics. In fact, records of marriage
license requests for the 1880s and 1890s show that only slightly
more than 10 percent of marriages among resident Cubans were solemnized by Catholic priests. Almost two-thirds were officiated by
Protestant ministers, with the remaining quarter by justices of the
peace. To promote Catholic baptisms and marriages, Key West's
Catholic priests offered the sacraments in private homes instead of at
church. Moreover, according to a Jesuit priest, "I never once asked
for money" to perform these services.[22] Despite such efforts, anti-
Catholicism was rampant, and the church of Rome was frequently
denounced as an arm of Spanish colonialism. The editors of Key
West's Cuban newspaper *El Republicano* warned the Catholic church
about its openly pro-Spanish sympathies, threatening that Cubans
would be forced to abjure the faith if their church continued to support the tyrants. In harsher terms, Methodist Cuban resident Manuel
Deulofeu scorned priests as corrupt and ignorant and their church as
a gangrene conducive to moral death.[23]

From the beginning, various Protestant denominations attracted
Cuban exiles, many of whom had grown disaffected with Catholicism and saw the churches as sources of spiritual support, community, identity, and education. Protestant services also became places
to manifest anti-Spanish feelings. According to Gerardo Castellanos,
"the pulpits offered evangelical sermons mixed with patriotism."
"One attended service with unction, to sing, to pray to God for

independence."[24] In 1870, Reverend William Gardner, who led Key West's Methodist church, placed an advertisement in *El Republicano* inviting residents to his Sunday school for both religious and English-language instruction. *El Republicano*'s editors applauded his efforts, describing Methodist services as "simple and imposing; cordial and solemn." The Catholic parish of St. Mary's responded with advertisements of its own and brought in a priest from New Orleans who could preach in both English and Spanish. One Catholic advertisement clarified that masses would not be political: "The Catholic Church is essentially beyond political debates." The church established a school for Cuban girls in 1873 and in 1879 a separate chapel, Our Lady of Charity of El Cobre, for Cubans to worship in. Decades later, Jesuit priests, the traditional anti-Protestant shock troops, were dispatched to Key West to counteract Protestant work among Cubans.[25]

In 1874, the Methodist church began a formal mission among the Key West Cubans under the leadership of Charles A. Fulwood and his Spanish-speaking assistant, a Canary Islander raised in Cuba named Francisco Diez. The mission's first formal pastor was Joseph E. A. Van Duzer, who died of yellow fever shortly after his arrival. A few months later, Cuban Enrique Benito (Henry) Someillán joined the congregation and began preaching; a few years later he was ordained as minister. Many years later Someillán served as Martí's Key West secretary.[26] By 1878, the mission had seventy-five members but lost many after the Ten Years' War ended. When the congregation was reorganized in 1884, it had only forty-eight members. By the eve of the Cuban War of Independence, however, Methodist membership had risen to eighty-one.

Although slower to establish work among Key West's Cubans, the Episcopal church was eventually more successful in attracting large numbers and creating independent congregations. Both J. L. Steele, rector of the local Church of St. Paul, and John F. Young, bishop of the diocese of Florida, belonged to the high-church tradition, which was familiar to Roman Catholic Cubans.[27] In December 1875, a group of influential and politically active Cubans petitioned Bishop Young to establish a Cuban congregation. Among them were

Juan Bautista Báez, a Cuban Episcopalian layman who was also a Freemason and a patriot; Carlos Manuel de Céspedes y Céspedes; tobacco manufacturer Teodoro Pérez; and several high-ranking members of the Cuban liberation army, including Colonel Fernando Figueredo Socarrás and Major General Alejandro Rodríguez.[28] Bishop Young supported the idea enthusiastically from the beginning and immediately asked Reverend Palma to come help organize the mission. Although Palma agreed to come, he found himself unable to make the trip and instead sent a member of the Santiago congregation. Before leaving Key West, Young appointed Báez as lay reader and placed him in charge of the Cuban congregation under the supervision of Reverend Steele of St. Paul's.[29] At about the same time, St. Paul's black communicants formed their own congregation, St. Peter's, under a lay reader surnamed Green.[30]

During Young's next episcopal visit (in 1877), Báez was admitted to the deaconate; and the Cuban congregation, still under the supervision of Reverend Steele, became the parish of St. John's. During the bishop's visit, Báez preached a sermon on the basic differences between the Catholic and Episcopal churches, which was followed by the confirmation of twenty-nine Cubans and the ratification of the confirmation of another thirty-five who had renounced the "Roman errors." Later that year a parochial school for Cuban boys began operations. Following St. Paul's model, the Cuban congregation was segregated racially, with black and mulatto Cubans attending separate services led by a lay reader surnamed Pérez. Reportedly, there were 1,000 to 1,500 black and mulatto Cubans in Key West, one-quarter to one-third of the emigré population.[31]

The proceedings of the annual councils of the Episcopal diocese of Florida detail St. John's development. In 1878, Young reported: "Mr Baez's work among the Cubans holds its own beyond my expectations. It is growing steadily in strength, and increasing in members and influence. . . . They are very anxious to have a church of their own." The parish report for 1878 listed 78 families and 259 individuals; fifty-nine infants were baptized, twenty-nine people confirmed, twenty-four marriages solemnized, and thirty-one burials carried out. Eighty-three children were enrolled in Sunday school. The following year's report showed a slight decrease owing to the departure of some exiles after the Ten Years' War.[32] Many more, however, decided to stay in Key West because of expanding employment opportunities. In 1880, Bishop Young announced: "St. John's Cuban Mission continues to be successful and prosperous." In 1879, Báez was advanced to the priesthood; and the following year he temporarily assumed the rectorship of both St. John's and St. Paul's, following the yellow-fever deaths of Reverend Steele in October 1878 and his successor, Charles A. Gilbert, in November 1880.[33] St. John's report for 1883 listed 63 families and 137 individual members for a total of 452 people. During that year, sixty-five people were baptized, the same number confirmed, thirty-nine married, and twenty-six buried. In comparison, the Baptists were somewhat slower in establishing missionary work among Key West's Cubans, beginning their efforts in late 1884, when Baptist preacher William F. Wood hired a young Cuban woman, Adela Fales, as an interpreter and teacher.[34]

Other U.S. Congregations

In addition to Key West and New York, there were sizable clusters of Cuban emigrés in New Orleans, Tampa, and Philadelphia. Large numbers of Cubans settled in Tampa during the 1880s and 1890s; and many of them joined the Methodist, Congregationalist, and other Protestant churches. In the early 1890s, Congregationalist pastor E. P. Herric began working among Cuban exiles and eventually established Immanuel Church for Cubans in Ybor City, Florida.[35]

The Philadelphia congregation had a noteworthy role in the development of Cuban Protestantism. In 1880, Episcopalian layman John P. Rhoads, treasurer of Philadelphia's Bible Society, came up with the idea of training exiled Cubans in Philadelphia to spread the faith on the island. With that goal in mind, he was instrumental in forming an Episcopalian congregation for Spanish speakers in Philadelphia under the spiritual leadership of Reverend Parmenio Anaya.[36]

Rhoads was not alone in his belief that Cuban exiles could spread Protestantism in their homeland. Supporters and leaders of various exile congregations also recognized the churches' potential for not only reaching the broader exile population but also multiplying those efforts when exiles returned home. The most optimistic saw the emigré congregations as the springboards of Protestantism into Latin America. Indeed, the seeds planted in Key West, New York, Philadelphia, and other places took root in 1879–95, when thousands of exiles returned to Cuba, among them a dozen or so ministers and lay readers who became the first native leaders of Protestantism on the island. The fact that they had embraced Protestantism in exile tied their faith to nationalism as well as anti-Catholic and anti-Spanish sentiments. Moreover, the Protestant exile communities were mostly composed of working-class Cubans. Thus, both extreme politicization and a working-class culture marked the next phase of Cuban Protestantism and continued to influence its development well into the twentieth century—arguably, until the present day.

Havana and Matanzas

In 1879, yet another chapter opened in the history of Protestantism in Cuba: Cuban-born ministers began leading Cuban congregations on Cuban soil. Protestant leaders in the United States, both Cuban and North American, had long recognized the potential of the Cuban missionary field and had invested resources and energy in ministering among exiles with the hope that soon they would return to the island and themselves minister among their fellow Cubans. As a promoter said, "in Key West the future Missionaries may, and doubtless will be trained ready, when the day of toleration comes, and the way is opened by the providence of God, to go and teach the Cubans in Cuba."[37]

At the end of the Ten Years' War, thousands of Cubans returned to their homeland, having in the meantime learned to vote for their own government officials, write freely for an uncensored press, and worship in Protestant churches. A sizable number of cigar workers returning from Key West founded a suburban neighborhood in Havana named Cayo Hueso. Thousands of others, however, remained in the United States. Key West's booming economy offered substantial salaries that could not be matched in depressed, postwar Cuba. In fact, Key West's total population actually grew from 5,657 in 1870 to 9,890 in 1880. Some 5,000 Cubans lived there in 1885, more than at any time during the Ten Years' War.[38]

After the war, colonial repression relaxed somewhat in Cuba, and optimism grew about the potential for real religious tolerance. Encouraged, the first Cuban Protestant missionaries began to arrive in 1879. As its representative, Florida's Methodist conference dispatched Aurelio Silvera, who had assisted Someillán in the Key West mission since the mid-1870s. On his arrival in Havana, he began to hold public services at the Hotel San Carlos, where years earlier Kenney had set up a chapel. Silvera, however, faced strong opposition and was forced to give up his efforts three years later.[39] At about the same time, Reverend Báez of Key West's St. John's Church began sporadic visits to Cuba, where he officiated at marriages and baptisms and carried out public services. It is certain that some former members of St. John's attended his services.[40]

More successful and longer-lasting missionary efforts began in 1882 and 1883 with the arrival of Alberto J. Díaz and Pedro Duarte y Domínguez, both Cuban Protestant lay workers sent by U.S. Bible societies as colporteurs (distributors of religious materials). A native of Guanabacoa, the thirty-year-old Díaz arrived in Havana on March 19, 1882, to explore the possibility of establishing a Protestant mission. He was a naturalized U.S. citizen who had fought against Spain during the Ten Years' War, serving as a medical officer with the rank of captain. Wounded in battle, he had escaped death by floating away on a piece of board. He drifted for twenty-four hours until he was spotted by a New York–bound vessel, whose crew fished him out of the ocean. In New York, Díaz worked as a reader in a tobacco factory; and while recovering from pneumonia, he converted to Protestantism. There is some confusion about Díaz's early Protestant affiliation. Some evidence points to a connection with Palma's Santiago Church, where he reportedly served as a vestryman. Other information, however, hints at a more intimate relationship with the Baptists. Several sources state that he was baptized on October 26, 1882, at Brooklyn's Gethsemane Baptist Church, which was led by

R. B. Montgomery. Díaz's sister, Minnie, was also active at that church.[41]

During Díaz's initial visit to Cuba in the spring of 1882, he held three religious conferences at 63 Bernaza Street. Although even his own family rejected his message at first, his work nevertheless sparked interest. Thus, when he returned to the United States, he reported positively to the leaders of the Philadelphia Bible Society and a local congregation that was sponsoring his ministry. In February 1883, Díaz returned to Havana as a colporteur, intending also to establish a permanent Protestant mission. The Bible Society of Philadelphia and its affiliated Female Bible Society sponsored his work.[42] On April 10, Díaz organized a nondenominational reformed church, which he named Getsemaní after the one he had attended in Brooklyn. It met at the El Pasaje building and reportedly attracted many former members of Santiago who were now back in Cuba. Díaz was a gifted preacher who could reach and energize large groups of followers. While not fully ordained, he nevertheless seems to have carried out full clerical duties, including the baptism of some three hundred converts during the first fifteen months of his ministry.[43]

In the meantime, another Protestant community was growing in Matanzas. Rhoads had recommended Duarte to the New York Bible Society, which sent him as a colporteur to his hometown of Matanzas. In July 1883, he arrived and founded on August 5 a Protestant mission named Fieles a Jesús in the working-class district of Pueblo Nuevo. Like Díaz, Duarte had fought against Spain during the Ten Years' War, managing to survive the infamous *Virginius* executions. He spent some time in exile in Key West, where he joined the Church of St. John's. He later moved to Philadelphia to pursue medical and theological studies and joined the Hispanic Episcopalian mission. When he arrived in Matanzas as a colporteur and licensed lay reader, Duarte was twenty-eight years old. A U.S. citizen, he was also a Freemason and founded a lodge in Matanzas soon after he arrived.[44] Báez, Duarte's pastor in Key West, visited the Matanzas congregation in September 1883 and officiated at various sacramental ceremonies. Before the end of the year, however, Duarte returned to Philadelphia to continue his theological studies. Nevertheless, he left his mark on Matanzas. During his sojourn there, he had been arrested. Successfully confronting the civil authorities on constitutional grounds, he thus publicized the religious tolerance legislation that had been in effect but unenforced since 1876.[45]

Since both Díaz and Duarte were colporteurs, much of their energy went into the importation and distribution of Bibles. With Díaz's brother, Alfredo, and a Presbyterian minister named A. J. McKim (who focused his efforts on the eastern part of the island), they brought close to 5,400 Bibles to Cuba and distributed another 5,000 or so by May 1885.[46]

Soon after the Cuban Protestants established a firm foothold under the leadership of Díaz and Duarte, Florida's Bishop Young began actively supporting their work. What Bishop Whipple was to the first Episcopalian missionary efforts during the 1870s, Bishop Young was to Protestant penetration during the mid-1880s. Young had had a long and friendly association with Key West's Cuban Protestants.[47] Thus, when 258 Matanzas Protestants signed a petition in 1883 requesting the establishment of a mission, Young enthusiastically offered his help. Basing his opinions on previous experiences with Cubans in Key West, he believed that Cuban society was particularly fertile ground for Protestant Christianity: "No people in the world have stronger religious instincts and predispositions than has the Spanish race." Addressing his church's tradition of avoiding interference in Christianized territories, Young argued that conditions in Cuba were different since the official church had abdicated its responsibilities. "The present religious condition of Cuba," he wrote, "is sad indeed to behold and contemplate"; the majority of Cubans "live and die without any religion, practically, save the lifeless formalities of the Church of Rome." He had nothing good to say about Catholic priests in Cuba, whom he described as undistinguished, immoral, and venal, having "forfeited all confidence and respect as ministers of Christ." In the island's population, Young saw "a million and a half of baptized Christians, who require only the evangelical teaching to become gradually built up into a temple of lively stones acceptable to God by Jesus Christ."[48]

After receiving the Matanzas petition, Young immediately approached the church's New York–based board of managers of foreign missions. The board, however, did not favor the project, particularly since funding for similar work in Mexico had borne little fruit. Disappointed but undaunted, Young sought other avenues, addressing a personal plea to all Episcopalian prelates and clergymen and to many laymen. These efforts paid off: the Cuba work received pledges of support amounting to 3,000 dollars each year.[49]

In January 1884, Young dispatched Báez to Cuba to take charge of the island's two Protestant congregations. Báez was also to remain the head of Key West's St. John's Church. He arrived in Matanzas on February 4, 1884, with his family and an organist and established a temporary home at 60 Santa Rita Street in Pueblo Nuevo, Matanzas, where Fieles a Jesús had remained active after Duarte's departure. Later that month, Young visited Matanzas and Havana, and Báez translated his sermons into Spanish. In Matanzas, Young confirmed forty-one people on one Sunday and twenty more on the following Sunday. Reportedly, more than four hundred people attended the services.[50]

In early March, Young and Báez visited Havana, where fifty-five of the city's Protestants received Episcopal confirmation. Young reported that "all [were] Cuban or Spaniard." Among Matanzas's and Havana's Protestants, there were several conspicuous former Catholics, including a former seminarist, a former nun candidate, and several church musicians and choir members. At this time Young also confirmed Díaz, who was then licensed as a lay reader and advanced as a candidate for holy orders. Following Báez's recommendations, Díaz adopted the mission services of the Episcopal church and the use of a surplice without a stole. Báez expressed his hope that henceforth Díaz's services would follow "churchly forms" and "Church principles."[51]

Havana's Protestant community was more economically diverse than Matanzas's and included a few wealthy individuals. Young reported that among the fifty-five he confirmed in Havana in 1884 there were seven doctors and dentists as well as lawyers, druggists, merchants, engineers, master mechanics, telegraph operators, and railroad conductors. One-half of the confirmed were women. In an 1884 letter, Báez reported that eleven upper-class families were involved in Protestant work.[52]

Shortly after his arrival in Cuba, Báez moved his family from Matanzas to Havana. From his new home, he oversaw Protestant work in both cities but left a lay reader surnamed Pi y Céspedes in charge of the Pueblo Nuevo mission and lay reader Alberto Oliva in charge of the Matanzas one (which came to be known as the San Pedro congregation). Nevertheless, Báez continued to make periodic visits to Matanzas. In August 1884, a year and a half after Díaz's arrival and thirteen months after Duarte's, Báez reported 400 believers in Pueblo Nuevo, 500 in Matanzas, 400 in Havana, 100 in Bejucal, 100 in Guanabacoa, and 150 in Santiago de las Vegas (where former Key West exile Manuel Deulofeu served as lay reader).[53]

In February and March 1885, Bishop Young paid a second visit to Cuba's Protestant congregations and confirmed 322 believers: eighty from Díaz's Getsemaní Church; ninety-six from Guanabacoa's mission; sixty from Jesús, María, y José; seventy-four from San Pedro's at Matanzas; ten from Havana's San Lucas; and two from the mission at Jesús del Monte. On the same occasion, Young married Díaz, whose congregation remained affiliated to the Episcopal communion.[54] At the time, Báez counted on the assistance of José Victoriano de la Cova, a thirty-year-old former Catholic seminarist who had converted to Protestantism while studying in Portland, Maine. Báez had met him at a Masonic lodge in Guanabacoa. For a while, de la Cova took charge of the missions at Guanabacoa and Jesús del Monte, districts settled largely by cigar makers.[55] Later he moved to Matanzas and directed the works there. Like Báez, de la Cova received a salary of fifty pesos per month; however, none of the other lay workers were compensated, including Báez's daughter, who served as organist and led the Sunday school. Báez's weekly preaching schedule included Sunday and Friday services in Havana; Mondays in Regla; Tuesdays in San Antonio de los Baños; Wednesdays in Guanabacoa; Thursdays in Jesús, María, y José; and Saturdays in Santiago de las Vegas, a town dominated by the tobacco industry. On occasions, he also preached in Matanzas.[56]

After only six months in Cuba, Báez was optimistic about the growth of Protestantism there: "With a sufficient number of suitable workers in the field, I do not hesitate to affirm that in a very short time fully two-thirds of the population of the Island will avow themselves adherents of our pure Catholic faith, the opulent as well as the middle classes." Although Báez's prediction was grandiose, a few thousand Cubans were indeed attracted to Protestantism during the 1880s. Díaz baptized close to three hundred people during the first fifteen months of his ministry, and Báez reported 3,000 converts during the first two years of his.[57]

Protestantism was attractive to Cubans on the island for some of the same reasons that it had appealed to Cubans in exile. As Louis A. Pérez, Jr., has pointed out economic dislocation, social displacement, and political discontent pushed thousands of Cubans to oppose Spain and its official church. For many anti-Catholics, Protestantism symbolized modernity, popular participation, and liberalism.[58] Moreover, the Protestant emphasis on personal reading of the scriptures, mutual support through prayer and fellowship, inspiring sermons in the vernacular, and participatory worship often filled spiritual and social needs that Catholicism did not.

Despite its growing popularity, Protestantism in Cuba continued to face obstacles. Some came from expected sources: intransigent Catholic priests and bigoted state officials. Missionary work also suffered chronically from inadequate support and uncertainty about its future. Moreover, it was plagued by internal divisions. In a moment of frustration, Báez summarized his challenges: "My struggle is fearful with the Roman clergy, with fanatics, with the little liberal laws of this Country, with thieves, with the Judas in our lines."[59]

Because Cuba's central government offered few guarantees concerning religious tolerance, local authorities were able to harass the Episcopalians throughout the mid-1880s, further politicizing the island's Protestants and intensifying their anti-Spanish sentiments. Like Duarte, Báez was jailed after a service attracted a crowd of about four hundred people. Díaz was arrested in 1883 and again in 1885, when he was attacked by an angry mob, left for dead, and briefly jailed in the town of Güines.[60] Both Díaz and Báez fought tenaciously to secure the rights of Protestant marriage and burial, making considerable gains with the help of sympathetic lawyers. Still, as Báez reported in 1886, "in Cuba we have no guarantee on the part of the government, only toleration."[61]

Unlike the church in Ponce, the Episcopalian missions in Havana and Matanzas depended heavily on outside sources of funding. Like their English-speaking predecessors in the 1870s, Cuba's Protestants in the mid-1880s were mostly working-class people who had returned to a depressed economy after years of exile. With few exceptions, affluent citizens avoided being associated with the missions for fear of social or economic consequences. The Protestant missions attracted a disproportionate number of working poor, many of color; and they flourished in working-class districts such as Pueblo Nuevo in Matanzas and Jesús del Monte and Santiago de las Vegas in Havana. Moreover, members lacked a culture of consistent and voluntary church giving. This was understandable: Cubans had come to view the Catholic church as a tax-collecting arm of an oppressive state. Collections at Havana's San Lucas Church, which gathered at El Pasaje, ranged from six to twelve pesos per month during the mid-1880s. According to Báez, Matanzas's congregations were even poorer, consisting "for the most part, of artisans, who depend upon the work of their hands for their support."[62]

Lack of funding not only made mission work difficult but its future uncertain. In response to the efforts of Bishop Young and other supporters, the Episcopal missionary society's board of managers had approved an initial allocation of 3,000 dollars. The following year, however, the allocation dropped to 1,000 dollars, supplemented only by gifts from individuals and a few northeastern congregations as well as Young himself. The diocese of Florida continued to pay Báez's salary using funds targeted for domestic missions.[63] Díaz's Getsemaní Church received support from the Female Bible Society of Philadelphia and from a congregation in the Philadelphia area. Between the time of his arrival and June 1884, funds received by his mission totaled more than 5,000 dollars.[64]

As discussed, the Episcopal church's reluctance to adequately invest in Cuba stemmed from its belief that missionary activity should only be carried out among non-Christianized people. In addition, because it was the establishment church of the United States, its missions policy tended to parallel the nation's foreign policy. As long as the U.S. government avoided confronting Spain about its despotic rule in Cuba, the Episcopalian hierarchy avoided confronting Cuba's Catholic clergy about its bigoted hold over the island's souls. Moreover, U.S. missionary organizations appeared to suspect the financial ability—even the honesty—of Cuban missionaries. At the request of the church's missionary society, Báez was subjected to a humiliating and unwarranted investigation conducted by Reverend F. D. Lyne, rector of St. Paul's Church in Key West, whose final report concluded that the mismanagement charges were false and the complaints "groundless." During the investigation, Young wrote to the society's secretary asserting "every confidence in Mr. Baez's integrity as well as earnestness." Young recognized, however, that "his management of financial affairs is his weakest element of character," adding that "his heart is too large for his purse, & his sympathies too free & general for our straightened circumstances." Báez's correspondence during and after the investigation reflects his humiliation. He alluded repeatedly to the many financial sacrifices that he and his family had endured for the work in Cuba. In a letter dated March 1886, he stated that he valued his honor "more than [his] life."[65]

Episcopalian works in Cuba suffered a severe blow in the fall of 1885, when the missionary society decided to cut its funding. Young traveled to New York City to lobby for reversal of the decision, but to no avail. Then on November 16, he died of pneumonia while still in the city. A contemporary source attributed the tragedy to his fatigue and frustration over the Cuba cause. To Cuban Protestants, Young was a martyr; and six Cuban laymen carried his casket to the hearse after the funeral.[66] Because Young's successor in the diocese of Florida, Bishop Edwin Gardner Weed, did not share his interest in Cuba, Bishop William B. Stevens of Pennsylvania assumed oversight of the work. Like Young, however, he also failed to gain the missionary society's support. Thus, in March 1886, the Cuban Guild was organized in Philadelphia to support the Cuban missions.[67]

Episcopalian missionary efforts faced even more difficulties when Díaz formally aligned himself with the Baptist church. He had been loosely linked with the Episcopal church from the beginning but had established a "reformed" church in which he reportedly carried out sacramental and other duties not in accordance with Episcopalian doctrine and practice. Although Bishop Young had confirmed and married him and had accepted him as a candidate for holy orders, Díaz and many of his followers continued to reject formal Episcopal oversight. Apparently, Báez had little control over what went on in the Getsemaní congregation; only in his early reports does he refer to it as Episcopalian. Díaz's independence from Báez and the Episcopalian church may have related to the relatively generous funding he received from the Female Bible Society of Philadelphia.[68]

In August 1885, Reverend William F. Wood, a former chaplain of the Union army and now pastor of Key West's Baptist congregation, visited Havana to learn more about Díaz's work and the possibility of expanding the Southern Baptist denomination into Cuba. He had learned about Díaz through Ángel Godínez, a Cuban member of his church. According to contemporary sources, Wood found Díaz and the Getsemaní congregation to be Baptist in their beliefs and reportedly carried out the island's first six baptisms by immersion, which took place secretly at night on the Havana shore. Getsemaní voted to affiliate itself with the Baptist church, and Díaz soon traveled to Key West for his ordination. The congregation officially became a Baptist church on January 26, 1886. De la Cova, another Episcopalian lay reader, also transferred to the Baptists; he had complained repeatedly about the inadequacy of Episcopalian funding.[69]

The Southern Baptist Convention was aggressive in its penetration of the Cuban field and generous in support of its missionaries. This denomination did not shy away from previously Christianized territories but was active in various so-called "papal fields," including Italy and Brazil. In their May 1886 convention, Southern Baptists placed Cuba under the management of their Home Mission Board. They offered Díaz an initial salary of 1,200 dollars and also hired de la Cova and Díaz's sister, Minnie. In addition, they also signaled support for the purchase of an adequate house of worship.[70]

Reverend Báez and the remaining Episcopalian lay workers resented Díaz's and de la Cova's move to the Baptists. Of de la Cova, Báez wrote that he should have been the last to complain, for he had received a monthly salary of fifty pesos while other lay workers received nothing in compensation.[71] The strongest attacks were reserved for Díaz. In a letter to the missionary society, fifteen Episcopalian laymen denounced Díaz as "ungrateful and disobedient" and accused him of having "done all in his power to crush [the Cuba mission] or rather its Vicar [Báez]." They also accused him of assuming "rights which correspond to an ordained minister, celebrating services, marriages and christenings which are *de facto* illegal, there by dishonoring the Mission." Díaz's critics went so far as to call him an instrument of Romanism and claim that he had conspired with a Catholic priest.[72]

On December 28, 1885, Báez received the disappointing news that the missionary society would no longer support the Cuban missions and would respond only to those financial agreements made before November 31, 1885. The news coincided with a robbery allegedly committed by Báez's maid, which left him "without means for the family."[73] At about the same time, de la Cova resigned from his post, rightly fearing that his lay reader's stipend was in jeopardy. Following Díaz to the Baptists, he took the bulk of his congregation with him. In the meantime, several of the missions' creditors and landlords were becoming impatient about money. Describing their growing dissatisfaction, Báez warned that failure to fulfill outstanding contracts and engagements would fuel the enmity of the Catholic clergy and anti-Protestant fanatics. On January 9, he called a meeting of all the vestries and broke the news that the work could not go forward; a week later he left for Key West with his family. Three lay workers remained on the island: Pablo Frías in Regla, Desiderio Herrera in Guanabacoa, and Deulofeu in Santiago de las Vegas.[74]

Because the missionary society had cut its funding for the Cuba work, Báez was personally responsible for nearly five hundred pesos in debts. To pay them off, he began working at a Key West cigar factory at forty dollars per month. He made it clear, however, that he might be unable to continue his Key West ministry if he had to remain at the factory. Yet Báez's misfortunes kept multiplying; on March 30 his home was destroyed in the great fire of 1886, which began at the Cuban patriotic hall of San Carlos and spread throughout the city, consuming six hundred buildings and eighteen cigar factories.[75]

Shortly after Báez left Cuba, the secretaries and wardens of Havana's and Matanzas's remaining Episcopalian chapels produced a detailed report summarizing the churches' membership, the number of sacraments administered, and other activities. The report included the chapels of San Lucas and Santiago in Havana, San Salvador in Regla, San Pablo in Guanabacoa, San Felipe in Santiago de las Vegas, and San Pedro Apóstol in Matanzas, also mentioning that San Esteban was being organized in San Antonio de los Baños. Of these, the largest were San Pedro (with 600 members and adherents) and San Lucas (with 426). Because so many of the congregations were located in working-class districts, they attracted a racially diverse population that included many blacks and mulattos. Cuban tobacco laborers of different races worked side by side in relative harmony and likewise worshiped together.[76] Thus, in contrast with Kenney's disjointed missionary efforts a decade earlier, the new Cuban congregations had achieved a sense of community.

Sacramental data compiled in 1886 for the previous two years show a tiny number of baptisms (42) among 1,876 congregants. Since the Episcopal church accepted Catholic baptisms, confirmations are better indicators of participation. The 1886 report recorded a total of 520 confirmations. It also reported a high number of marriages (102) despite the many social and legal obstacles to non-Catholic unions. Nearly half of these marriages took place in the San Lucas congregation. The high number of marriages shows that the congregation included a growing number of families and women, in contrast with Kenney's congregation during the 1870s. The number of deaths registered in the report is strikingly small, certainly a reflection of the lingering fears associated with non-Catholic burial. Only six deaths were registered in two years, all of them in Havana, which had a Protestant cemetery. Doubtless many other Protestants died in

Havana and elsewhere, but their surviving relatives had them buried as Catholics.[77]

Between Báez's departure in January 1886 and the return of Duarte in 1887, Cuba's Episcopalian missions remained under the care of lay leaders who toiled with minimal financial support from the Cuba Guild. Three congregations now operated in Matanzas; one of them, Philadelphia, served blacks. In Havana, five congregations survived; in 1888, two were under the care of Evaristo P. Collazo, a former cigar worker. One of Havana's congregations, Belén, met at a Masonic temple, while El Calvario in Jesús del Monte had forty adherents who met at a private home and held a Sunday school for twenty children. Lay reader J. P. Trías superintended three congregations in and around Havana. Duarte supervised both Trías's and Collazo's work but himself remained in Matanzas.[78]

In 1887, Bishop Stevens died after a short tenure as overseer of Cuba's missionary activities. Bishop Ozi W. Whitaker replaced him. He visited Cuba in February 1889, confirming thirty-eight in Havana and forty-eight in Matanzas. In 1888, the American Church Missionary Society assumed responsibility for funding the work, and the Cuba Guild became its auxiliary.[79]

In 1889, another Episcopalian, Manuel F. Moreno, was dispatched to Cuba to replace lay reader Collazo. A member of Palma's Santiago Church in New York, Moreno took charge of Havana's two remaining Episcopalian congregations: Belén and El Calvario in Jesús del Monte. He later started an English-speaking mission in El Cerro named Grace Chapel. Belén continued to meet at the Masonic temple until moving to a more spacious location at 105 Prado, where two hundred worshipers gathered on Sunday mornings and another two hundred attended evening services. In 1892, Moreno advanced to the priesthood and a year later was ordained as presbyter. In 1893, another Episcopalian priest arrived, Arthur H. Mellen, who took charge of Belén and Grace chapels. A Cuban lay reader, José Ramón González de la Peña, assisted Mellen and directed the work of Jesús del Monte.[80]

Meanwhile, in Matanzas, Episcopalian work moved forward under Duarte's supervision. In 1889, his congregation purchased a

FIGURE 7. Pedro Duarte and orphans in front of the Fieles a Jesús Chapel, Matanzas, 1899. Courtesy of the Archives of the Episcopal Church USA.

building at 60 San Juan de Dios for 2,200 pesos. There Duarte established a school named El Precursor. In 1894, a chapel was constructed on the property's patio, the first structure built in Cuba specifically for Protestant worship. Significantly, it was erected more than two decades after Puerto Rico's first. Another Episcopalian mission was established in the predominantly black and mulatto town of Bolondrón, southwest of Matanzas, in 1890.[81]

Southern Baptist missionary work expanded faster and more successfully than did the chronically underfunded work of the Episcopalians. Membership rolls increased sharply and steadily from 301 members in 1887, to 1,493 in 1889, to 2,261 in 1893. Women constituted a large and active portion of the membership, and they were well organized into ten-member cells under the direction of Díaz's mother and sisters. In 1890, there were at least seven Baptist missions in and around Havana. Díaz pastored over Getsemaní, the largest congregation; José R. O'Halloran was in charge of the work at Los Puentes; while de la Cova and Ángel Godínez tended the missions of El Pilar and Regla, respectively. Other missions operated in Calle Neptuno, San Miguel del Padrón, and Guanabacoa. Various Baptist schools were established in the late 1880s and early 1890s with the goal of educating Havana's youth and increasing the denomination's "hold upon the better classes." Meanwhile, in March 1887, Reverend Wood and Adela Fales organized a Baptist congregation in Cienfuegos, a port city 145 miles southeast of Havana, with the backing of Jamaican Baptists. Another North American, E. Pendelton Jones, was appointed by the Southern Baptist Convention in 1893 to oversee all the Cuban missions. He left the island a few months later, however, due to ill health.[82]

In 1889, the Southern Baptist Home Mission Board spent 65,000 dollars to buy El Circo Teatro Jané, centrally located at the corner of Zulueta and Dragones streets. Built in 1881, the building accommodated 3,000 people, and today it is still used as a Baptist church. Because of prohibitions against outdoor religious activities, including baptisms, Díaz built a baptistry inside the new church: a realistic representation of a river, with running water flowing across a platform lined with rocks and grass.[83]

In 1890, Reverend Collazo was expelled from the Baptist church for unknown reasons and joined the Presbyterians. That year the Presbyterian minister Anthony T. Graybill went to Cuba to oversee Collazo's work. Four years later, another North American Presbyterian, H. B. Pratt, arrived in Cuba to start a mission in Santa Clara. Before the end of the century, Presbyterian works were established in Havana, Santa Clara, Sagua la Grande, Camajuaní, and Caibarién. After a failed attempt earlier in the decade, Southern Methodists sent Aurelio Silvera and Henry B. Someillán to Havana in 1883, where they set up a chapel at the Saratoga Hotel. Although Someillán returned to Key West, Silvera remained on the island for some time and, before departing, organized the Methodist mission El Tabernáculo. He reported "preaching to large congregations." In 1888, a missionary named John James Ransom volunteered to head the congregation, which at the time was led by layman Francisco González Cala. Clemente Moya, one of the first Cuban converts in Key West, served as El Tabernáculo's pastor between 1890 and 1892. Average attendance at Methodist services was fifty-four. In 1892, Miguel Pérez Arnaldo briefly worked among the city's Methodists and was succeeded by Isidoro E. Barredo and Juan Martínez. In 1892, Deulofeu began helping the Methodists in the city and became active in the tobacco workers' strikes of 1893 and 1894.[84]

Catholic reaction to Protestant activities intensified in direct relation to the success of Protestant penetration, particularly after the Cuba work was no longer limited to chaplaincy for foreign Protestants. The continuing secularization of Cuban society and the colonial administration during the 1880s and 1890s further frustrated the Catholic church hierarchy, which became increasingly defensive about its power over birth registration, marriages, and burials. In and around Havana, priests reportedly turned to defamation and coercion to keep Cubans from participating in Protestant services and activities. Priests continued to argue—and they were partly right—that Protestants were revolutionary and that their message was more political than religious. They sabotaged some Protestant efforts in Havana, where the concentration of Catholic priests was far greater than on the rest of the island. Allegedly, Báez's short-lived work in El

Cerro came to a halt because priests forced the owner of the hall where the services were being held to terminate the lease. Likewise, priests in Guanabacoa, across the bay from Havana, reportedly pushed lay reader de la Cova to the brink of bankruptcy when they threatened to impose religious sanctions on Catholics sending their children to his school. In 1888, a mob surrounded a Baptist meeting place during a women's prayer gathering and hurled stones and epithets. A year later, the mayor and several policemen broke up a Sunday service in the suburban town of Marianao. In 1890, the appointment of Captain-General Camilo Polavieja, whose religious zeal had earned him the nickname "Christian general," intensified the persecution of Protestants and Freemasons. A permanent inspector was appointed that year to inspect and regulate Protestant places of worship; and as a result, Díaz and two other Baptist missionaries were arrested in Guanabacoa for alleged violations of zoning laws. Also in 1890, Francisco Arriaga, a former Catholic priest now affiliated with the Baptists, was imprisoned for the alleged defamation of Puerto Rico's Catholic bishop.[85]

The struggle for control over final resting places and mortal remains remained at the heart of religious conflict during the last two decades of the nineteenth century. In Guanabacoa, priests reportedly went house to house threatening to deny burial to anyone associating with the Protestants. The bishop of Havana did, in fact, threaten to excommunicate anyone who buried a relative in a non-Catholic cemetery. As a result, according to Duarte, some frightened residents of Matanzas were trying to prevent their loved ones from attending Protestant chapels. Báez responded by offering to bury free of charge anyone denied a Catholic burial.[86]

Not surprisingly, securing lots for Protestant burial became a priority for Bishop Young as well as Báez, Díaz, and Duarte. Significantly, both the Baptist and Episcopalian churches bought property for cemeteries long before they bought or built permanent places of worship. According to a Southern Baptist minister, "a cemetery in Havana is of more importance to our Baptist cause than a house of worship." Young was scandalized by the state of Protestant burials when he first visited Matanzas in 1884: "For the first time in my life,

I saw and realized what is implied in the phrase 'the burial of a dog.'" He encouraged the Protestants of Matanzas to write and sign a petition for the erection of a Protestant cemetery, which he forwarded to the city's governor. Not finding any legal obstacle to the request, the governor permitted its construction. Matanzas Protestants acquired a lot in 1887 thanks to a four-hundred-dollar donation from a Philadelphia woman. It measured 164 by 250 feet and was adjacent to the Catholic cemetery. As late as 1895, it had not yet been built.[87]

The Baptists were far more successful at securing a burial ground for their brethren. In 1887, Díaz puchased a six-acre lot near Colón Cemetery, which was officially inaugurated in April of that year. Three years later it was expanded, and a chapel was erected inside. The first person buried in the Baptist cemetery was a man from Kentucky who had been ordered to be buried outside the walls of Colón. As in similar cases in Ponce fourteen years earlier, the dead man's remains were exhumed and reburied in the Protestant burial ground. The second person buried there was Díaz's own infant daughter. Nicknamed El Jardín de las Flores, the Baptist cemetery attracted not only Protestants but other non-Catholics as well; even Catholics purchased tombs there. According to contemporary estimates, between one third and one half of all the city's burials in 1888–89 took place in the Baptist cemetery. The labor leader and Freemason Enrique Roig San Martín was buried there, an event that included a procession of 4,000 mourners. Some contemporary critics were quick to point out that the burial ground produced a steady flow of income for Díaz and his church. Díaz's own reports reflect a yearly income of 1,693 dollars stemming from the sale and rental of burial plots. Other Baptist cemeteries were built at about the same time in Guanabacoa and San Miguel del Padrón. By 1891, a total of 4,139 people had been buried in Havana's three Baptist cemeteries. By that time, another Protestant burial ground had been built in Cienfuegos by the Presbyterian congregation.[88]

Catholic authorities objected to separate cemeteries as visible symbols of the right of Protestants to live and die in Cuban territory. The issue was no longer a matter of secular potter's fields for foreign heretics but real cemeteries owned by Protestant churches for the

FIGURE 8. Ossuary, Havana, 1890. Courtesy of the Ramiro Fernández Collection, New York.

burial of Catholic-born, Catholic-baptized people over whom the Catholic church believed it had spiritual jurisdiction. As with a petition for the erection of a Chinese cemetery in 1883, Catholic authorities argued that plots had already been set aside for the burial of non-Catholics in Havana, Matanzas, and other locations. Therefore, Chinese, Protestant, and other non-Catholic cemeteries were not necessary.[89] Indeed, the southwestern corner of the Colón Cemetery measuring 873 by 310 feet, with its own walls and a separate entrance, had been set aside for non-Catholic burials. Between 1875 and 1879, an average of 101 non-Catholic burials were performed there each year, reportedly at a cost of only three pesos each.

Construction in the non-Catholic part of Colón was finished in July 1883.[90]

During the 1880s and 1890s, particularly in localities without Protestant burial grounds, Catholic clerics continued to exercise control over cemeteries and wield the threat of burial denial as a form of spiritual terrorism.[91] Several incidents during that period illustrate ongoing tensions over cemetery control. The priest of the parish of Batabanó denied burial in consecrated ground to a woman who had committed suicide. Reportedly, the alcalde responded by agitating a mob that forced its way into the cemetery and buried the body. Likewise, in Santa Clara a mob of three hundred people buried a woman who had been denied entrance into consecrated ground because of her civil marriage. A similar incident took place in Güines, where mourners of another civilly married woman jumped over the cemetery's fence and buried her in defiance of a priest's orders. In 1888, the Catholic priest of Los Puentes forcibly took control of a cadaver that mourning relatives had intended to bury in the Baptist cemetery. Nearly 1,500 angry parishioners surrounded the church to demand the body's return.[92] In 1897, ten corpses were buried outside the walls of Matanzas's cemetery because the local priest had refused to grant interment licenses.[93] Although less successful in maintaining the absolute control it had possessed before the 1870s, the Catholic church continued to demand that walls be erected to separate non-Catholic tombs from Catholic ones.[94]

With the growth of non-Catholic cemeteries and the expansion of Protestantism among the island's native population, new challenges emerged concerning Catholic control over funerals and burials. As Bishop Manuel Santander reminded the captain-general, the church continued to claim that "the corpses of Catholics belong to the Catholic Church; and no judge, nor anyone can legally or illegally deprive the church of this right." When Díaz opened the Baptist cemetery, Catholic representatives diligently worked to prevent the burial of Catholics there. Reportedly, priests stopped hearses at the gates of the cemetery and continued to use coercion and threats among the townspeople. At one point, the bishop of Havana ordered the road to the Baptist cemetery destroyed, and Díaz had to have another one built.[95]

In their own cemeteries, Díaz, O'Halloran, and other Protestant ministers continued to bury the corpses of people they identified as

Protestants. Nevertheless, Catholic clerics from parish priests to bishops repeatedly complained that Catholics were being buried as Protestants in violation of church law and public decency. To say the least, jurisdiction over dead bodies was a tricky matter. Protestants and Catholics had conflicting definitions of religious affiliation: Catholics insisted that all those baptized as Catholics remained members of the church forever, unless excommunicated, while Protestants maintained that a simple public act of worship sufficed to establish Protestant affiliation. Although a dead person's will should have been enough to determine the resting place of his or her remains, in many cases that person's desires may have not been made clear, or survivors may have not respected them. Thus, there were many clashes over burials. One such case involved the body of Petronila Seijas, the daughter of Francisco Seijas, who had reportedly joined the Baptist congregation some time before his daughter's death. According to Bishop Santander, Díaz and O'Halloran "forced" Seijas to have his daughter buried in the Protestant grounds.[96] In another incident, the parish priest of El Cerro raised an angry protest after the Protestant burial of Rosario Martínez. The priest claimed that he had administered last rites shortly before her death. Nevertheless, her position in regards to the Protestant church remains unclear, including whether or not she wanted Catholic last rites or had expressed a preference for a particular place of burial.[97] In yet another case, when a man named Felipe Morales died and was buried in the Baptist cemetery, the ecclesiastical governor of the diocese of Havana claimed the body and demanded that it be exhumed and reburied in a Catholic cemetery.[98] In a letter to the captain-general, the diocese's bishop expressed his anguish over such scandals and demanded the immediate closing of the Protestant burial ground.[99]

The clash among the cemeteries escalated a price war. Protestant burials were notably cheaper than Catholic ones. According to Catholic reports, ministers were charging seven pesos for burials in the Protestant burial grounds. In 1888, however, the bishop of Havana claimed that cost should not be a pretext for burying someone as a Protestant; his "parish priests are behaving with exemplary generosity to the extent that one of them has given in a month burial licenses for fifty-five corpses and has charged for only two."[100]

Whatever the case, one thing to come out of the price wars was lower burial prices for everyone.

While Protestant missionary work in Cuba had never been easy, the outbreak of the War of Independence in 1895 virtually shut it down. Because the anti-Catholic and anti-Spanish sentiments of Cuba's Protestant leaders were no secret, tolerating their activities—mild as the tolerance may have been—became a matter of national security. Moreover, the war, arguably the most brutal in the hemisphere's modern history, created unprecedented levels of bloodshed and destruction; and missionary work under such conditions became almost impossible.

On February 24, known as the day of El Grito de Baire (the start of the war against Spain), the civil governor of Matanzas ordered Duarte to leave the island within twenty-four hours. Duarte went into exile in Key West, where he took over the rectorship of St. John's after Báez's death. He later moved to Tampa, where he worked at a cigar factory and formed a revolutionary club. In 1892, Duarte had founded a revolutionary committee; and in 1894, he began to conspire with Juan Gualberto Gómez, Martí's righthand man in Havana. Baptist minister de la Cova also went into exile and led a congregation in Tampa, where he set up relief stations for Cuban refugees. Díaz managed to stay in Cuba until April 1896, when he was accused of treason, arrested, and forced once again to leave his homeland in fear for his safety. His U.S. citizenship spared him from facing a firing squad. He went to Tampa and later to Mexico and New York, where he worked for the American Bible Society. During the war, Díaz's congregation set up Red Cross stations to take care of reconcentrados and other war victims. O'Halloran and Francisco Bueno also left Cuba and established similar stations in Key West. Collazo, too, was forced to flee, and his Cuban Presbyterian missions were closed down; he joined the ranks of the liberation army.[101] In 1895, Methodist ministers Deulofeu and Moya went into exile, leaving behind a functioning preaching station in the artisan neighborhood of Concordia under the care of Isidoro E. Barredo. Someillán, who visited Cuba during the war, received orders to return to the United States in January 1898. Shortly after the start of the war, Havana's Episcopalian ministers Mellen and Moreno also left the island, not only because of the political situation but because the missionary society again decided to cut its funding for Cuba's missions.[102] The Episcopal church continued to support the U.S. policy of avoiding even the slightest perception of support for the cause of Cuban independence. The missionary society's 1896 annual report defended this false neutrality: "Of the issue of war, we cannot speak. One thing is sure. When it is over, when peace once more comes to Cuba, then we shall have, in the providence of God, such an opportunity and opening to proclaim the liberty of the Gospel of Jesus Christ, throughout its confines, as we have never had in times past."[103] By the summer of 1896, all that was left of the Protestant work in Havana were tiny cells of Protestants congregating quietly under a handful of lay leaders. González Peña gathered a few of Havana's Episcopalians for secret midnight services; he was jailed twice during the war. Baptist services and prayer meetings went on under the leadership of Minnie Díaz and three other women missionaries. According to contemporary reports, the Baptist congregations "had diminished" and had "few men . . . most of them . . . old." In Matanzas, "all is silent as concerns the sound of the Gospel." Fieles a Jesús Chapel had been turned first into a theater and later into a refuge for reconcentrados, and "dead bodies had lain for days in the vestry."[104]

In sum, the various Cuban Protestant congregations of the 1880s and 1890s developed a distinctively Cuban character. They were led by Cuban ministers and lay workers, who carried out services in Spanish for an overwhelmingly Cuban membership. As Louis A. Pérez, Jr., has written, "Protestant churches in Cuba had assumed the full form and function of local religious institutions without much to suggest the existence of a foreign connection, addressing concerns and issues that were largely Cuban, immediate, and local, and under the direction of Cubans." These congregations were profoundly influenced by their working-class composition and racial diversity. Several Protestant leaders of the 1880s and 1890s (Báez, Díaz, and Duarte, among them) worked in cigar factories while in exile, and many of their church members were also cigar workers. These circumstances were mirrored in the congregations' social and political radicalism and their benevolent and unionist organization.[105]

Epilogue

On February 17, 1898, in the
third year of the bloody Cuban War of Independence, the U.S.S.
Maine exploded and sank in the Bay of Havana, killing 260 sailors
and officers. In keeping with Cuba's ancient restrictions, Spanish
authorities denied Commander Charles D. Sigsbee's requests to
read the Protestant burial service over the dead; and services had to
be held behind closed doors. A few of the fallen sailors were buried
in Havana's Baptist cemetery.[1] Following the sinking of the *Maine*,
U.S. public opinion swayed toward intervention; and beginning in
May 1898, U.S. warships began attacking Spain's Pacific and
Caribbean possessions.

Understandably, Cuba's and Puerto Rico's Protestant minorities
welcomed U.S. military intervention and the consequent extinction of
Spanish colonialism. For their part, U.S. Protestant leaders saw the
war as a great opportunity to expand their missionary efforts. On July
28, 1898, Alexander Horton, sexton of Ponce's Holy Trinity Church,
tolled the bell in celebration as U.S. troops marched through the joyous city. Two months later, Reverend Bean of the Vieques Protestant
congregation invited the invading forces to come to All Saints
Church before officially taking command of the island. The troops
marched to the church, where prayers were said and hymns sung. The
aging pastor dedicated the U.S. flag, which was later raised at
the customs house, reportedly "in the midst of a hundred amens."

Some of Puerto Rico's Protestants in the Aguadilla region joined anti-Spanish guerilla activities after the invasion.[2]

In Cuba, meanwhile, several Protestant clergymen fought side by side with U.S. soldiers. Díaz joined the troops of General Nelson A. Miles, a fellow Baptist. Duarte, who had been in exile since 1895, returned to the island in time for General James H. Wilson's formal occupation of Matanzas. Duarte was deputized to raise the U.S. flag and deliver the welcoming speech. Two other Episcopalian clergymen returned to Cuba in 1898—Moreno, who now focused his efforts in Bolondrón, and Mancebo, who began a mission in Santiago. González de la Peña had remained in Havana and was ordained as a deacon in 1900. Baptist O'Halloran returned in 1898, starting works in Santiago and Guantánamo; and shortly after the war, Methodist Someillán, Presbyterian Pedro Rioseco, and Congregationalist J. M. Fernández also returned to establish missionary works in various parts of the island.[3]

After the war, the United States retained temporary control of Cuba and indefinite control of Puerto Rico, thus dramatically shifting regional and international tensions concerning religion. Almost overnight, the Catholic church lost its privileged political position. While Catholicism remained the faith of the majority, it was no longer the state religion. At the same time, Protestant churches benefited from more liberal religious legislation and from the convergence of missionary objectives and U.S. imperialism. As Louis A. Pérez, Jr., has concluded, this convergence, while mutually beneficial, had "no suggestion of conspiracy, or even the need for formal collaboration, [but was] rather a convergence of ideological constructs and shared cultural norms."[4]

Thus, new political alignments formed within a new hegemony. In Puerto Rico, Hispanofile Catholicism became a sign of nationalism in the face of expanding U.S. control and cultural influence. The Federal party of Luis Muñoz Rivera grew increasingly discontent with U.S. rule, shedding its anticlericalism and becoming increasingly hostile to North American missionary efforts.[5] In Cuba, the political equation was complicated by lingering anti-Spanish sentiments as well as socially and politically radical Protestant communities composed of

Cubans of all races. Both North American Protestant missionaries and Cuban political leaders found themselves contending with this population. Díaz, for one, became active in politics, aggressively campaigning for liberal candidates. His behavior, according to some, turned his church into a "nest of conspiracies." Moreover, both the Catholic church and some nationalists accused Protestants of imperialism, heralding Catholicism as the truly Cuban faith.[6] Remarkably, Cuba's first president, Tomás Estrada Palma, often labeled an annexationist, was a Protestant with Quaker links.

In both Cuba and Puerto Rico, U.S. military authorities issued decrees that reduced or eliminated the traditional privileges of the Catholic church. One of the first decrees ended the government's financial support for the church, and later decrees secured non-Catholic burials and civil marriages.[7] Because the United States had long-term plans for direct colonial rule in Puerto Rico, its decrees there went beyond those in Cuba. For example, divorce was legalized in Puerto Rico in 1899 but not until 1918 in Cuba.[8] In fact, Governor Leonard Wood, who ruled Cuba from 1899 to 1902, was generous to the Catholic church, supporting ample compensation for church properties that had been secularized decades earlier under Spanish rule. A Cuban Baptist minister accused General Wilson of siding with the Catholic church against the Protestants: "He ignores us completely and all his attentions are on the side of the Romanists." General Wood's predecessor, General John R. Brooke, faced similar accusations. C. D. Daniel, who arrived in Cuba in 1901 to superintend the work of the Southern Baptist Home Mission Board, wrote emphatically: "the military leaders here pander to Romanism and have frequently treated gospel workers with contempt."[9] Perhaps these accommodations in Cuba were an attempt to use the Catholic church as an instrument for social control. Because Puerto Rico was under direct colonial rule, the United States did not need the church to play that role there. Moreover, Protestants in Cuba had for decades been politically active in ways that had no counterpart in Puerto Rico.

Immediately after the war, dozens of U.S. missionaries representing virtually all the major Protestant denominations began to arrive in Cuba and Puerto Rico. In Cuba, they found functioning clusters of Protestants led by Cuban clergymen and laymen. In Puerto Rico, they encountered a defunct Anglican congregation in Ponce and a struggling one in Vieques. Several of the Protestant denominations (the Southern Baptists, the Episcopalians, the Southern Methodists, and the Southern Presbyterians) had already established a foothold in Spanish Cuba, while others were new to the region.

Before 1898, the Cuban Baptists overseen by the Home Mission Board of the Southern Baptist Convention had been the most successful Protestant denomination on the island. After the war, Díaz returned to his work in Havana, and de la Cova and O'Halloran resumed missionary activities in Matanzas and Oriente, respectively. Francisco Bueno started a Southern Baptist mission in Cienfuegos, and seven other Baptist ministers (all but two of them Cuban) joined the work before 1901.[10] In November 1898, the missionary boards of the southern and northern branches of the Baptist church met to coordinate missionary efforts in the newly acquired territories. They agreed that Southern Baptists would focus on western Cuba, while the Northern Convention would carry out its work in Cuba's eastern section and in Puerto Rico.[11]

The Episcopalian church, which had also established a foothold in Spanish Cuba, dispatched several North American clergymen to the island after the war. The works of González de la Peña in Havana, Duarte in Matanzas, and Moreno in Bolondrón came under the direct supervision of clergymen such as William H. Neilson, W. H. McGee, and Andrew T. Sharpe.[12] In 1901, the church's general convention designated Cuba as a foreign missionary district, and Albion Knight was elected as the island's first Episcopal bishop. Bishop Young, the late bishop of Florida and an ardent supporter of the Cuba work, had confirmed Knight and later made him a deacon and a priest.[13]

Of the other Protestant missions sweeping into Cuba, perhaps the most aggressive and successful were the Southern Methodists under the leadership of Florida's Bishop Warren Aiken Candler. The first four Methodist ministers sent to the island included two Cubans (Someillán and Barredo) and two North Americans (George N. MacDonell and H. W. Baker).[14] The Congregationalist church sent E. P. Herrick, former pastor of the Cuban congregation of Ybor City, as its first missionary; and the first Congregationalist church in Havana was reportedly composed largely of former congregants of the Florida mission. In 1901, Someillán left the Methodists and joined the Congregationalists.[15] In 1899, the Southern Presbyterian church began missionary work in Cárdenas and other places where Collazo had labored before 1898. Its first missionary was John Gillespie Hall. Thus, by 1903, all the major Protestant denominations were present in some part of Cuba.[16]

In Puerto Rico, the Anglican communities in Ponce and Vieques continued to operate under the jurisdiction of the bishop of Antigua until 1901, when they were formally transferred to the American Episcopal church. As part of the transfer agreement, the Episcopal church paid 750 dollars for the properties and agreed to retain Bean as the rector of All Saints. Blind and infirm, he led the congregation until his retirement in 1905; he died in 1907.[17] Episcopalian services began in San Juan in early 1899, first under chaplain Henry A. Brown and later under George B. Pratt, who established the St. John the Baptist mission. In 1902, James H. Van Buren was elected bishop of Puerto Rico, which also included jurisdiction over Cuba.[18] By 1900, Northern Baptists, Congregationalists, Disciples of Christ, Northern Methodists, Lutherans, and other denominations had sent missionaries to Puerto Rico. Some of San Juan's first Protestant services were interdenominational gatherings at the city's theater.[19]

To avoid chaos and destructive competition, representatives of the major Protestant denominations met on several occasions to coordinate efforts and carve out territory. An early meeting took place in May 1898. In March 1899, missionaries gathered in Puerto Rico and on a map dissected the island into spheres of influence. The Baptists received the east-central region; Congregationalists received the eastern end; the United Brethren received the south near Ponce; the Disciples of Christ received part of the west-central region; the Northern Methodists received the southeast and shared a section of the west-central region with the Presbyterians. San Juan and Ponce were to remain open to all denominations.[20] These arrangements have received much criticism, even the outrageous suggestion that they were ploys to control the agricultural production of various geo-

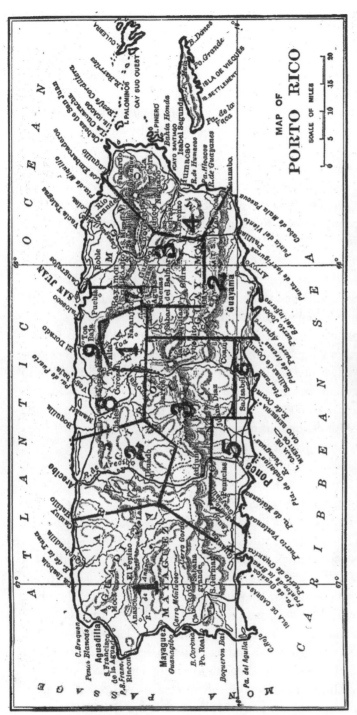

THE DIVISION OF MISSION FIELDS IN PORTO RICO

1. Presbyterian (also San Juan)
2. Methodist
3. Baptist
4. Congregational
5. United Brethren
6. Christian Church
7. Lutheran
8. Christian Alliance
9. Church of Christ

FIGURE 9. Division of Puerto Rico into denominational spheres of influence. From *Missionary Review of the World*, n.s., 28, no. 8 (August 1915): 577.

graphic regions. But in fact there is no evidence of sinister motivations; they were simply strategies to control competition.[21] Nevertheless, competition continued, which led to further agreements and the formation of the Federation of the Evangelical Churches of Porto Rico in 1905 and later the establishment of the Evangelical Union of Puerto Rico in 1916.[22]

Similar coordination took place in Cuba. In 1902, representatives of several denominations met in Cienfuegos and assigned spheres of influence. Northern and Southern Baptists retained their earlier agreement concerning the eastern and western sections of the island. The Society of Friends (Quakers) and the Northern Methodists focused on the east, while Presbyterians, Southern Methodists, and Congregationalists focused on the west. The Episcopalians retained Matanzas and Santiago. Havana and other large cities remained open to all denominations.[23]

On both islands, church membership among the various Protestant groups grew rapidly during the first years of the twentieth century. By 1903, Protestant membership in Cuba hovered at close to 3,000, with membership in Puerto Rico slightly higher. Rolls on both islands reached 10,000 by 1910. In Cuba, the Methodists were the most successful denomination, while the Presbyterians and the Baptists attracted the highest numbers in Puerto Rico.[24]

Relief efforts account for much of the success of Protestant missionary efforts at this time. When the missionaries arrived, the region was staggering from the effects of several years of war and the accompanying social and economic dislocation.[25] In Cuba, hundreds of thousands of reconcentrados had been forcibly uprooted from their homes and livelihoods, and a shockingly large number of them died. An estimated 250,000 children were orphaned by the war, and the island had one widow for every two wives—the world's highest ratio.[26] Faced with this situation, Cuban and North American missionaries emphasized relief efforts, offering the islanders food, shelter, and medicine. In 1898 and 1899, they established dozens of orphanages, clinics, and feeding stations. In Puerto Rico, where the war had been limited to a few skirmishes between U.S. and Spanish soldiers, Protestant missionaries also carried out relief efforts and established several hospitals. On both islands, they set up educational institutions ranging from day schools to technical colleges.[27]

On both islands, the growth of Protestantism was influenced by previous experiences under Spanish rule. In Cuba, Protestantism continued to appeal predominantly to members of the working class, many of them Cubans of color. In 1899, Reverend de la Cova described Matanzas's Methodist congregation: "[they] belong to the lowest class of this country: many of them reconcentrados, and, as a rule ignorant." Fifteen years later, Bishop Knight said: "the native people who are being reached belong only to what is ordinarily known as the lower class of people. They are naturally the poorer classes."[28] Thus, Cuba's native-born Protestant clergymen, the majority of them politically radical and oriented toward associations of mutualistic benevolence, were uneasy with the North Americans who assumed leadership of the missions. The end of Spanish domination and the control of yellow fever due to improvements in sanitation allowed North American churchmen to settle in Cuba and superintend the work of Cuban missionaries, who had endured many hardships to lay the foundations of Protestant work. Díaz, Duarte, Someillán, O'Halloran, Barredo, Emilio Planas, and other Cuban clergymen all clashed with their leadership and eventually resigned from their posts.[29] These heirs of a culture forged in tobacco factories and patriotic halls could not coexist with representatives of an imperial nation increasingly influenced by business and financial interests on the island.

In Puerto Rico, Protestant developments after 1898 continued to retain some of the social and political patterns of Ponce's plantation model. In San Juan, for example, two Episcopalian churches were established. St. John's served the predominantly well-to-do white population of natives and foreigners. Its members included many families who had once been associated with Ponce's Holy Trinity Church: the Lees, the Spinosas, the Finlays, the Basantas, and the Dodds. St. Luke's, located in the working-class district of Puerta de Tierra, served Puerto Rican and Antillean laborers of color. Similarly, San Juan's Methodist mission began by offering three separate services: one for North American whites, one for English-speaking blacks, another for Spanish speakers. Thus, the racial segregation of Ponce's congregation was continued through the establishment different congregations.[30]

The roots of Protestantism in nineteenth-century Cuba and Puerto Rico and among Cuban exiles influenced the march of Protestantism during the twentieth century and will likely continue to do so during the twenty-first. Those roots have also shaped common and scholarly perceptions of the region's Protestants. Significantly, Puerto Rico's Protestants have historically been more conservative and pro–United States than have their counterparts in Cuba. Likewise, while Puerto Rico's social scientists have generally castigated Protestant churches as anti-national tools of empire, their Cuban colleagues celebrate the Protestant patriots of yesteryear.

As I have demonstrated throughout this book, however, political-religious convergences are often precarious. The passage of time usually exposes them as alliances of convenience and circumstance. Today, as Cuba faces inevitable transitions after half a century of tyranny, the Catholic church remains the island's only nonstate institution with a semblance of authority and independence. Its ministers have valiantly—albeit cautiously—denounced the excesses and shortcomings of the Communist regime. The island's Protestant churches, on the other hand, remain fragmented and silent, co-opted by the state. As Cuba anticipates future changes, including a torrent of foreign missionaries, Catholics and Protestants remain profoundly divided, lacking a common agenda for facing the opportunities and challenges to come. In Puerto Rico, where recent research demonstrates that church-attending Protestants outnumber church-attending Catholics, the relations between Catholics and Protestants continue to be marked by tension and mutual suspicion. When a Puerto Rican Catholic evaluator of this book's manuscript labeled it a "Protestant book" and saw that perspective as a "disadvantage," I was reminded that the intolerance my fellow Protestants faced under colonial Spain is not altogether gone.

NOTES

Unless otherwise noted, the author has translated all Spanish quotations to English.

Introduction

1. Hans-Jürgen Prien, "Protestantismo, liberalismo y francmasonería en América Latina durante el siglo xix," 15–23; Prien, *Historia del Cristianismo en América Latina,* 718. Latin America's first Protestant congregations emerged in Rio de Janeiro (1819) and Buenos Aires (1825); others followed in Caracas, Lima, Montevideo, and Santiago de Chile. Studies on early Protestantism in Latin America include Jean-Pierre Bastian, *Breve historia del protestantismo en América Latina;* Virginia Garrard Burnett, "Protestantism in Rural Guatemala"; Martín Norberto Dreher, "Protestantismo de inmigración en Brasil"; and Evelia Trejo, "La introducción del protestantismo en México."
2. For example, see Daniel R. Rodríguez, *La primera evangelización norteamericana en Puerto Rico;* Emilio Pantojas García, *La Iglesia Protestante y la americanización de Puerto Rico,* 4 and passim; A. G. Quintero Rivera, *Conflictos de clase y política en Puerto Rico,* 46–49; and Margaret E. Crahan, "Religious Penetration and Nationalism in Cuba," 204–24. For a critique of such interpretative frameworks, see Bastian, "Introducción," and "Las sociedades protestantes y la oposición a Porfirio Díaz en México, 1877–1911," both in Bastian, ed., *Protestantes, liberales y francmasones,* 9–10, 132–64.
3. See Sidney W. Mintz and Eric R. Wolf, "An Analysis of Ritual Co-Parenthood," 342, 353.
4. See, for example, Manuel Moreno Fraginals, *El ingenio*; Fraginals, "Iglesia e ingenio," 11–28; Fernando Picó, *Libertad y servidumbre en el Puerto Rico del siglo xix,* 115–52; Picó, "Iglesia y esclavitud en el Caribe hispano," in *Al filo del poder: subalternos y dominantes en Puerto Rico,* 93–95.
5. For example, although the bishop of Santiago, Antonio María Claret y Clará, advocated for slaves' rights during the mid-1850s, other prelates actively defended slavery and even the continuation of the slave trade. Significantly, the Puerto

Rican–born presbyter, José Gutiérrez del Arroyo, was at one point Ponce's and perhaps Puerto Rico's wealthiest landowner and one of the island's largest slave owners. See Arthur F. Corwin, *Spain and the Abolition of Slavery in Cuba,* 115; Manuel P. Maza Miquel, *Entre la ideología y la compasión,* 72; Picó, "Iglesia y esclavitud," 97; Ivette Pérez Vega, *El cielo y la tierra en sus manos,* 16, 45–50.

6. See, for example, documents in Archivo Histórico Diocesano de la Archidiócesis de San Juan (hereafter cited as AHDASJ), Justicia, Procesos Legales, Soltería, Ponce, bundle J-182; and Archivo del Arzobispado de La Habana (hereafter cited as AALH), Expedientes Ultramarinos, and Matrimonios Ultramarinos; and various anti-Protestant articles and documents published in *El Boletín Eclesiástico de Puerto Rico* and *El Boletín Eclesiástico del Obispado de La Habana.*

7. Fernando Ortiz Fernández, *Contrapunteo cubano del tabaco y el azúcar.*

CHAPTER 1   *Religion and Political Struggle*

1. Alec R. Vidler, *The Church in an Age of Revolution,* 113, 146, 151, 159; Pope Gregory XVI (1831–46) considered prohibiting railroad construction in his territories to keep modern ideas from spreading. See Manuel P. Maza Miquel, *Entre la ideología y la compasión,* 31.

2. José Manuel Cuenca Toribio, *Estudios sobre la iglesia española del siglo xix,* 69, 74–75; Raymond Carr, *España,* 231–50; William J. Callahan, *Church, Politics, and Society in Spain,* 149–50, 191–92; Jerónimo Bécker, *Historia de las relaciones exteriores de España durante el siglo xix,* 2:213–14.

3. Carr, *España,* 231, 236; Almudena Hernández Ruigómez, *La desamortización en Puerto Rico,* 135–37; Vicente Carcel Orti, *Iglesia y revolución en España,* 106; Callahan, *Church,* 186.

4. Mario A. Rodríguez León, *Los registros parroquiales y la microhistoria demográfica en Puerto Rico,* 68–69; Maza Miquel, *Entre la ideología,* 64; Eduardo Torres-Cuevas, *Polémica de la esclavitud,* 36–39, 50; Ivette Pérez Vega, *El cielo y la tierra en sus manos,* 45; Justo L. González, *The Development of Christianity in the Latin Caribbean,* 46–47; Manuel P. Maza Miquel, "Iglesia cubana," in Maza Miquel, ed., *Esclavos, patriotas y poetas a la sombra de la cruz,* 41–43.

5. Jorge David Díaz Reyes, "Estudio sobre el clero de Caguas, siglo xix," 67–138; Maza Miquel, "Iglesia cubana," 47.

6. Fernando Picó, *Libertad y servidumbre en el Puerto Rico del siglo xix,* 131–32.

7. "Informe de Dn. Pedro Hernández Morejón . . . ," (September 15, 1864), Library of Congress (hereafter cited as LC), Del Monte Collection, box 4, file 529; Manuel Moreno Fraginals, *El Ingenio,* 1:33; Robert L. Paquette, *Sugar Is Made with Blood,* 61; Fernando Picó, "Iglesia y esclavitud en el Caribe hispano," in *Al filo del poder: subalternos y dominantes en Puerto Rico,* 93–94; Maza Miquel, *Entre la ideología,* 72. In a revealing deposition for the Junta de Información, Nicolás Azcárate claimed that Catholic missionary establishments could not be harmonized with the regimentation of plantation life; see Arthur F. Corwin, *Spain and the Abolition of Slavery in Cuba,* 199.

8. High-ranking state functionaries in the Cuban municipality of Manzanillo refused to comply with ecclesiastical demands that their slaves be baptized. Archivo

Nacional de Cuba (hereafter cited as ANC), Gobierno Superior Civil, bundle 738, file 25104. Even many of the slaves belonging to the clergyman Nicolás Alonso de Andrade on his estate in Puerto Nuevo, near San Juan, "were baptized only in their deathbeds and by the generous hand of a fellow slave." See Picó, "Iglesia y esclavitud," 98–99; also see Centro de Investigaciones Históricas de la Universidad de Puerto Rico (hereafter cited as CIH), *El proceso abolicionista en Puerto Rico: documentos para su estudio*, 1:152–55. Based on a sample consisting of 40 percent of the slave population of Puerto Rico in 1872, 98 percent were single. See Benjamín Nistal Moret, cited by Picó, "Iglesia y esclavitud," 100. Also see Rodríguez León, *Registros*, 82; H. B. Auchinloss, "La fabricación del azúcar en Cuba," in Juan Pérez de la Riva, *La isla de Cuba en el siglo xix vista por los extranjeros*, 205–6; Salvador Brau, "Las clases jornaleras de Puerto Rico," in *Ensayos*, 30. See "Regulation on Education, Treatment, and Occupation which the Masters of this Island [Puerto Rico] Should Give to the Slaves," by Miguel de la Torre (1826), in Kal Wagenheim and Olga Jiménez de Wagenheim, *The Puerto Ricans*, 45; and Slave Code of 1842 in Paquette, *Sugar*, 267–72.

9. This was so despite an 1849 law that required Chinese laborers to receive religious instruction. See *The Cuba Commission Report*, 23, 109–15.

10. Richard Robert Madden, *The Island of Cuba*, 161–63; Antonio Carlo Napoleone Gallenga, *The Pearl of the Antilles*, 155; Fredrika Bremer, *The Homes of the New World*, 2:309; [John George F. Wurdemann], *Notes on Cuba*, 209; Benjamin Moore Norman, *Rambles by Land and Water*, 38; Anthony Trollope, *The West Indies and the Spanish Main*, 135; [William Henry Hurlbert], *Gan-Eden*, 168; James Rawson, *Cuba*, 31; James William Steele, *Cuban Sketches*, 180, 200; Leví Marrero, *Cuba*, 14:168; [Julia Louisa Matilda Woodruff] pseud. J.L.M. Jay, *My Winter in Cuba*, 165; Demoticus Philalethes, *Yankee Travels through the Island of Cuba*, 52, 222; James Mursell Phillippo, *The United States and Cuba*, 405; Lewis Leonidas Allen, *The Island of Cuba*, 10; Picó, *Libertad y servidumbre*, 127; Pedro Deschamps Chapeaux, *El negro en la economía habanera del siglo xix*, 198; Abiel Abbot, *Letters Written in the Interior of Cuba*, 63.

11. Church property was secularized in 1836, 1841, and 1855. The first was implemented in Cuba in 1841 and the last in Cuba in 1862 and Puerto Rico in 1865. When properties were valued in 1838, the regular clergy's properties were estimated at 179,000 pesos in Puerto Rico and 4,330,000 pesos in Cuba. See Francisco Tomás y Valiente, *El marco político de la desamortización en España*, 73–77, 97, 106; Francisco González del Valle, *La Habana en 1841*, 209; Almudena Hernández Ruigómez, *La desamortización en Puerto Rico*, 135–37, 179, 208; also see José M. García Leduc, "La iglesia y el clero católico de Puerto Rico (1800–1873)," 175; Juan Martín Leiseca, *Apuntes para la historia eclesiástica de Cuba*, 153; Marrero, *Cuba*, 14:111; and David Lockmiller, "The Settlement of the Church Property Question in Cuba," 488–89; Law of suppression of convents of 1837 in AHDASJ, Gobierno, bundle G-125. The ratio of priests to souls in Cuba in 1846 was 1 to 673; in 1861 it was 1 to 476. According to census figures, there were 779 "religiosos" in Cuba in 1860, and 401 of them lived in Havana. For information about the number of priests, see Paquette, *Sugar*, 62; [Wurdemann], *Notes*, 47; Archivo Histórico Nacional, Madrid (hereafter cited as AHN), Ultra-

mar, bundle 2030, file 8; Franklin W. Knight, *Slave Society in Cuba during the Nineteenth Century*, 107–8; Hernández Ruigómez, *Desamortización*; and García Leduc, "Iglesia," 213.

12. Regent of the Audiencia of Puerto Príncipe to the captain-general, February 28, 1843, ANC, Gobierno Superior Civil, bundle 717, file 23765; "Resumen del censo de población de la Isla de Cuba del año 1841," reproduced in Cuba, National Commission of Statistics, Institute of Statistical Research, *Los censos de población y viviendas de Cuba*, tome 1, 2:18; file in ANC, Gobierno Superior Civil, bundle 726, file 24283; Archbishop Claret to Monsignor Casadevall, November 24, 1851, quoted in Reyneiro G. Lebroc, *Cuba*, 127, note 591. In another letter Claret complained directly to a high-ranking official about the many filthy churches with ragged and dirty ornaments and about the starving condition of the priests; Archbishop Claret to the Spanish minister of justice, December 24, 1851, Lebroc, *Cuba*, 127, note 592; also see 1885 report on the clergy in Santiago in Manuel P. Maza Miquel, *El alma del negocio y el negocio del alma*, 18.

13. An 1858 law severely restricted the clergy's power to collect sacramental and other fees. See royal decree of 1858 in Francisco Ramos, *Prontuario de disposiciones oficiales*, 132–35; also see García Leduc, "Iglesia," 292, 337; and Lidio Cruz Monclova, *Historia de Puerto Rico*, 1:468.

14. See Luis Martínez-Fernández, *Torn between Empires*, especially chap. 3.

15. The patronato real was established through the Bula Universalis Ecclesiae of 1508. See Maza Miquel, "Iglesia cubana," 26; and Cruz Monclova, *Historia*, 1:332.

16. Minister Pidal to the British minister in Madrid, August 19, 1850, Public Record Office, Kew, U.K. (hereafter cited as PRO), Foreign Office (hereafter cited as FO), 72/866; Spanish minister of state to Captain-General Concha, September 20, 1850, AHN, Ultramar, bundle 4645, cited in Lebroc, *Cuba*, 128, note 592.

17. Concha, cited in Lebroc, *Cuba*, 128, note 598; Mariano Torrente, *Bosquejo económico político de la isla de Cuba*, 1:202; 2:12; Torrente, "Memoria del 28 de septiembre de 1852," in España, Ministerio de Ultramar, *Cuba desde 1850 a 1873*, 170.

18. Félix de Bona, *Cuba, Santo Domingo y Puerto Rico*, 98; circular by the governor of Puerto Rico, May 12, 1848, in Cruz Monclova, *Historia*, 1:285; president of the Junta de Comercio of Puerto Rico to the Spanish secretary of state, May 19, 1846, Archivo General de Puerto Rico (hereafter cited as AGPR), Audiencia Territorial, Real Acuerdo, box 16, file 52; also see Cruz Monclova, *Historia*, 1:371; and British consul at San Juan to Lord Palmerston, December 24, 1846, PRO, FO, 72/886. In Cuba, planters who hired foreign mechanics demanded exemptions from the requirement to be Catholic. Miguel Tacón, *Correspondencia reservada del Capitán General don Miguel Tacón con el gobierno de Madrid*, 46–47, 291; lieutenant governor of Sagua la Grande to the captain-general, February 27, 1852, ANC, Gobierno Superior Civil, bundle 791, file 26861.

19. See, for example, Marcos Antonio Ramos, *Panorama de protestantismo en Cuba*, 138–39. Also see Francisco J. Ponte Domínguez, *La masonería en la independencia de Cuba*, 13–15.

20. [J. C. Davis] pseud. O.D.D.O., *The History of the Late Expedition to Cuba*, 33.

21. Gaspar Betancourt Cisneros, *Thoughts upon the Incorporation of Cuba into the American Confederation in Contra-position to those Published by Don José Saco*, 28; Gaspar Betancourt Cisneros and John S. Thrasher, *Addresses Delivered at the Celebration of the Third Anniversary in Honor of the Martyrs of Cuban Freedom*, 6–7.

22. José Antonio Saco, "Ideas sobre la incorporación de Cuba en los Estados Unidos," in *Contra la anexión*, 96; [Cristóbal F. Madan], *Contestación a un folleto titulado*, 6–7; Domingo del Monte to Saco, July 18, 1850, and Gaspar Betancourt Cisneros to Saco, April 3, 1849, both in Saco, *Contra la anexión*, 223, 209; Antonio González Ponce de Llorante, *¿Qué es la anexión?*, 38–39.

23. [Madan], *Contestación*, 5–7; [Cristóbal F. Madan] pseud. Un Hacendado, *Llamamiento de la isla de Cuba a la Nación Española*, 217; [Porfirio Valiente] pseud. Un Cubano, *La anexión de Cuba y los peninsulares en ella*, 11–12; Betancourt Cisneros, *Thoughts*, 18.

24. Joan Casanovas, *Bread, or Bullets!*, 72–73; Martínez-Fernández, *Torn between Empires*, 187–98; Enrique José Nemesio Piñeyro y Barry, *Morales Lemus y la revolución de Cuba*, 77; untitled article, *El Siglo*, March 23, 1865; Raúl Cepero Bonilla, "'El Siglo' (1862–1868)," in *Obras históricas*, 275; Ramos, *Panorama*, 139.

25. CIH, *Proceso abolicionista*, 2:30–31; statement by Cuban delegates, Madrid, 1867, LC, Del Monte Collection, box 4, file 534; Segundo Ruiz Belvis, José Julián Acosta, and Francisco Mariano Quiñones, *Proyecto para la abolición de la esclavitud*, 53.

26. Zeno's deposition of November 20, 1866, and de Armas's deposition of December 2, 1866, both in Un emigrado cubano, *Información sobre reformas en Cuba y Puerto Rico*, 50, 57; Corwin, *Spain and the Abolition*, 198.

27. Jaime Luciano Balmes (1810–48) was a Catalan ultramontanist theologian. See his *European Civilization: Protestantism and Catholicity, Compared in their Effects on the Civilization of Europe*. Vidler, *Church*, 151; "El protestantismo, VII," *La Verdad Católica* 1, no. 37 (January 11, 1863): 146. See *El Boletín Eclesiástico de Puerto Rico* 9, no. 22 (November 15, 1867): 270–72; "El protestantismo, VII," *La Verdad Católica* 1, no. 37 (January 11, 1863): 146; and "Estudio sobre Lutero," *El Boletín Eclesiástico de Puerto Rico* 6, no. 8 (April 15, 1864): 89; "Seis confesiones de la Fe," *El Boletín Eclesiástico de Puerto Rico* 2, no. 16 (August 15, 1860): 191–92; "La caridad protestante," *La Verdad Católica* 1, no. 7 (June 15, 1862): 27–28; and captain-general of Cuba to the overseas minister, September 13, 1856, AHN, Ultramar, bundle 4646, file 17, doc. 2.

28. The twelve-part series "El protestantismo" began in *La Verdad Católica* 1, no. 29 (November 16, 1862). All of the articles began with an out-of-context quote from the Psalms: "Todos sus pensamientos y palabras son en favor de la iniquidad" [All of its thoughts and words work for evil ends]. See "El protestantismo, II," *La Verdad Católica* 1, no. 31 (November 30, 1862): 123; *El Boletín Eclesiástico de Puerto Rico* 1, no. 29 (November 16, 1862): 270–71; "El protestantismo, I," *La Verdad Católica* 1, no. 29 (November 16, 1862): 115; "Contradicciones protestantes," *El Boletín Eclesiástico de Puerto Rico* 4, no. 17 (September 1, 1862): 205.

29. "El protestantismo, II," *La Verdad Católica* 1, no. 31 (November 30, 1862): 124.
30. *El Boletín Eclesiástico de Puerto Rico* 2, no. 13 (July 1, 1860): 150–51; "El protestantismo, III," *La Verdad Católica* 1, no. 32 (December 7, 1862): 127; *El Boletín Eclesiástico de Puerto Rico* 2, no. 17 (August 29, 1860): 197.
31. Letter from Tacón, March 5, 1836, and Tacón to the Spanish secretary of state, August 31, 1835, in Tacón, *Correspondencia*, 223–24, 177–79; David Murray, *Odious Commerce*, 147, 157; Marrero, *Cuba*, 9:73; royal order by the Spanish secretary of state, October 27, 1841, and the governor of Santiago to the intendant of El Cobre, July 8, 1842, both in ANC, Asuntos Políticos, bundle 41, files 19 and 42. Also see the Spanish consul at Kingston to the captain-general of Cuba, October 17, 1853, ANC, Asuntos Políticos, bundle 48, file 33; Corwin, *Spain and the Abolition*, 73; and Paquette, *Sugar*, 155.
32. David Turnbull to the captain-general of Cuba, September 16, 1841, ANC, Gobierno Superior Civil, bundle 744, file 25346; Emma Aurora Dávila Cox, *Este inmenso comercio,* 160–61; Howden to Claudio Antón de Luzuriaga, April 4, 1855, and D. R. Clarke to Palmerston, January 26, 1850, both in PRO, FO, 72/885; Malmesbury to Howden, April 23, 1852, AHN, Estado, bundle 8565; acting consul Kennedy to the captain-general of Cuba, May 7, 1850, PRO, FO, 72/886.
33. Julius W. Pratt, "The Ideology of American Expansion," in Avery Craven, ed., *Essays in Honor of William Dodd*, 335–52; [Richard Burleigh Kimbal], *Cuba, and the Cubans*, 158, 194; George W. Williams, *Sketches of Travel in the Old and New World*, 7, 35, 43–44; Spanish minister in Washington, D.C., to the Spanish secretary of state, August 30, 1852, Archivo del Servicio Histórico Militar, Madrid (hereafter cited as ASHM), Ultramar, bundle 90.
34. U.S. Senate, Senator George E. Pugh of Ohio speaking on the acquisition of Cuba, 35th Cong., 2d sess., *Congressional Globe* 28 (February 10, 1859): part 1, p. 940; U.S. Senate, Senator Zachariah Chandler of Michigan speaking on the acquisition of Cuba, 35th Cong., 2d sess., *Congressional Globe* 28 (February 17, 1859): part 2, p. 1080–1; John P. Hale, *The Acquisition of Cuba*, 13–15; John J. Perry, *The Filibuster Policy of the Sham Democracy*, 3–4. U.S. Senate, Senator Stephen R. Mallory of Florida speaking on the acquisition of Cuba, 35th Cong., 2d sess., *Congressional Globe* 28 (February 25, 1859): part 2, pp. 299, 1330.

CHAPTER 2   *The Roman Catholic Grip*

1. Consul Andrew K. Blythe to William Cass, July 20, 1857, National Archives, Washington, D.C., and College Park, Md. (hereafter cited as NA), General Records of the Department of State, Record Group (hereafter cited as RG) 59, Diplomatic Dispatches, Havana, microfilm T20, reel 36; George C. Backhouse to his aunt, August 3, 1853, in John Backhouse Papers, Special Collections Department, Perkins Library, Duke University, Durham, N.C. (hereafter cited as Backhouse Papers); Alexander Gilmore Cattell, *To Cuba and Back in Twenty-Two Days*, 34; James Mursell Phillippo, *The United States and Cuba*, 211; John Joseph Gurney, *A Winter in the West Indies*; Richard Henry Dana, Jr., *To Cuba and Back*,

30; Lidio Cruz Monclova, *Historia de Puerto Rico*, 2:416–17; Howden to Palmerston, September 22, 1851, PRO, FO, 83/159.

2. See the royal order to all archbishops and bishops of the Indies, July 13, 1559, in Alejandro Tapia y Rivera, ed., *Biblioteca histórica de Puerto Rico*, 400–401. Limpieza de sangre was a requirement for university admission and for entering certain professions, including the priesthood. This requirement was finally abolished in Spain on May 16, 1865, and in the colonies by the decree of March 20, 1870. See the limpieza de sangre proceedings of Felipe Betances (father of Ramón Emeterio Betances) in AGPR, Varios 2, box 142; and the 1870 decree in Tapia y Rivera, ed., *Biblioteca*, 384–86.

3. See the 1815 Cédula de Gracias, in Cayetano Coll y Toste, ed., *Boletín histórico de Puerto Rico*, 1:297–304; and "Real Cédula de 21 de octubre de 1817, sobre aumentar la población blanca de la isla de Cuba," ANC, Gobierno Superior Civil, bundle 1657, file 82745. Also see D. C. Corbitt, "Immigration in Cuba," 280–308. The intention of these laws was to attract Catholic settlers from Ireland, France, Corsica, Louisiana, Italy, and other Catholic countries. See the Spanish minister in Washington, D.C., to the Spanish vice-consul at Savannah, Georgia, March 8, 1859, Duke University, Perkins Library, Special Collections Department, Papers of Spain, Ministry of Foreign Affairs, Savannah Consulate.

4. In a circular dated 1839, the archdeacon of Santiago, Juan Pacheco, recognized that foreign immigration could enrich the island but warned priests to be alert for the slightest spark of the "deadly fire" of strange cults. Juan Pacheco, *Circular al venerable clero del Arzobispado de Santiago de Cuba*, 6; [John George F. Wurdemann], *Notes on Cuba*, 166; U.S. Consular Agent Minvielle to Consul Edward Conroy, March 22, 1872, NA, Records of Foreign Service Posts, RG 84, San Juan, vol. 7117.

5. Havana's British consul-general reported in 1852 that applicants were allowed two years to document the fact that they were Catholic; past this grace period no further verification occurred to ensure that the requested documentation had been gathered. Joseph T. Crawford to Lord Palmerston, January 22, 1852, PRO, FO, 72/886. Copy of the oath of domiciliation in NA, RG 59, Havana, microfilm T20, reel 24; see Jorge Luis Chinea Serrano, "Racial Politics and Commercial Agriculture," 269; also see the listing of undomiciled foreigners residing in Matanzas (1844) in Archivo Histórico Provincial de Matanzas (hereafter cited as AHPM), Gobierno Provincial, Negociado de Orden Público y Policía, bundle 58, file 6001.

6. On Cabildos, see Philip A. Howard, *Changing History*. Regarding similarities between Catholicism and African religions, Mary Turner has stated: "In general slave workers found many recognizable elements in Catholic religious ritual: religious specialists who interceded with the gods, ranks of spirits deified in their miraculous deeds, spiritual powers embodied in statues, medallions, relics, feasts and processions, sacred clothing and special utensils." See her "Religious Beliefs," in *General History of the Caribbean*, 3:307. Syncretism also occurred among slaves who were proselytized by Protestant missionaries in the British West Indies. Because these missionaries remained vigilant about African retentions, the syncretic outcome among Jamaican slaves, for example, were more formal and

attitudinal than foundationally theological. See Mary Turner, *Slaves and Missionaries*, 57–59.

7. Documentation on banned books in Biblioteca Nacional José Martí (hereafter cited as BNJM), Colección Manuscritos Morales, files 18 and 54.A.

8. Francisco Ramos, *Prontuario de disposiciones oficiales*, 122–25; James William Steele, *Cuban Sketches*, 140; [Wurdemann], *Notes*, 1; Una Roberts Lawrence, *Cuba for Christ*, 142–43.

9. Tacón to the Spanish secretary of state, August 31, 1835, in Miguel Tacón, *Correspondencia reservada del Capitán General don Miguel Tacón*, 177–79; David Murray, *Odious Commerce*, 119; Marcos Antonio Ramos, *Panorama de protestantismo en Cuba*, 109, 65–67; John Coleman to the Female Bible Society of Philadelphia, April 12, 1855 (copy), in Archives of the Episcopal Church, Austin, Tex. (hereafter cited as AEC), Cuba Scrapbook; Eliza McHatton Ripley, *From Flag to Flag*, 129–30.

10. Ángel L. Gutiérrez, *Evangélicos en Puerto Rico en la época española*, 21–23; Donald T. Moore, *Puerto Rico para Cristo*, 8; Guillermo A. Baralt, *Esclavos rebeldes*, 72.

11. Cruz Monclova, *Historia*, 1:644–45; *El Boletín Eclesiástico de Puerto Rico* 9, no. 22 (November 15, 1867): 270–71; *El Boletín Eclesiástico de Puerto Rico* 11, no. 8 (April 15, 1870): 58. See "Reglamento de periódicos," Archivo Histórico Municipal de Ponce (hereafter cited as AHMP), bundle 84, file 2; and documentation on censored books in Cuba in BNJM, Colección Manuscritos Morales, files 18 and 54.A.

12. For example, in 1821 the parish priest of Toa Alta, José María Martínez, received 100 pesos from 200 baptisms, 106 pesos for 25 weddings, and 54 pesos for burials. José M. García Leduc, "La iglesia y el clero católico de Puerto Rico (1800–1873)," 338, 394.

13. Steele, *Cuban Sketches*, 173–74, 184.

14. Very occasionally, priests refused to baptize particular children, which had more to do with the proposed godparents than with the children. One priest in Bayamo, Cuba, refused to baptize an infant brought in by a man named Pedro Castus because he had a concubine. See the governor of the Oriental Department to the captain-general, October 28, 1856, ANC, Gobierno Superior Civil, bundle 729, file 24418. Nine percent of all baptisms among blacks in Havana (1859) were adult baptisms; see Félix Erenchún, *Anales de la isla de Cuba*, 1910. Also see Verena Martínez-Alier, *Marriage, Class, and Colour in Nineteenth-Century Cuba*, 83; and Turner, "Religious Beliefs," 308. See Antonio Cuesta Mendoza, *Historia eclesiástica del Puerto Rico colonial*, 232; Jorge D. Flinter, *Examen del estado actual de los esclavos de la isla de Puerto Rico*, 38.

15. Godparents, who usually enjoyed higher economic status than did parents, were expected to cover many of the costs associated with the baptismal celebration, including, in some instances, the distribution of gold and silver coins for the ceremony's attendants. On baptismal fees, see Pedro Tomás de Córdova, *Memorias geográficas, históricas, económicas y estadísticas de la Isla de Puerto Rico*, 3:37–38; Samuel Hazard, *Cuba with Pen and Pencil*, 119; [Wurdemann], *Notes*, 168; Cuesta Mendoza, *Historia eclesiástica*, 233. Also see the baptisms of Asians

in Archivo Parroquial de la Iglesia Salvador del Mundo, El Cerro, Havana (here-after cited as APISM), Libros de bautismos; José García de Arboleya, *Manual de la Isla de Cuba*, 181; and Sidney W. Mintz and Eric R. Wolf, "An Analysis of Ritual Co-Parenthood."

16. Cartilla de Domingo Rosaín de 1824 para parteras con instrucciones [1824 manual for midwives by Domingo Rosaín], cited in Pedro Deschamps Chapeaux, *El negro en la economía habanera del siglo xix*, 170; Slave Code of 1842 reproduced in Robert L. Paquette, *Sugar Is Made with Blood*, 267–72; Cuesta Mendoza, *Historia eclesiástica*, 233; Fernando Picó, *Libertad y servidumbre en el Puerto Rico del siglo xix*, 127; Charles Walker, letter of May 3, 1836, "Charles Walker's Letters from Puerto Rico," 44–47; Mario A. Rodríguez León, *Los registros parroquiales y la microhistoria demográfica en Puerto Rico*, 79.

17. Nélida Agosto Cintrón, *Religión y cambio social en Puerto Rico*, 37. On masters' responsibilities for sacramental expenses, see Cédula de Carlos III, May 31, 1789, cited in "Testimonio del expediente formado para averiguar las causas que influyen en el frecuente *suicidio de los esclavos*," AHN, Ultramar, bundle 4655, file 816; also see García Leduc, "Iglesia," 187; CIH, *El proceso abolicionista en Puerto Rico*, 1:152–55; Dana, *To Cuba*, 124; Fernando Picó, "Iglesia y esclavitud," in *Al filo del poder*, 98–100.

18. See Mintz and Wolf, "Analysis."

19. Picó, *Libertad y servidumbre*, 128. Provisions existed for the so-called ecclesiastic divorce, which allowed for the separation of the marriage partners without the dissolution of the marriage bond but did not permit remarriage. See Silvia M. Arróm, *La mujer mexicana ante el divorcio eclesiástico*, 17. On age requirements, see the law of June 20, 1862, AGPR, Real Audiencia, Tribunal en Pleno, box 3, file 15. This law did not fully apply to Cuba and Puerto Rico "because of the greater precociousness of physical development that takes place in tropical climates, which accelerates and precipitates for both sexes, but particularly among women, the plenitude of capabilities"; quoted in Ramón de Armas y Sáenz, *Ley de disenso paterno aplicada a las islas de Cuba y Puerto-Rico por real decreto de 3 de febrero de 1882*, 20; also see "Ley de disenso paterno," *El Boletín Eclesiástico del Obispado de La Habana* 2, no. 6 (March 16, 1882): 41. In Cuba, interracial marriages were allowed without special licences by the archbishop of Cuba (1853) and by the colonial government (1881). On restrictions on interracial marriages, see Martínez-Alier, *Marriage*, 40; Arthur F. Corwin, *Spain and the Abolition*, 115; and Dana, *To Cuba*, 120. On impediments to marriage, see Asunción Lavrin, "Sexuality in Colonial Mexico," in *Sexuality and Marriage in Colonial Latin America*, 56.

20. Damián López de Haro, *Constituciones sinodales*, 187–88; José Martín de Herrera, *Auto del Excmo. é Illmo. Señor arzobispo metropolitano facultando a los párrocos para tramitar expedientes matrimoniales*, 5; Ramos, *Prontuario*, 140–41; Córdova, *Memorias*, 3:37–38; Steele, *Cuban Sketches*, 178; Demoticus Philalethes, *Yankee Travels*, 243; Cuesta Mendoza, *Historia eclesiástica*, 239; and Félix Manuel Ortiz Medina, "Análisis de los registros de matrimonios de la Parroquia de Yabucoa," 87; see records of bans in AHDASJ, Justicia, box 140; also see APISM, Libro primero de matrimonios de españoles.

21. Real Cédula sobre arreglo y dotación de Culto y Clero [royal decree on church allocations] (1858), in Ramos, *Prontuario*, 132–35; also see 140; testimony of Father Pedro Pizá and the parish priest of Arroyo, Puerto Rico, in Henry K. Carroll, *Report on the Island of Porto Rico*, 658–59, 697. Salvador Brau, "La Campesina," in *Ensayos*, 114.

22. See Rodríguez León, *Registros*, 122. Reduced dispensation costs established in 1857 for Puerto Rico ranged between 150 pesos for second degree of affinity down to 10 pesos for second degree with fourth degree. On costs, see Martín de Hererra, *Auto*, 9; AGPR, Audiencia Territorial, Real Acuerdo, box 20B, file 20; testimony of Father Juan Perpiñá y Pibernat, in Carroll, *Report*, 708; and García Leduc, "Iglesia," 384. In the Puerto Rican parish of Yabucoa, 199 of 590 marriages (1813–50) were between contractors with some degree of consanguinity; Ortiz Medina, "Análisis," 199. Also see Brau, "Campesina," 114; Picó, *Libertad y servidumbre*, 128–29; and Martínez-Alier, *Marriage*, 87.

23. López de Haro, *Constituciones*, 187–88; AGPR, Audiencia Territorial, Real Acuerdo, box 20A, file 10; and communication by the bishop of Puerto Rico, November 1, 1865, in Francisco Ramos, *Apéndice al prontuario de disposiciones oficiales*, 189–90. Also see AALH, Matrimonios Ultramarinos. Widows wishing to remarry had to prove that their late husbands had been dead for 301 days or longer, which made sure that they were not carrying their late husbands' children. Also see *The Cuba Commission Report*, 22–23, 134.

24. Circumstances warranting leniency included absence of potential marriage partners of equal condition, a woman's having reached the age of twenty-four or not having a sufficient dowry, a widow or single woman's having too many children and the groom's promise to support them, cohabitation, sexual activity, pregnancy, suspicion of intercourse, and "whenever there is a danger that those wishing to marry, even at the highest degrees [of consanguinity] due to a denial of dispensation will approach a non-Catholic minister for the celebration of the marriage." See "Instrucciones sobre dispensas matrimoniales," *El Boletín Eclesiástico del Obispado de La Habana* 3, no. 17 (September 30, 1883): 214–17. Also see the document on marriage dispensations, 1857, in AGPR, Audiencia Territorial, Real Acuerdo, box 20B, file 20.

25. García Leduc, "Iglesia," 397–98; Martínez-Alier, *Marriage*, 50; Salvador Brau, "Las clases jornaleras de Puerto Rico," in *Ensayos*, 32. See the circular of April 2, 1855, in Ramos, *Prontuario*, 19–20; letter of the Spanish overseas minister to the governor of Puerto Rico, October 4, 1866, in Ramos, *Apéndice*, 90; García de Arboleya, *Manual*, 119; Ramón Marín, *Las fiestas populares de Ponce*, 221; and the document of September 30, 1874, on cohabitation in Ponce in AGPR, Gobernadores Españoles, box 534. For a discussion on campaigns against cohabitation in Puerto Rico, see Félix V. Matos Rodríguez, *Women and Urban Change in San Juan, Puerto Rico*, 96–100.

26. Circular by Bishop Gil Esteve, December 23, 1852, AHDASJ, Gobierno, Circulares, 1813–99. The soltería proceedings of Jorge Y. Finlay and Emilia Francisca Van Rhyn of 1866 cost 53 pesos and 38 cents. See AHDASJ, Justicia, Procesos Legales, Soltería, Ponce, bundle J-182; and Cuesta Mendoza, *Historia eclesiástica*, 239.

27. According to Asunción Lavrin, "the state was primarily interested in the worldly bonds, and it focused on the legal issues surrounding sexual behavior and the institution of marriage. Among them, the establishment of the legitimacy of the marital union to secure the allocation of inheritance and the division of benefits among spouse and offspring was of cardinal importance. The church established a sacramental bonding connecting the material with the spiritual. Its goals were to place all actions expressing sexuality within a teleological objective: the salvation of the soul." Lavrin, "Introduction," *Sexuality and Marriage*, 3.

28. The Juntas de Vagos y Amancebados were established in Puerto Rico by Governor Miguel López de Baños. Each municipal junta had the local parish priest as one of its permanent members. See García Leduc, "Iglesia," 16; Matos Rodríguez, *Women*, 28, 96–100. See also circulars by Puerto Rico's governors on the subject of amancebados, January 23, 1845, April 2, 1855, and July 24, 1855, in Ramos, *Prontuario*, 18–19.

29. Philalethes, *Yankee Travels*, 149; Christopher Schmidt-Nowara, *Empire and Antislavery*, 105; Slave Code of 1842, reproduced in Paquette, *Sugar*, 267–72; Picó, *Libertad y servidumbre*, 138.

30. Ortiz Medina, "Análisis," 87. On the case of Marciala Saleces, see AGPR, Audiencia Territorial, Real Acuerdo, box 18, file 10.

31. For Havana (1842), see [Wurdemann], *Notes*, 169; for Bayamón (1879), see Mario A. Rodríguez León, *Bayamón: notas para su historia*, 2:10–13. Numbers in Ponce (1883) were 1,252 births, 113 marriages, and 1,406 deaths; see "Estadística eclesiástica de la diócesis de Puerto Rico, Parroquia de Ponce, año 1883," in AHDASJ, Disciplina, Padrones, Estadística, 1872–83, bundle P-61. Also see Córdova, *Memorias*, 2:32, 33, 95, 209, 255, 274, 406; Carroll, *Report*, 218; Cuba, Statistics Commission, *Cuadro estadístico de la siempre fiel isla de Cuba [1846]*, 34, 97, 212; and Erenchún, *Anales*, 1908.

32. In Ponce in 1876, there were 600 legitimate births and 609 illegitimate ones; in 1883, there were 595 legitimate births and 657 illegitimate ones. See Marín, *Fiestas*, 221; and "Estadística eclesiástica de la diócesis de Puerto Rico, Parroquia de Ponce, año 1883," in AHDASJ, Disciplina, Padrones, Estadística, 1872–83, bundle P-61. On Loíza (1835–44), see Rodríguez León, *Registros*, 82. Also see Carroll, *Report*, 35.

33. In 1844, there were forty illegitimate births and twenty-two legitimate ones in Vieques; see Parroquia de Vieques, Libro de Bautismos, microfilms in CIH. According to a census of 1845, only one of five residents of Vieques was married; CIH, Papeles de Vieques, 733. See declaration by Presbyter Francisco Torres, 1851, and an undated letter from the captain-general of Puerto Rico (circa 1851), in CIH, Papeles de Vieques, 820–21, 213.

34. In 1865, there were fourteen illegitimate births and twenty legitimate ones; see Parroquia de Vieques, Libro de Bautismos, microfilms in CIH.

35. Manuel Hernández González, *La emigración canaria a América*, 108–12; Father Perpiñá y Pibernat's testimony, in Carroll, *Report*, 655.

36. In Puerto Rico in 1867, there were 41,737 slaves, of which only 1,099 were married; for the same year the rate of marriage among Puerto Rico's whites was 70 percent and among blacks 25 percent. See CIH, *Proceso abolicionista*, 2:168–70;

Rafael María de Labra y Cadrana, *La brutalidad de los negros*, 29; Benjamín Nistal, quoted in Picó, *Al filo*, 100; CIH, Papeles de Vieques, 733; and Carroll, *Report*, 655.

37. Cuba, *Cuadro estadístico [1846]*, 34, 145, 212; AHPM, Gobierno Provincial, Negociado de Orden Público, bundle 31, file 3141; Erenchún, *Anales*, 1902–3; Dana, *To Cuba*, 124; Aline Helg, *Our Rightful Share*, 28.

38. An 1852 law established that at least one-fifth of all imported coolies had to be female, but the law was not obeyed. More than 99 percent of all Asian laborers imported to Cuba were male; in Matanzas (1877), there were 20,028 male coolies and only 26 females. See *Cuba Commission*, 10, 22–23, 115, 134; and Laird W. Bergad, *Cuban Rural Society in the Nineteenth-Century*, 254.

39. Estela Cifre de Loubriel, *Catálogo de extranjeros residentes en Puerto Rico en el siglo xix*, xlix; Martínez-Alier, *Marriage*, 64.

40. Jay Kinsbruner, *Not of Pure Blood*, 89.

41. Fernando Ortiz Fernández, *Hampa afro-cubana*, 120.

42. Philalethes, *Yankee Travels*, 251; regulations for Ponce's cemetery, in Ramón E. López Crespo, "El desarrollo histórico del cementerio de las calles Simón de la Torre y Frontispicio Ponce, Puerto Rico, 1843–1918," 30; López de Haro, *Constituciones*, 181–83; circular by the provisor and general vicar of the bishopric of Puerto Rico; and the appeals judge of Aguadilla to the regent of the Real Audiencia, May 26, 1866, AGPR, Real Audiencia, Tribunal en Pleno, box 44, file 9; *Cuba Commission*, 109–10. Also see *El Boletín Eclesiástico de Puerto Rico* 8, no. 10 (May 15, 1866).

43. For information on funeral costs in Cuba, see García de Arboleya, *Manual*, 316–17. A social stigma was attached to the label *pobres de solmenidad*. See Manuel P. Maza Miquel, *Entre la ideología y la compasión*, 381.

44. As established by an 1866 attempt to regulate and standardize funeral fees in Puerto Rico, a first-class funeral service with deacons, candelabra, incense, vigil, and chanted mass with music cost sixteen and one-quarter pesos. For nine and a half pesos, one could get a second-class funeral without music or deacons. Funeral processions from the home of the deceased to the church and from the church to the cemetery cost eight and eighteen pesos, respectively. See the overseas minister to the governor of Puerto Rico, October 4, 1866, in Ramos, *Apéndice*, 90–92; Córdova, *Memorias*, 3:37–38; Walker, letter of April 7, 1836, "Charles Walker's Letters," 42–44.

45. García de Arboleya, *Manual*, 267–69; George W. Williams, *Sketches of Travel in the Old and New World*, 38; Deschamps Chapeaux, *El negro*, 76–77; Francisco González del Valle, *La Habana en 1841*, 397.

46. Steele, *Cuban Sketches*, 185; U.S. Consul Helm to William Cass, April 28, 1860, NA, RG 59, Havana, microfilm T20, reel 40; [Wurdemann], *Notes*, 168; 1842 document in ANC, Gobierno Superior Civil, bundle 715, file 23628.

47. Bishop of Havana to the captain-general, July 29, 1847, ANC, Gobierno Superior Civil, bundle 745, file 25604; Julián Zulueta to the captain-general, March 4, 1854, ANC, Gobierno Superior Civil, bundle 727, file 24299; petition to build a cemetery in the plantation of Agustín Esponda of Sancti Spiritus, ANC, Gobierno Superior Civil, bundle 366, file 17522. Also see Miguel Barnet, *Biografía de un*

cimarrón, 27, 59; the document pertaining to Alboy's demands, in AGPR, Audiencia Territorial, Real Acuerdo, box 26C, file 7; and CIH, *Proceso abolicionista*, 1:206–7.

48. Case of Juan Bautista Sanz, September 1836, in ANC, Gobierno Superior Civil, bundle 714, file 23574; Wajay case, in Rafael González to the governor and captain-general, February 26, 1853, ANC, Gobierno Superior Civil, bundle 727, file 24299; case of Nueva Bermeja, priest of Nueva Bermeja to the civilian governor, April 1, 1854, ANC, Gobierno Superior Civil, bundle 727, file 24299. Also see the 1842 document in ANC, Gobierno Superior Civil, bundle 715, file 23628.

49. Miguel Estorch, cited in Inés Roldán de Montaud, "Origen, evolución y supresión del grupo de negros 'emancipados' en Cuba," 581; Crawford to Lord Clarendon, June 1, 1855, AHN, Estado, bundle 8048; Paquette, *Sugar*, 135; Crawford to Lord Clarendon, January 3, 1855, in Great Britain, Parliament, House of Commons, *British Parliamentary Papers [Slave Trade]* (hereafter cited as *BPP*), vol. 41, class B, p. 563; Gustave D'Hespel D'Harponville, *La reine des Antilles*, 279–80. Also see the bishop of Havana to the captain-general of Cuba, September 5, 1855, ANC, Gobierno General, bundle 337, file 16254; Vice-Consul Savage to Seward, April 23, 1864, NA, RG 59, Havana, microfilm T20, reel 47; and García Leduc, "Iglesia," 394. Also see ANC, Gobierno General, bundle 258, file 13376.

50. Marrero, *Cuba*, 14:83–88; Domingo Rosaín, *Necrópolis de La Habana*, 15; Ismael Testé, *Historia eclesiástica de Cuba*, 3:167; 5:415–16; López Crespo, "Desarrollo histórico," 11.

51. In 1867, the bishop of Havana determined that Asians were people of color and therefore should not be buried next to whites in niches or vaults; decree by Bishop Jacinto María Martínez of Havana, July 1867, LC, Del Monte Collection, box 4, folder 4, doc. 42. Frederika Bremer, *The Homes of the New World*, 2:414–15; Rosaín, *Necrópolis*, passim; Emilio Roig de Leuchsenring, *La Habana: apuntes históricos*, 61–63; Walker, letter of April 7, 1836, "Charles Walker's Letters," 42–44. The subscription for Ponce's second cemetery included donations from Protestants such as James Gilbee and Guillermo Oppenheimer. See AHMP, "Índice del cementerio antiguo," 1:143; and López Crespo, "Desarrollo histórico," 18.

52. William Cullen Bryant, *Letters of William Cullen Bryant*, 3:31; Nicolás Tanco Armero, "La Isla de Cuba," 134; Steele, *Cuban Sketches*, 185; Marrero, *Cuba*, 14:89; Erenchún, *Anales*, 1794. Referring to funerals among Caribbean slaves, Mary Turner has stated: "Funeral rituals, however, reflected not only belief in immortality and the role of the dead in the fortunes of the living, but also the belief that death was related to the reality of social conflict. Funeral rituals consequently incorporated divination techniques; the body directed the coffin bearers along the road it chose, forced them to stop or to run, and pushed the coffin from their shoulders to identify enemies"; Turner, "Religious Beliefs," 298. The bishop of Havana once justified such restrictions, stating that "this practice, imported from countries with totally different religious circumstances, gave a profane character to one of the most pious and sublime ceremonies of the Holy Religion of Jesus Christ." See AHN, Ultramar, bundle 1705, file 43; and Ramos, *Prontuario*, 89. Also see the royal order of 1857, in Ramos, *Apéndice*, 30; Juan García de Palacios, *Sínodo de*

Santiago de 1681, 90. On the ban on night burials, see ANC, Gobierno Superior Civil, bundle 769, file 26424; the bishop of Havana to the captain-general, November 1851, ANC, Gobierno Superior Civil, bundle 746, file 25637; and the case of religious and civil authorities of Mayagüez, in AGPR, Audiencia Territorial, Real Arreglo, box 22A, file 41.

53. Robert W. Gibbes, *Cuba for Invalids*, 51; Richard J. Levis, *Diary of a Spring Holiday in Cuba*, 90; Steele, *Cuban Sketches*, 185; [William Henry Hurlbert], *Gan-Eden*, 136–37; [Wurdemann], *Notes*, 31; journal letters of Ledyard Lincklean and Mrs. Lincklean (February–March 1857), New York Historical Society (hereafter cited as NYHS); Edward Kenney to Bishop Whittingham, November 25, 1873, Maryland Diocesan Archives [Episcopal Church], Baltimore (hereafter cited as MDA), Cuba folder 4.

54. Secretary of the government to the municipal government of Havana, July 5, 1860, ANC, Gobierno General, bundle 101, file 4825; *El Siglo* (October 1, 1865); *La Voz de Cuba* (August 9, 1870).

55. Testé, *Historia eclesiástica*, 5:415–19; Martín Socarrás Matos, *La Necrópolis Cristóbal Colón*, 19, 32; Roig de Leuchsenring, *La Habana*, 61–63; "Reglamento de 1867," ANC, Gobierno General, bundle 101, file 4825.

56. This was Ponce's second cemetery, which was built by public subscription between 1838 and 1843; its size doubled when it was expanded in 1867. See AGPR, Obras Públicas, Obras Municipales, box 289, bundle 54B, file 2; AHMP, bundle 43, file 4; and "Índice del cementerio antiguo," 1:143; and López Crespo, "Desarrollo histórico," 27–55.

57. Bremer, *Homes*, 2:414–15; [Wurdemann], *Notes*, 29; Gibbes, *Cuba*, 51; [Hurlbert], *Gan-Eden*, 136–37; journal letters of Ledyard Lincklean and Mrs. Lincklean (1857), NYHS; documents pertaining to the expansion of Ponce's cemetery (1864), AGPR, Obras Públicas, Obras Municipales, box 289, bundle 54B, file 2. Also see Lewis Leonidas Allen, *The Island of Cuba*, 17; and the diary of Reverend William Norwood (hereafter cited as Norwood diary), March 28, 1844, Virginia Historical Society, Richmond; Bryant, *Letters*, 3:30–31; D'Hespel D'Harponville, *Reine*, 105; Joseph J. Dimock, *Impressions of Cuba in the Nineteenth Century*, 69–70; and Walker, "Charles Walker's Letters," 42.

58. *Cuba Commission*, 110; Bryant, *Letters*, 3:39. [Wurdemann], *Notes*, 32; Steele, *Cuban Sketches*, 185; journal letters of Ledyard Lincklean and Mrs. Lincklean (1857), NYHS; AGPR, Obras Públicas, Obras Municipales, box 289, bundle 54B, file 5.

59. Capitán pedáneo of Quemados to the captain-general, February 20, 1847; and doctors' reports of February 20, 1847, both in ANC, Gobierno Superior Civil, bundle 721, file 24004.

60. Philalethes, *Yankee Travels*, 251; López Crespo, "Desarrollo histórico," 30; Ramos, *Prontuario*, 90–91.

61. Governor of Puerto Rico to the bishop of Puerto Rico, July 1, 1876, AHN, Ultramar, bundle 2061, file 26; the bishop of Havana to the captain-general of Cuba, January 2, 1888, ANC, Gobierno General, bundle 107, file 5016; "Doctrina de Benedicto XIV y de las congregaciones Romanas," *El Boletín Eclesiástico del Obispado de La Habana* 3, no. 17 (September 30, 1883): 141; López de Haro,

Constituciones, 181–82; the bishop of Havana to the captain-general, January 2, 1888, ANC, Gobierno General, bundle 107, file 5016.

62. Walker, letter to his uncle and aunt, December 22, 1835, "Charles Walker's Letters," 38–41. Andújar case documents in AHN, Ultramar, bundle 2060, file 31.

63. Capitán pedáneo of Ceiba Mocha to the governor of Matanzas, April 10, 1858, AHPM, Gobierno Provincial, Cementerios, bundle 13, file 5; Antonio Medina Fernández, "Historia de la localidad," copy in Museo del Cerro; transcribed document dated June 2, 1870, in BNJM, Colección Pérez, file 331.

64. Letter of the appeals judge of Aguadilla, Puerto Rico, to the regent of the Real Audiencia, May 26, 1866, AGPR, Real Audiencia, Tribunal Pleno, AGPR, box 44, file 9; ANC, Gobierno Superior Civil, bundle 738, file 25054; captain-general of Cuba to the bishop, April 26, 1852, and the governor of Bejucal to the captain-general, March 2, 1852, ANC, Gobierno Superior Civil, bundle 725, file 24257; inspector of the Plaza de Armas of Matanzas to the governor of Matanzas, July 20, 1836, AHPM, Gobierno Provincial, Negociado de Orden Público, bundle 58; capitán pedáneo of Nueva Carcel to the captain-general, August 18, 1842, ANC, Gobierno Superior Civil, bundle 717, file 23732; jail guard to the civilian lieutenant governor, June 22, 1854, ANC, Gobierno General, bundle 315, file 15292.

65. "Testimonio del espediente formado para averiguar las causas que influyen en el frecuente *suicidio de esclavos*," AHN, Ultramar, bundle 4655, file 816; report by guard, May 13, 1881, AHPM, Gobierno Provincial, Negociado de Orden Público, bundle 17, file 1702; Paquette, *Sugar*, 71; Turner, "Religious Beliefs," 297; Abiel Abbot, *Letters Written in the Interior of Cuba*, 44; D'Hespel D'Harponville, *Reine*, 270–71; Bremer, *Homes*, 2:332; [Wurdemann], *Notes*, 262–63.

66. *Cuba Commission*, 42, 49, 50, 70, 82, 100–109; commander of El Cerro to the president of the political governorship, June 20, 1847, ANC, Gobierno Superior Civil, bundle 721, file 24006; Juan Pérez de la Riva, "Demografía de los culíes," in *El barracón*, 67; Ripley, *From Flag to Flag*, 178; Dana, *To Cuba*, 44; Levis, *Diary*, 90.

67. D'Hespel D'Harponville, *Reine*, 451; lieutenant governor of Cárdenas to the captain-general, February 2, 1861, ANC, Gobierno Superior Civil, bundle 734, file 24769; case of the foreigner Leded Warren who died on February 20, 1838 and was not buried in the church cemetery of Salvador del Mundo, APISM, Libro primero de defunciones; Archivo Parroquial de la Iglesia Nuestra Señora del Pilar, El Cerro (hereafter cited as APNSP), Libro cuarto de defunciones; also see Dimock, *Impressions*, 113.

68. Steele, *Cuban Sketches*, 184; testimony of Mr. Cartagena, president of the Board of Public Works, January 24, 1899, in Carroll, *Report*, 663; John F. Young, "Cuba," *Spirit of Missions* 49 (October 1884): 490.

69. Lieutenant governor of Cárdenas to the captain-general, February 2, 1861, ANC, Gobierno Superior Civil, bundle 734, file 24769; documents on Andújar's case, AHN, Ultramar, bundle 2060, file 31; order of February 8, 1862, ANC, Gobierno Superior Civil, bundle 738, file 25054; the bishop of Havana to the captain-general, August 31, 1850, ANC, Gobierno Superior Civil, bundle 723, file 24178.

70. U.S. Consul Jourdan to Seward, July 19, 1866 and attached copy of decree by governor Marchesi, NA, RG 84, San Juan, vol. 7228; petition, March 15, 1864,

ANC, Gobierno General, bundle 102, file 4829; ANC, Gobierno Superior Civil, bundle 729, file 24423.

71. Young, "Cuba," 486–87; the presbyter of Vieques to the bishop of Puerto Rico, June 22, 1875, AHDASJ, Gobierno, Correspondencia Parroquia-Obispo, 1847–1927, bundle G-29.

72. Some Yoruba rites practiced by slaves and others in Cuba required the use of human remains, which were readily available from most cemeteries. Brains, bone, hair, and other remains were employed in a variety of ways: in cannibalistic rituals, to cure illnesses, to combat infertility, and to gain supernatural powers over other human beings and evil spirits. See Ortiz Fernández, *Hampa*, 57–59. Also see Steele, *Cuban Sketches*, 185; and the diary of J. B. Dunlop (1810–11), NYHS.

73. APISM, Libro segundo de defunciones. Sample years are 1851 and 1855–56. See López de Haro, *Constituciones*, 176.

74. Commander of San Antonio to the civilian governor, December 28, 1846, ANC, Gobierno Superior Civil, bundle 719, file 23905; lieutenant governor of Santiago to the civilian governor, September 22, 1847; the bishop of Havana to the captain-general, September 27, 1847, both in ANC, Gobierno Superior Civil, bundle 721, file 24020.

75. Decrees by Cuba's captain-general, June 12 and August 20, 1848, ANC, Gobierno Superior Civil, bundle 724, file 24246.

76. Priest of Monserrate Parish of Havana to the capitán juez pedáneo of Barrio Colón, August 2, 1847; the capitán juez pedáneo of Barrio Colón to the civilian governor, August 2, 1847; the civilian governor to the capitán juez pedáneo of Barrio Colón, August 4, 1847, all in ANC, Gobierno Superior Civil, bundle 721, file 24007. Also see the bishop of Havana to the captain-general, September 14, 1849, ANC, Gobierno Superior Civil, bundle 723, file 2415.

77. José Hernández to the captain-general, July 2, 1851, ANC, Gobierno Superior Civil, bundle 724, file 24247.

78. The mayor of Roque to the governor of Matanzas, November 24, 1888, AHPM, Gobierno Provincial, Cementerios, bundle 13, file 14; the bishop of Havana to the captain-general, September 14, 1849, ANC, Gobierno Superior Civil, bundle 723, file 2415.

79. Royal order of March 19, 1848, in Ramos, *Prontuario*, 89–90; "Reglamento de 1867," ANC, Gobierno General, bundle 101, file 4825. On requests to embalm dead U.S. citizens (1841, 1843), U.S. Consul Calhoun to the captain-general, November 26, 1841, and U.S. Consul Campbell to the captain-general and unsigned permission slip, both dated December 30, 1843, in ANC, Gobierno Superior Civil, bundle 1530, files 70685 and 70691. Also see Erenchún, *Anales*, 1792. Various documents on exhumations and U.S. consul to the captain-general, February 26, 1849, ANC, Gobierno Superior Civil, bundle 1535, file 70885.

Chapter 3   *Crypto-Protestants and Pseudo-Catholics*

1. French and other foreign settlers in Vieques reportedly lived for many years on the island without seeking domiciliation; see the governor of Puerto Rico to the minister of government, November 18, 1851, CIH, Papeles de Vieques, 209–10.

2. See Luis Martínez-Fernández, *Fighting Slavery in the Caribbean*, 4–6, 20–21.
3. Havana's population includes all of its rural and urban districts. The actual city of Havana had a population of 158,587 in 1860; of these 2,688 were non-Spanish foreigners. In Matanzas the foreign population in 1888 was 1,336. See Cuba, Statistics Commission, *Cuadro estadístico de la siempre fiel isla de Cuba [1846]*, 69, 77; Félix Erenchún, *Anales de isla de Cuba*, 1902–3; "Register of Americans [in Cuba] from January 1, 1871 to December 31, 1871," NA, RG 84, Havana, c.14.1; *Censo de población de 31 de diciembre de 1887 a 1ro. de enero de 1888, provincia de Matanzas*; Gustave D'Hespel D'Harponville, *La reine des Antilles*, 106; Edward Kenney to Bishop Whittingham, April 1, 1876, MDA, Cuba folder 5; Edward Kenney, report of 1874, in [Edward Kenney], *Report of Our Mission in Cuba*, 12.
4. Domiciliation files for 1855, ANC, Gobierno Superior Civil, bundle 796, file 27003; registry of nondomiciled foreigners in AHPM, Gobierno Provincial, Negociado de Orden Público y Policía, bundle 58, file 6001. Also see AHPM, Expedientes de Ferrocarriles, bundle 6, files 389, 390. The 1871 register of U.S. citizens in Cuba identifies 737 individuals by occupation. The dominant categories were merchants (38 percent), machinists (31 percent), skilled or semiskilled artisans (13 percent), and professionals (9 percent). Out of the total 737, only 37 (5 percent) are identified as planters, agriculturalists, property owners, or farmers. Information on occupations from "Register of Americans [in Cuba] from January 1, 1871 to December 31, 1871," NA, RG 84, Havana, c.14.1.
5. Robert L. Paquette, *Sugar Is Made with Blood*, 187; Edward Kenney to Bishop Whittingham, April 1, 1876, MDA, Cuba folder 5. In 1852, some Cuban planters requested an exemption of domiciliation and Catholicity requirements. See lieutenant governor of Sagua la Grande to the captain-general, February 27, 1852, ANC, Gobierno Superior Civil, bundle 791, file 26861. Consul Helm was quoted in Louis A. Pérez, Jr., *On Becoming Cuban*, 23.
6. Roberto Gómez Reyes, "Informe histórico sobre la casa #256 de la Calle Tulipán entre Santa Catalina y Falgueras. Cerro," Museo del Cerro, file 4.1.10. Also see Martínez-Fernández, *Fighting Slavery*, chap. 2.
7. Ponce's population in 1867 was 29,857; see *La Gaceta de Puerto Rico* 70 (September 17, 1868): 4. Also see Francisco A. Scarano, *Sugar and Slavery in Puerto Rico*, chap. 2; and Guillermo A. Baralt, *Buena Vista*, chap. 1. According to religious tax assessments based on wealth (1858), Ponce's assessment was 12,040 pesos, San Juan's 7,679 pesos, and the entire island's 105,000 pesos. See *La Gaceta de Puerto Rico* (February 21, 1861): 3.
8. See Luis Martínez-Fernández, *Torn between Empires*, chap. 3.
9. According to an 1838 census, of a total of 277 immigrants, thirty-eight were from St. Thomas, twenty from the United States, twelve from Germany, six from Great Britain, and four from Scotland. See "Padrón de extranjeros, Ponce, 1838," AGPR, Gobernadores Españoles, box 14, Ponce; also see "Padrón de Extranjeros, Ponce, 1868," AHMP, bundle 53, box 51, file 24; Eduardo Newmann, *Verdadera y auténtica historia de la ciudad de Ponce*, 85; and Ramón Marín, *Las fiestas populares de Ponce*, 203.
10. Scarano, *Sugar and Slavery*, 81–82; Francisco A. Scarano, "Sugar and Slavery in

Puerto Rico," 445–49; Ivette Pérez Vega, "Las oleadas de inmigración sobre el sur de Puerto Rico," 114–23; and Jorge Luis Chinea Serrano, "Racial Politics and Commercial Agriculture," 325–26.

11. José María Archebald owned Hacienda Cintrona, Tomás Davidson owned Hacienda Consuelo, William Lee owned Hacienda Constancia, Thomas G. Salomons owned Hacienda Santa Cruz, Gilbee owned Hacienda Fortuna; see "Padrón de productos y capitales, Ponce, 1869–70," and "Riqueza territorial, 1871–72," AHMP, bundle 31, box 30A, and bundle 31, box 30C; "Renovación del ayuntamiento de Ponce 1872," AGPR, Gobernadores Españoles, Municipios, Ponce, box 555; Andrés A. Ramos Mattei, *La hacienda azucarera*, 22; Albert E. Lee, *An Island Grows*, 3. Also see Secretaría del Gobierno Superior Civil de la Isla de Puerto Rico, *Registro central de esclavos (6to. Depto.),* microfilm in CIH.

12. "Register of Americans [in Cuba] from January 1, 1871 to December 31, 1871," NA, RG 84, Havana, c.14.1; "Gobierno Superior Civil de la Provincia de Puerto Rico, Registro de Extranjeros, 22 de agosto, 1870–11 de junio, 1875," LC, Puerto Rican Collection, box 8.

13. Significantly, Ponce's mail from San Juan arrived by sea via Guayama or Mayagüez instead of over land. See George Coggeshall, *Voyages to Various Parts of the World*, 138; Scarano, *Sugar and Slavery*, 123; Marín, *Fiestas populares*, 239; and Lee, *Island*, 12. During the second half of the nineteenth century, Puerto Rico's trade with the Lesser Antilles decreased when the island increased its direct trade with Europe. See Martínez-Fernández, *Torn between Empires*, chap. 2; Charles De Ronceray to Cass, January 14, 1860, in U.S. Department of State, San Juan Consulate, *Despachos de los cónsules norteamericanos en Puerto Rico*, 421–23.

14. In 1853, the U.S. consul at San Juan reported that there were no U.S. citizens in the districts of Arecibo, Aguadilla, and Naguabo to serve as consular agents. In 1866, the eight-man U.S. consular corps in Puerto Rico included only two U.S.-born agents and three who were not even naturalized. Reportedly, when the vice-consulship in Ponce had to be filled in 1866, an Englishman was appointed because no U.S. citizen was available. When the U.S. consular agent at Vieques resigned in 1870, a Danish subject, Henry N. Longhrez, had to be appointed in his place because there was no U.S. resident there. See Consul George Latimer to William Marcy, July 22, 1853, U.S. Department of State, *Despachos*, 308. Also see Jourdan to Seward, July 2, and December 31, 1866, NA, RG 84, San Juan, vol. 7228; dispatch of April 18, 1870, NA, RG 59, San Juan, microfilm M76, reel 15.

15. The Basantas and the Van Rhyns were key families in Ponce's complex foreign social web. The Basantas were connected by marriage to the González, Salich (of Yauco), Van Rhyn, Mirailh, Lee, Toro, and Finlay families and by compadrazgo to the Dodds, Lees, and Finlays. The Van Rhyns were linked by marriage to the Basantas, Weichers, Mirailhs, Eckelmans, Oppenheimers, and Finlays and by compadrazgo to the Dodds, Eckelmans, Lees, Finlays, Penders, and Oppenheimers. See Lee, *Island*, 3, 9–10. Also see Archivo Parroquial de Ponce, Libros de Matrimonios y Libros de Bautismos (microfilms in CIH); and Archivo Parroquial de la Iglesia Santísima Trinidad, Ponce (hereafter cited as APIST), books 1 and 6.

16. The best source on West Indian immigration to nineteenth-century Puerto Rico is Chinea Serrano, "Racial Politics," chap. 2 and pp. 185, 206, 253–58, 260, 284–86, and 325–26. Of a population of 277 foreigners (in 1838), race was determined for 208: 127 whites and 81 mulattos. See "Padrón de extranjeros, Ponce, 1838," AGPR, Gobernadores Españoles, box 14, Ponce; Scarano, *Sugar and Slavery*, 97; Emma Aurora Dávila Cox, *Este inmenso comercio*, 343–44, 110.

17. Andrés A. Ramos Mattei, "La importación de trabajadores contratados para la industria azucarera puertorriqueña," in Francisco A. Scarano, ed., *Inmigración y clases sociales en el Puerto Rico del siglo xix*, 134; CIH, Papeles de Vieques, 23, 24, 46, 620–22, 745–55; Antonio Rivera Martínez, *Así empezó Vieques*, 12–14.

18. The island remained virtually depopulated, with a total of 122 residents in 1828. A merchant mariner who sailed by the island in 1831 assumed that it was uninhabited and described its "lonely, solitary appearance." See report on Vieques circa 1840, and "Informe de Ramón Aboy, 14 de septiembre de 1828," both in CIH, Papeles de Vieques, 745–55, 462–63; Pedro Tomás de Córdova, *Memorias geográficas, históricas, económicas y estadícas*, 2:411; Coggeshall, *Voyages*, 265. Also see report of the governor of Vieques (1839) and report of the governor of Puerto Rico (1841), in CIH, Papeles de Vieques, 720–21, 686–89.

19. Saínz took charge of a population of nearly 667 free persons and 369 slaves; close to one-third of the total population consisted of French citizens. Throughout the following decade, friction often erupted between Spanish officials and the remaining French property owners. See the minister of the navy to the minister of state, January 10, 1841, and an undated document signed by Saínz circa 1851, both in CIH, Papeles de Vieques, 653–57, 211–15; also see 725–26 and 733.

20. The intendant of Puerto Rico to the minister of the treasury of the first overseas secretariat, quoting the governor of Puerto Rico, CIH, Papeles de Vieques, 145–46. Data on marriages from report of January 20, 1864, in AHDASJ, Gobierno, Corrrespondencia, Parroquia-Gobernador Eclesiástico, Vieques, 1854–1912, bundle G-45.

21. The population of Vieques in 1846 was 1,275; in 1866 it was 5,040; see *La Gaceta de Puerto Rico* 70 (September 17, 1868); Consul Hyde to Seward, March 4, 1865, in U.S. Department of State, *Despachos*, 667; and "Censo de libertos (1873)" in CIH, *Proceso abolicionista*, 2:157.

22. The 1870 regulations were strict and unyielding toward workers but lax and flexible toward planters. For example, they allowed planters to force workers to labor on holidays, if needed, and established that the work day was generally from sunup to sundown but could be extended "well into the night" during the harvest. Although the workers could not shorten their contract terms, masters could lay off workers at any time as long as they paid them half the salaries they would have normally earned. See "Reglamento de peones de 12 de agosto de 1870," CIH, Papeles de Vieques, 848–49; "Reglamento para los jornaleros extranjeros (1874)," AHN, Ultramar, bundle 315, file 15; and Ramos Mattei, "Importación," 134–35. Also see the governor of Puerto Rico to the overseas minister, March 5, 1864, CIH, Papeles de Vieques, 312–18.

23. In fact, this population came from diverse places in the Windward and Leeward islands. An 1874 document with a sample of thirty-seven workers lists thirteen

from Nevis, seven from St. Kitts, seven from Barbados, five from Tortola, three from Antigua, one from Anguila, and one from St. Vincent. Some contract workers also came from the Danish West Indies. Among the 683 transient workers of color in Vieques in 1871, there were 591 men and 92 women. See Robert Rabin Siegal, "Los tortoleños" (copy in Archivo Histórico de Vieques [hereafter cited as AHV]), 11–12; Ramos Mattei, "Importación," 135–36; Consul Hyde to Seward, March 4, 1865, in U.S. Department of State, *Despachos*, 667; census of 1871 in *La Gaceta de Puerto Rico* 135 (December 28, 1872): 3; church membership list of the All Saints Church of Vieques (started in 1883), Archivo Parroquial de la Iglesia de Todos los Santos, Vieques (hereafter cited as APITS).

24. Andrew K. Blythe to Cass, July 20, 1857, NA, RG 59, Havana, microfilm T20, reel 36; Pérez, *On Becoming Cuban*, 23. Estimate for Puerto Rico based on an average of sixteen men per ship and navigation statistics in Charles De Ronceray to Cass, July 29, 1859, U.S. Department of State, *Despachos*, 390.

25. Blythe to Cass, June 10, and July 20, 1857; and Charles Helm to Cass, May 5, 1860, NA, RG 59, Havana, microfilm T20, reels 36 and 40; William J. Karras, "Yankee Carpenter in Cuba, 1848," 17–23; Abiel Abbot, *Letters*, 19; Benjamin Moore Norman, *Rambles by Land and Water*, 3. One U.S. physician who organized health trips to Cuba advised that the "invalid should hasten to a southern clime, before the first cold spells of winter have aggravated his affection. He who resides in the more northern states, should leave his home in September." See [John George F. Wurdemann], *Notes on Cuba*, 3.

26. Julia Ward Howe, *A Trip to Cuba*, 112; Abbot, *Letters*, 27; George W. Williams, *Sketches of Travel in the Old and New World*, 8; Richard Henry Dana, Jr., *To Cuba and Back*, 3–15; Ramón Hernández Poggio, *Aclimatación é higiene de los europeos en Cuba*.

27. Quoted from Samuel Hazard, *Cuba with Pen and Pencil*, 378–79; also see Leví Marrero, *Cuba*, 14:58; De Ronceray to Cass, January 6, 1860, NA, RG 84, San Juan, vol. 7228; D'Hespel D'Harponville, *Reine*, 335–38; Maturin M. Ballou, *Due South: Or Cuba Past and Present*, 209; David Turnbull, *Travels in the West*, 218.

28. Questionnaire answered by the governor of Puerto Rico enclosed with dispatch number 31 of December 24, 1850, PRO, FO, 72/886.

29. British Consul-General Crawford to Lord Palmerston, January 22, 1852, PRO, FO, 72/866; John G. Taylor, *The United States and Cuba*, 297; Turnbull, *Travels*, 67. Also see domiciliation papers of George Booth and Guillaume Perrone, ANC, Gobierno Superior Civil, bundle 1656, file 82742, and domiciliation papers of David Clark, bundle 787, file 26754; testimony of Luis Mariátegui on behalf of Juan Emilio Beylle, AALH, Matrimonios Ultramarinos, file 25, January 1841; and domiciliation declarations in AGPR, Gobernadores Españoles, Extranjeros, boxes 89–114.

30. [Wurdemann], *Notes*, 166; Grace M. Backhouse to Catherine Backhouse, January 6, 1854, and George C. Backhouse to his aunt, August 3, 1853, both in Backhouse Papers; declaration of Jorge Y. Finlay (1866) on professing "la Religión A. C. R.," AHDASJ, Justicia, Procesos Legales, Certificados de Soltería, Ponce, bundle J-182; and declaration of María Callaghan of February 7, 1852, on being "C.A.R.", ANC, Gobierno Superior Civil, bundle 791, file 26855. For more on the Back-

houses, see Martínez-Fernández, *Fighting Slavery*. See Acting Consul Kennedy to Lord Palmerston, June 21, 1850, and Consul-General Crawford to Lord Palmerston, January 22, 1852, both in PRO, FO, 72/886; and Dávila Cox, *Este inmenso comercio*, 162.

31. Williams, *Sketches*, 21.

32. This was the case with Mr. Otway, a fictional character in Gertrudis Gómez de Avellaneda y Arteaga, *Sab*. Although he had converted to Catholicism, he remained a heretic in the eyes of Puerto Príncipe's gossips (41). Also see Matthew D. Bagg, *Journal of Two Months Residence in St. Thomas, Santa Cruz & Porto Rico and the Voyage Thither and Thence [1851–1852]*, 42.

33. Coggeshall, *Voyages*, 145–46.

34. The Spanish minister of justice to the president of the Spanish council of ministers, April 29, 1853, CIH, Papeles de Vieques, 267–72. Also see the case of Philip Boylan, A. Mallory, and Edward Gibson, in PRO, FO, 72/885 and 72/886; and especially Crawford to the Earl of Clarendon, March 30, 1855, 72/885, and Crawford to Lord Palmerston, January 22, 1852, 72/886.

35. Granville to Howden, January 10, 1852, AHN, Estado, bundle 8565; Howden to Claudio Antón de Luzuriaga, April 4, 1855, PRO, FO, 72/885; Howden to Pedro Pidal, August 10, 1850, PRO, FO, 72/886.

36. Norwood diary, March 21, 1844; Lewis Leonidas Allen, *The Island of Cuba*, 10, 23; Dana, *To Cuba*, 20–21; Hazard, *Cuba*, 120–21, 127–30, 431; Ballou, *Due South*, 159; Norman, *Rambles*, 38; Carlton H. Rogers, *Incidents of Travel in the Southern United States and Cuba*, 89; diary of Grace Backhouse, April 3, 1853, Backhouse Papers; diary of Elizabeth West Nevins, March 7, 1859, NYHS; Bagg, *Journal*, 36; Charles Walker, "Charles Walker's Letters," 38–41; Frederika Bremer, *The Homes of the New World*, 2:375; Abbot, *Letters*, 76; Williams, *Sketches*, 6.

37. Coggeshall, *Voyages*, 13; Bagg, *Journal*, 42.

38. Diary of George Backhouse, March 24–25, 1853, and diary of Grace Backhouse, April 12, 1854, both in Backhouse Papers; [Julia Louisa Matilda Woodruff], *My Winter in Cuba*, 56–58, 156; Taylor, *United States*, 295; [Wurdemann], *Notes*, 194; Dana, *To Cuba*, 38; Ballou, *Due South*, 37, 145; Norman, *Rambles*, 35; Abbot, *Letters*, 62, 76, 103; James Mursell Phillippo, *The United States and Cuba*, 405; James William Steele, *Cuban Sketches*, 176–77, 183, 200; Williams, *Sketches*, 38, 43–44; Bremer, *Homes*, 2:302; Steele, *Cuban Sketches*, 180; Rogers, *Incidents*, 145.

39. The Anglican and Episcopalian Book of Common Prayer's articles of faith included a rejection of both the dogma of purgatory and the miracle of transubstantiation. They also held the primacy of faith over works as vehicles for salvation and allowed priests to marry. See Williams, *Sketches*, 38–39, 43–44; Demoticus Philalethes, *Yankee Travels through the Island of Cuba*, 219; Bremer, *Homes*, 2:302; and [Woodruff], *My Winter*, 172.

40. John Joseph Gurney, *A Winter in the West Indies*, 211; Rachel Wilson Moore, *Journal of Rachel Wilson Moore*, 32.

41. See Martínez-Fernández, *Fighting Slavery*, 114–15; George C. Backhouse to his aunt, August 3, 1853; diary of George Backhouse, March 25, 1853; and diary of

Grace Backhouse, March 25–27, April 24, June 10, November 20, 1853, February 12, April 9, June 12, and November 19, 1854, all in Backhouse Papers. Also see [Woodruff], *My Winter*, 157.

42. Letter signed by George A. Leakin, March 16, 1906, and copy of the diary of Henry B. Whipple, March 20, 1871, both in AEC, Cuba Scrapbook; Henry B. Whipple, *Lights and Shadows of a Long Episcopate*, 358–60; Marcos Antonio Ramos, *Panorama de protestantismo en Cuba*, 78; Hiram H. Hulse, "The History of the Church in Cuba," 249; Leopoldo J. Alard, "Proceso histórico de la Iglesia Episcopal en Cuba," 5.

43. Jerry Fenton, *Understanding the Religious Background of the Puerto Rican*, 5; Agosto Cintrón, *Religión*, 45; Enrique Rodríguez-Bravo, "Origen y desarrollo del movimiento protestante en Puerto Rico," 18–20; Donald T. Moore, *Puerto Rico para Cristo*, 9–11.

44. Ramos, *Panorama*, 78; diary of Grace Backhouse, October 29, 1853, October 28, 1854; February 4, 11, and March 4, 18, 1855; Grace Backhouse to Mary Backhouse, June 30, 1853, all in Backhouse Papers; Rogers, *Incidents*, 173–75; Amelia Matilda Murray, *Letters from the United States, Cuba and Canada*, 2:64, 77; Norwood diary, March 24, 1844.

45. Grace Backhouse to Mary Backhouse, June 30, 1853; and diary of Grace Backhouse, October 29, 1853, both in Backhouse Papers. Also see Alard, "Proceso," 5; Hulse, "History," 249; and Whipple, *Lights and Shadows*, 359.

46. See Archivo Parroquial de Ponce, Libros de Bautismos (1866–72) and Índice de Bautismos Católicos de Ponce, 1850–1931 (microfilms in CIH).

47. John Nott to the bishop of Puerto Rico, June 16, 1840; and Robert McPherson documents, both in AHDASJ, Justicia, Procesos Legales, Papeles de Extranjeros, bundle J-229. Also see documentation pertaining to Basanta and Mirailh (1870), in AHDASJ, Justicia, Procesos Legales, Certificaciones de Soltería, Ponce, bundle J-187. El Cerro cases appear in Lourdes Sampera González, "Breve reseña sobre la Parroquia el Salvador del Mundo del Cerro," Museo del Cerro, file 6.1.1. On Pardo, see Chinea Serrano, "Racial Politics," 244. The profession of Catholicity included accepting that the Roman Catholic church was the only one established by Christ and believing in the miracle of transubstantiation, the seven sacraments, purgatory, the veneration of the saints and their images, and the authority of ecclesiastical tradition. See Francisco Javier Hernández, *Colección de bulas, breves, y otros documentos relativos a la iglesia de América y Filipinas*, 2:756–57.

48. Grace Backhouse to Catherine Backhouse, March 3, 1854, in Backhouse Papers. A few years later, Julio Runge and Fanny Tolmé decided to baptize another of their children, Gustavo, with Catholic rites. See APISM, Libro tercero de Bautismos, 144; and Kenney report of 1874, in [Kenney], *Report of Our Mission*, 12.

49. APISM, Libros de Bautismo; Archivo Parroquial de Vieques, Libros de Bautismo (microfilms in CIH).

50. Grace Backhouse to Mary Backhouse, June 30, 1853; Grace Backhouse to Catherine Backhouse, March 25, 1855; diary of Grace Backhouse, October 28–30, 1853, and October 30, 1855; and certified copy of the baptismal certificate of John Sandham Backhouse, all in Backhouse Papers.

51. Whipple, *Lights and Shadows*, 359; Whipple's diary (copy), March 20, 1871, in AEC, Cuba Scrapbook.

52. Baptism entries of George Clarke (1854), Henry Walter Basanta (1855), and Rosita Mary Wellcome (1862), in the All Saints Church of St. Thomas, Baptismal Registers (microfilms at the Florence Williams Public Library, St. Croix); Lee, *Island*, 5.

53. See circular by Bishop Gil Esteve, December 23, 1852, AHDASJ, Gobierno, Circulares, 1813–99; also see files in AHDASJ, Justicia, Procesos Legales, Certificados de Soltería, bundles J-181 and J-182; and AALH, Matrimonios Ultramarinos.

54. Process to verify soltería y catolicidad of Augusto Lion and Elena Catalina Salomons (1862); witnesses were Bernardo Eckelman, Emilio Overmann, and a man surnamed Degetau. Roberto Graham and Ysabel Spense married as Catholics and were witnessed by Tomás A. Dodd, Guillermo Lee, and Jorge Finlay, all of whom said they were Catholics. On August 18, 1868, Juan Herman Van Rhyn and Juana Francisca Mirailh were married as Catholics. Jorge Ysidoro Finlay and Emilia Francisca Van Rhyn underwent proceedings of soltería y cristiandad; his witnesses were Ramón Berartain, Juan Sullivan, and Francisco Antonsanti; hers were Pedro Minvielle and James Gallagher. The process was completed on June 8, 1866, and they married on July 5. The process of soltería of Guillermo Oppenheimer and Ana María Salomons took place in 1864. Carlos Juan Oppenheimer and Ana María Van Rhyn married as Catholics on June 18, 1865. See AHDASJ, Justicia, Procesos Legales, Certificaciones de Soltería, Ponce, bundles J-181 and J-182, and Archivo Parroquial de Ponce, Libros de Matrimonios (microfilms in CIH).

55. See AHDASJ, Justicia, Procesos Legales, Certificaciones de Soltería, Ponce, bundle J-182; also see Steele, *Cuban Sketches*, 178. On Bernardo Eckelman as witness of soltería y catolicidad for Jorge Federico Weichers, see (1862), AHDASJ, Justicia, Procesos Legales, Certificaciones de Soltería, Ponce, bundle J-181. Documentation on Basanta and Mirailh (1870) appears in bundle J-182.

56. Ángel L. Gutiérrez, *Evangélicos en Puerto Rico*, 31–33.

57. Kenney's report of 1874, in [Kenney], *Report of Our Mission*, 12; and Kenney to Bishop Whittingham, November 25, 1873, MDA, Cuba folder 5. The files Expedientes Ultramarinos of the archbishopric of Havana, in which marriages among foreigners were registered, and the marriage records of El Cerro's parishes contain few names from Protestant countries. See the baptism of Carolina Smith (1862) before her marriage to Javier Molina y García, APISM, Libro de Bautismos 4, pp. 2–3, and Libro de Matrimonios 2. Also see Acting Consul Kennedy to John Bidwell, January 8, 1850, PRO, FO, 72/771.

58. On Dr. Faber, see Emilio Roig de Leuchsenring, *Médicos y medicina en Cuba*, 48; and Martínez-Fernández, *Fighting Slavery*, 78.

59. All Saints Church of St. Thomas, Marriage Records (microfilms at the Florence Williams Public Library of St. Croix); Lee, *Island*, 3, 9.

60. See José Ignacio Rodríguez, "Sobre los matrimonios que van a celebrarse en los Estados-Unidos [I and II]," and Isidro Carbonell y Padilla, "Sobre los matrimonios

que van a celebrarse en los Estados-Unidos," both in *Revista de Jurisprudencia* 3, no. 1 (1858): 267–74; 358–62; 432–42; Antonio de las Barras y Prado, *Memorias, La Habana a mediados del siglo xix*, 83–84; [Woodruff], *My Winter*, 128; and Verena Martínez-Alier, *Marriage, Class, and Colour*, 88. On the marriage of Luis Bonafoux and Clemencia Quintero of Guayama, St. Thomas (1852), see AGPR, Audiencia Territorial, Real Acuerdo, box 34, file 19. Also see parish priest of Vieques to the bishop of Puerto Rico, March 12, 1857; AHDASJ, Gobierno, Correspondencia Parroquia-Obispo, Vieques, 1847–1927, bundle G-29; and Dutch Reformed church of Christiansted, St. Croix, Books of Marriages (microfilms at the Florence Williams Public Library of St. Croix).

61. See Rodríguez, "Sobre los matrimonios," 358–62; circular of March 1, 1854, in Ramos, *Prontuario*, 313; "Instrucción sobre dispensas matrimoniales," *El Boletín Eclesiástico del Obispado de La Habana* 3, no. 17 (September 30, 1883): 214–17; and document dated October 5, 1860, in AGPR, Audiencia Territorial, Real Acuerdo, box 34, file 19.

62. Hernández Poggio, *Aclimatación*, 67–70; Ángel José Cowley, *Ensayo estadístico-médico de la mortalidad de la Diócesis de La Habana durante el año 1843*; Jorge Le-Roy y Cassá, *Estudios sobre la mortalidad de La Habana durante el siglo xix y comienzos del actual*; William H. Robertson to Marcy, July 27, 1854, NA, RG 59, Havana, microfilm T20, reel 28; Robert Francis Jameson, *Letters from the Havana, during the Year 1820*, 59, 119 (emphasis in the original). On Puerto Rico, see De Ronceray to Cass, December 3, 1860, U.S. Department of State, *Despachos*, 308; Córdova, *Memorias*, 1:201–7; and consular agent W. Russell to the U.S. secretary of state, July 24, 1878, NA, RG 59, Ponce, microfilm M76, reel 28.

63. "1857 Sick to Hospitals of Havana from American Vessels," NA, RG 59, Havana, microfilm T20, reel 39. Also see APIST, book 1; and Lee, *Island*, 31–33.

64. Steele, *Cuban Sketches*, 185–86; [William Henry Hurlbert], *Gan-Eden*, 136–37.

65. Blythe to Cass, July 20, 1857, NA, RG 59, Havana, microfilm T20, reel 36.

66. Jaeger to Seward, January 4, 1862, NA, RG 59, consular despatches, Santo Domingo, microfilm T56, reel 4; U.S. consul at Havana to the captain-general, February 26, 1849, ANC, Gobierno Superior Civil, bundle 1535, file 70885. Williams, *Sketches*, 55; Dana, *To Cuba*, 102–3.

67. Alfonso Lockward, ed., *Documentos para la historia de las relaciones dominico americanas*, 64–69.

68. There is some evidence that dying Protestants sought to leave the Spanish islands. It is also plausible that surviving relatives may have smuggled the remains of their loved ones onto neighboring islands for proper burial. Ponce resident Robert Bennet was buried in St. Thomas on February 1, 1867. The burial records state "lately arrived here for the benefit of his health." Ponce, however, was by most accounts healthier than St. Thomas. See All Saints Church of St. Thomas, Register of Burials (microfilms at the Florence Williams Public Library of St. Croix).

69. Steele, *Cuba Sketches*, 174; Howe, *Trip*, 178.

70. Ramos, *Panorama*, 77; Jourdan to Seward, July 19, 1866, NA, RG 84, San Juan, vol. 7228; Jourdan to Seward, June 2, 1866, U.S. Department of State, *Despachos*, 707; Jourdan to C. H. Verges, June 1, 1866, NA, RG 84, San Juan, vol. 7223.

71. Rodríguez León, *Registros*, 148; "Crónica religiosa: una conversión," *El Boletín Eclesiástico de Puerto Rico* 1, no. 9 (October 1, 1859): 219.

72. APISM, Libro cuarto de Bautismos, 27–28; Ramiro Guerra y Sánchez, *Guerra de los Diez Años, 1868–1878*, 2:29; Ramos, *Panorama*, 140.

73. Petition by Roura and Hernández to the bishop of Puerto Rico, April 28, 1887, AHDASJ, Justicia, Procesos Legales, Validación de Matrimonios, Ponce, bundle J-218.

74. See APISM, Libros de Matrimonios, and Archivo Parroquial de Ponce, Libros de Matrimonios and Libros de Bautismos (microfilms in CIH); and Henry K. Carroll, *Report on the Island of Porto Rico*, 668, 694.

75. Archivo Parroquial de Ponce, Libros de Defunciones (1857–82) (microfilms in CIH). The Salomons's mausoleum was transplanted to the Protestant section in 1878 and is probably the one still visible today in ruins. See AHMP, "Índice del cementerio antiguo," 1:166. Also see capitán pedáneo of San Lázaro to the captain-general, December 22, 1849, ANC, Gobierno Superior Civil, bundle 745, file 25568; and letter of 1853, quoted in Mariano Torrente, *Política ultramarina que abraza todos los puntos referentes a las relaciones de España con los Estados Unidos, con Inglaterra y las Antillas, y señaladamente con la isla de Santo Domingo*, 198–99. Also see Lee, *Island*, 6; and Blythe to the secretary of state, February 24, 1857, NA, RG 59, Havana, microfilm T20, reel 36.

76. Blythe to Cass, July 20, 1857, and Thomas Savage to the assistant secretary of state, September 9, 1858, NA, RG 59, Havana, microfilm T20, reels 36 and 39; Consul Jourdan to Cass, July 19, 1866, NA, RG 84, vol. 7228; "Minuta sobre cementerio protestante de noviembre 8, 1841," ANC, Gobierno Superior Civil, bundle 744, file 25546; Howe, *Trip*, 178; Alexander Jones, *Cuba in 1851*, 30.

77. Diary of J. B. Dunlop, NYHS; "Minuta sobre cementerio protestante de noviembre 8, 1841," ANC, Gobierno Superior Civil, bundle 744, file 25546; Marrero, *Cuba*, 14:88; the capitán pedáneo of San Lázaro to the captain-general, August 31, 1845, September 4, 1845, and December 22, 1849; and Ángel Cowley of the Board of Sanitation to the civilian governor, February 17, 1847, ANC, Gobierno Superior Civil, bundle 745, file 25568. Also see Ángela Oramas, *Cemenerios de La Habana*, 26–29.

78. U.S. consul Robert Campbell to the captain-general, December 30, 1843, ANC, Gobierno Superior Civil, bundle 1530, file 70691; Dr. Belot to Helm, April 28, 1860, with Helm to Cass, April 28, 1860, NA, RG 59, Havana, microfilm T20, reel 36.

79. David Turnbull to the captain-general of Cuba, September 16, 1841, ANC, Gobierno Superior Civil, bundle 744, file 25346; Ángel Cowley of the Sanitation Board to the civilian governor, February 17, 1847, and the capitán pedáneo of San Lázaro to the captain-general, August 31, 1845, ANC, Gobierno Superior Civil, bundle 745, file 25568.

80. Diary of J. B. Dunlop, NYHS; quote from Richard J. Levis, *Diary of a Spring Holiday in Cuba*, 109.

81. John F. Young, "Cuba," *Spirit of Missions* 49 (October 1884): 486–87; governor of Matanzas to the parish priest of Matanzas, September 15, 1841, AHPM, Gobierno Provincial, Orden Público y Policía, bundle 74, file 8349.

82. Coggeshall, *Voyages*, 144–45; Jourdan to Seward, July 19, 1866, NA, RG 84, San Juan, vol. 7228.

83. Documents pertaining to Clifford's case, in AHMP, bundle 35, file 14; Marín, *Fiestas populares*, 231–32.

84. "Asiento de difuntos protestantes habidos en la isla de Vieques desde 1 de Septiembre de 1845," Registro del Gobernador de Vieques 1838–1845, CIH, vol. 4 (copy in AHV).

85. Turnbull to the captain-general of Cuba, September 16, 1841, ANC, Gobierno Superior Civil, bundle 744, file 25346; Moore, *Journal*, 208; Kenney to Bishop Whittingham, November 25, 1873, MDA, Cuba folder 4; Miguel Aldama to Domingo del Monte, April 9, 1844, in Domingo Figuerola-Caneda, ed., *Centón epistolario de Domingo del Monte*, 6:21; Consul Blythe to the secretary of state, February 24, 1857, NA, RG 59, Havana, microfilm T20, reel 36.

86. Abbot, *Letters*, 17; Jourdan to Seward, February 3, and May 6, 1867, NA, RG 84, San Juan, vol. 7228; request of license to ship the remains of E. H. Harkness to the United States (July 20, 1878), AHPM, Gobierno Provincial, Orden Público, bundle 81, file 9127; Helm to Cass, April 21, 1860, NA, RG 59, microfilm T20, reel 40; request to embalm and ship the remains of G. W. Tarkington, U.S. consul to the captain-general, February 26, 1849, ANC, Gobierno Superior Civil, bundle 1535, file 70885; also see bundle 1530, file 706585. In a related and widespread form of abuse, government officials charged excessive intestate death fees and mercilessly looted the estates of dead foreigners. According to the irate U.S. consul of Matanzas, "the Harpies here have pounced upon the foreigner's effects even before the breath was out of his body—aye before the spirit had left." He reported that such practices represented a great source of revenue and bound himself "to drive the vultures from the dead carcass[es] of my fellow countrymen." See Consul Edward Morrel to Marcy, June 29, and July 5, 1855, NA, RG 46, U.S. Senate, 34B-B15; letter from Spanish secretary of state, April 23, 1856, AGPR, Audiencia Territorial, box 27, file 21.

Chapter 4   *War and Religion*

1. Raymond Carr, *España, 1808–1975*, 304, 334; William J. Callahan, *Church, Politics, and Society in Spain*, passim; Vicente Carcel Orti, *Iglesia y revolución en España (1868–1879)*, 225–30; Cayetano Coll y Toste, ed., *Boletín histórico*, 12:123; *La Voz de Cuba* (November 4, 1870); decree of January 22, 1875, with C. Cushing to Hamilton Fish, February 2, 1875, U.S. Department of State, *Papers Relating to Foreign Affairs* (hereafter cited as *PRFA*) (1875), 1099; Jerónimo Bécker, *Historia de las relaciones exteriores*, 3:200.

2. Roberto H. Todd, "La Iglesia Episcopal de Ponce," 20; Ángel Luis Ortiz Díaz, "La manifestación anticlerical en Puerto Rico entre 1870–1900," 42; Juan Bautista Vilar, *Un siglo de protestantismo en España*, 27–30.

3. A decree dated September 23, 1869, extended religious tolerance to all inhabitants of the Spanish Antilles. The Spanish constitution was momentarily extended to Puerto Rico on September 4, 1873, but not to Cuba, where war raged on. See Governor Sanz to the regent of the Real Audiencia of Puerto Rico, October 18,

1869, AGPR, Real Audiencia, Tribunal en Pleno, box 11, bundle 2; Lidio Cruz Monclova, *Historia de Puerto Rico*, vol. 2, part 1, pp. 331–33.

4. Callahan, *Church*, 258; José Manuel Cuenca Toribio, *Estudios sobre la iglesia española del siglo xix*, 93; "Circular royal order, regulating religious liberty and non-Catholic worship in Spain [October 23, 1876]," with A. Augustus Adee to Fish, October 25, 1876, U.S. Department of State, *PRFA* (1876), 482–87; José A. Rodríguez García, *De los requisitos previos para contraer matrimonios*, 37; Víctor Burset, "The First Fifty Years of Protestant Episcopal Church in Puerto Rico," 22; Leopoldo J. Alard, "Proceso histórico de la Iglesia Episcopal en Cuba," 26; Kenney Report of 1877 in [Edward Kenney], *Report of Our Mission in Cuba*, 5.

5. Arthur F. Corwin, *Spain and the Abolition of Slavery in Cuba*, 218, 229.

6. Reece B. Bothwell González, ed., *Puerto Rico*, 2:29–35; Cruz Monclova, *Historia*, vol. 2, part 1, pp. 216–21, 83–85.

7. Ramón de Arautegui to the U.S. consul, April 20, 1871, NA, RG 84, Havana, c. 8.1.

8. Minvielle to Conroy, NA, RG 84, Ponce, vol. 7191; *La Gaceta de Puerto Rico* (October 19, 1869).

9. Cruz Monclova, *Historia*, vol. 2, part 1, pp. 382–91.

10. Carlos A. Tamayo, "Historia de la Iglesia Episcopal de Cuba," 6. Consul Hall to the U.S. secretary of state, October 24, 1871, NA, RG 59, Havana, microfilm T20, reel 65; Ramón de Arautegui to the U.S. consul, April 20, and November 4, 1871, NA, RG 84, Havana, c. 8.1.

11. Letter by the three bishops to the king of Spain, March 15, 1876, AHDASJ, Gobierno, Correspondencia, 1805–1920, bundle G-16; [Jacinto María Martínez], *Los voluntarios de Cuba y el Obispo de La Habana*, 16; "Carta Pastoral de los Prelados de Santiago," October 15, 1885, in *El Boletín Eclesiástico del Obispado de La Habana* 7, no. 2 (January 27, 1886): 61–65.

12. Cruz Monclova, *Historia*, vol. 2, part 1, p. 209; "El triunfo de la Iglesia en Cuba," *Revista Católica* 3, no. 49 (January 22, 1876): 832; Ramiro Guerra y Sánchez, *Guerra de los Diez Años*, 1:228; Manuel P. Maza Miquel, *Entre la ideología y la compasión*, 84; [Martínez], *Voluntarios*, 30–39, 50.

13. Ismael Testé, *Historia eclesiástica de Cuba*, 3:249–50, 4:83–84; Juan Martín Leiseca, *Apuntes para la historia eclesiástica de Cuba*, 188; Francisco González del Valle, "El clero cubano en la Revolución Cubana," 161–79; Francisco González del Valle, *El clero cubano y la independencia*, 122–29.

14. [Francisco Vicente Aguilera], *Notes about Cuba*, 46; Consul Conroy to the U.S. secretary of state, February 18, 1873, NA, RG 84, San Juan, vol. 7230; Primo de Rivera to the Spanish overseas minister, July 26, 1873, AHN, Ultramar, bundle 5113, file 23, doc. 2; Cruz Monclova, *Historia*, vol. 2, part 1, p. 215.

15. Bishop Jacinto María Martínez to the superior civil governor, April 15, 1871, in [Martínez], *Voluntarios*, 307–9; also see 147, 167–73; Maza Miquel, *Entre la ideología*, 46, 85; González del Valle, *Clero cubano*, 62; "El triunfo de la Iglesia en Cuba," *Revista Católica* 3, no. 49 (January 22, 1876): 832–33.

16. "Los masones en Filipinas," *El Boletín Eclesiástico de Puerto Rico* (February 15, 1875): 43; "La regla de fe protestante. IV," *La Verdad* (June 14, 1874); Miguel Gastón y Gastón, "El catolicismo y los cultos disidentes en la época actual," *La*

Juventud Católica 1, no. 2 (November 26, 1871): 18–20; "Libertad de pensar," *El Boletín Ecleciástico de Puerto Rico* 13, no. 10 (May 15, 1871): 113. Also see *La Juventud Católica* 2, no. 9 (May 12, 1872): 203; "El protestantismo en España," *La Juventud Católica* 2, no. 15 (August 18, 1872): 303; "El matrimonio civil," *La Voz de Cuba* (April 21, 1871); and "El protestantismo en Suiza," *La Voz de Cuba* (September 10, 1874).

17. "Prospecto," *La Juventud Católica* 1, no.1 (November 12, 1871): 1–2; R. M. de A., "El catolicismo y los voluntarios de Cuba," *La Juventud Católica* 2, no. 22 (November 25, 1872): 1–2.

18. Cruz Monclova, *Historia*, vol. 2, part 1, pp. 390–92, 89; José Pérez Moris, *Historia de la insurrección de Lares*, 344.

19. "Educación—Instrucción, II," *La Voz de Cuba* (July 28, 1870); "El Suicidio," *La Voz de Cuba* (December 12, 1874); Antonio López de Letona, *Isla de Cuba: reflexiones sobre su estado social, político y económico*, 53; "Educación—Instrucción, I," *La Voz de Cuba* (July 27, 1870); "Educación—Instrucción, III," *La Voz de Cuba* (August 30, 1870); *La Voz de Cuba* (August 4, 1870); *La Gaceta de La Habana* (November 17, 1871); Edward D. Fitchen, "Primary Education in Colonial Cuba," 104–20.

20. Some Cuban separatists who opposed the island's annexation to the United States were anti-Protestant. See, for example, J. G. Havá, "A 'un habanero,'" *La Propaganda Política* (September 10, 1870) [New Orleans], in LC, Rare Book Room, Broadside Collection, no. 316.

21. Tamayo, "Historia," 71; Marcos Antonio Ramos, *Panorama de protestantismo en Cuba*, 93–94, 99, 141.

22. Gerardo G. Castellanos García, *Motivos de Cayo Hueso*, 247–48; Juan Ramón de la Paz y Cerezo, "Síntesis cronológica de la historia de la iglesia episcopal en Cuba" (copy), Archivo de la Catedral Episcopal Santísima Trinidad, Havana (hereafter cited as ACEST); Ramos, *Panorama*, 99, 140–43; Guerra y Sánchez, *Guerra*, 2:29; [Oliver Wilson Davis], *Sketch of Frederic Fernández Cavada*, 56.

23. Raúl Cepero Bonilla, *Azúcar y abolición*, 126–27; Guerra y Sánchez, *Guerra*, 1:125, 308, 265; Francisco J. Ponte Domínguez, *La masonería en la independencia de Cuba*, 24–29; Junta Cubana, *Facts about Cuba Published under the Authority of the N.Y. Cuban Junta*, 27; Philip S. Foner, *A History of Cuba and Its Relations with the United Sates*, 2:163; González del Valle, *Clero cubano*, 119; González del Valle, "Clero," 159.

24. Gerald Eugene Poyo, "Cuban Emigré Communities in the United and the Independence of Their Homeland," 9; Joan Casanovas, *Bread, or Bullets!*, 103; Spanish consul at Kingston to the captain-general of Cuba, November 8, 1872, AHN, Ultramar, bundle 4726, file 145; George A. Lockward, *El protestantismo en Dominicana*, 261; Ramos, *Panorama*, 91.

25. *La Revolución* (May 5 and October 6, 1869); "El Reverendo Mr. Newman," *La Revolución* (April 17, 1869).

26. Un habanero, *Probable y definitivo porvenir de la Isla de Cuba*, 9–10.

27. Cruz Monclova, *Historia*, vol. 2, part 1, p. 404; Marín, *Las fiestas populares de Ponce*, 222; *El Eco del Pueblo* 2, no. 1 (August 30, 1873).

28. Principios del Partido Liberal Reformista (1886), in Bothwell González, ed.,

Puerto Rico, vol. 1, part 1, p. 170; Román Baldorioty de Castro quoted in Edward J. Berbusse, *The United States in Puerto Rico*, 198; Salvador Brau, *Ecos de la batalla*, 9.

29. Puerto Rico's first Masonic meetings also took place in Ponce in 1873; San Juan's first took place in 1885. See Jourdan to Seward, March 6, 1869, NA, RG 84, San Juan, vol. 7230; Jerry Fenton, *Understanding the Religious Background of the Puerto Rican*, 5; Gutiérrez, *Evangélicos*, 27, 33; Samuel Silva Gotay, *Protestantismo y política en Puerto Rico*, 8; José A. Sierra Martínez, *Camuy*, 79–82; Mariano Vidal Armstrong, *Ponce*, 55.

30. Corwin, *Spain and the Abolition*, 141, 157; Cruz Monclova, *Historia*, 1:380; Luis Manuel Díaz Soler, *Historia de la esclavitud negra en Puerto Rico*, 131; Christopher Schmidt-Nowara, *Empire and Antislavery*, 117.

31. Maza Miquel, *Entre la ideología*, 120; Manuel P. Maza Miquel, *El alma del negocio y el negocio del alma*, 79; José Sedano y Agramonte, *Ley Provisional del Matrimonio Civil y su reglamento*; José Manuel Mestre, *Sobre el matrimonio civil*; "Real Decreto, haciendo extensivo á Cuba y Puerto Rico el Matrimonio Civil de 18 de Junio de 1870," *El Boletín Eclesiástico del Obispado de La Habana* 3, no. 7 (April 15, 1883): 53.

32. Maza Miquel, *Entre la ideología*, 135.

33. The total number of deaths during the war has been estimated at more than 500,000. See Philip S. Foner, *The Spanish-Cuban-American War and the Birth of American Imperialism*, 1:113; John L. Offner, *An Unwanted War*, 112; Susan Schroeder, *Cuba*, 76.

34. Louis A. Pérez, Jr., "North American Protestant Missionaries in Cuba," in *Essays on Cuban History*, 55; Louis A. Pérez, Jr., *On Becoming Cuban*, 101.

35. Maza Miquel, *Entre la ideología*, 185–86.

36. Ibid., 215, 225.

37. Bishop Santander to the nuncio at Madrid, April 1898; archbishop of Santiago de Compostela to the Spanish troops in Cuba, circa 1896; and bishop Santander to Mariano Rampolla, May 16, 1896, all in González del Valle, *Clero cubano*, 14, 144, 13; Ortiz Díaz, "Manifestación anticlerical," 127–28.

38. Harold Greer, "Baptists in Western Cuba," 64; González del Valle, *Clero cubano*, 169–71.

39. Pérez, "North American," 62.

40. Manuel Deulofeu, *Historical and Biographical Notes on the Cuban Mission*, 32.

41. José Martí, Antonio Maceo, and Máximo Gómez were Freemasons. See Aline Helg, *Our Rightful Share*, 64.

42. Francisco J. Ponte Domínguez, *Pensamiento laico de José Martí*, 45, 50; Emilio Roig de Leuchsenring, *Martí y las religiones*, 23–27.

43. Roig de Leuchsenring, *Martí y las religiones*, 35, 56–57; José Martí, *Martí y la Iglesia Católica*, 17–18; Roberto D. Agramonte, *Martí y su concepción del mundo*, 405, 471; Ramos, *Panorama*, 52–53.

44. Rafael Cepeda, "Joaquín de Palma y Pedro Duarte," 4–5; Ramos, *Panorama*, 92; Agramonte, *Martí*, 470; Roig de Leuchsenring, *Martí y las religiones*, 53–55; Pérez, "North American," 58.

45. Quoted in Pérez, "North American," 57.

46. Hostos quoted in H. Hoetink, *The Dominican People, 1850–1900*, 150; Lockward, *Protestantismo*, 281; Berbusse, *United States*, 22; Rafael Peralta Brito and José Chez Checo, *Religión, filosofía y política en Fernando A. de Meriño*, 29; Gutiérrez, *Evangélicos*, 66–67.

CHAPTER 5   *Puerto Rico's First Protestant Congregations*

1. Minvielle to Conroy, November 2, 1869, NA, RG 84, Ponce, vol. 7191; *Gaceta de Puerto Rico* (October 19, 1869); Sanz to the regent of the Real Audiencia of Puerto Rico, October 18, 1865, AGPR, Real Audiencia, Tribunal en Pleno, box 11, file 2. See letter by F. J. Finlay, November 29, 1869, describing the activities of October 19, 1869, in Víctor Burset, "The First Fifty Years of Protestant Episcopal Church in Puerto Rico," 17–19.
2. Minvielle to Conroy, November 2, 1869, NA, RG 84, San Juan, vol. 7191; letter by F. J. Finlay, November 29, 1869, describing the events of October 19, 1869, in Burset, "First Fifty Years," 17–19; Charles L. Colmore, "The Beginnings of the Church in Puerto Rico," 398.
3. The document's signers were William E. Lee, Daniel Basanta, Thomas G. Salomons, George F. Weichers, Thomas A. Dodd, Joseph Henna, John A. Finlay, Charles H. Daly, George F. Finlay, and Peter Minvielle. See Colmore, "Beginnings," 398; Juan Jorge Rivera Torres, *Documentos históricos de la Iglesia Episcopal Puertorriqueña*, 11. Minvielle to Conroy, November 2, 1869, NA, RG 84, Ponce, vol. 7191. A copy of the appeal is reproduced in Roberto H. Todd, "la Iglesia Episcopal de Ponce," 20.
4. Letter by F. J. Finlay, November 29, 1869, describing the events of October 19, 1869, in Burset, "First Fifty Years," 17–19; Lidio Cruz Monclova, *Historia de Puerto Rico*, vol. 2, part 2, p. 853; program for 125th anniversary of la Iglesia Santísima Trinidad (mimeographed leaflet), APIST.
5. Minvielle to Conroy, November 2, 1869, and March 22, 1872, NA, RG 84, Ponce, vol. 7191, and San Juan, vol. 7117. James F. Finlay was U.S. consul during the early 1840s. A letter addressed to Puerto Rico's governor by a group of Protestants included the signatures of Bernardo Eckelman, vice-consul of the German empire; A. Ganslandt, vice-consul of Denmark; T. Bronsted, vice-consul of Sweden and Norway; and the U.S. consular agent; see letter by Ponce's Protestants to the captain-general, June 21, 1874, AHN, Ultramar, bundle 2061, file 20; and APIST, book 1.
6. Jorge Luis Chinea Serrano, "Racial Politics and Commercial Agriculture," 210, 253–56, 260, 284–86; Emma Aurora Dávila Cox, *Este inmenso comercio*, 343–44.
7. Mariano Vidal Armstrong, *Ponce*, 44; on similar tensions in the U.S. south among Baptists, see Paul Harvey, *Redeeming the South*, 10, 34.
8. Minvielle to Conroy, November 2, 1869, NA, RG 84, Ponce, vol. 7191.
9. Charles H. Daly to Samuel Denison, February 27, 1870, in AEC; letter transcribed in Rivera Torres, *Documentos*, 11–13.
10. Letter to the corregidor by Father José Balbino David, cited in Antonio Rivera Martínez, "La primera iglesia evangélica en Puerto Rico" (mimeographed mono-

graph in CIH), 9; letter by F. J. Finlay, November 29, 1869, describing the events of October 19, 1869, in Burset, "First Fifty Years," 17–19.

11. Letter by F. J. Finlay, November 29, 1869, describing the events of October 19, 1869, in Burset, "First Fifty Years," 17–19; Albert E. Lee, *An Island Grows*, 17, 5; Todd, "Iglesia," 20, 98.

12. See Mary Turner, *Slaves and Missionaries*.

13. Daly to Denison, February 27, 1870, in AEC; letter in Rivera Torres, *Documentos*, 11–13.

14. Valentín Basanta was born in Trinidad; his wife, Adelaide Wainwright, was from Bermuda. William E. Lee and his wife, Sarah Louisa Baggs, were born in St. Croix. Lee's son, Thomas Edward Lee, was born in St. Thomas. James Francis Finlay was born in St. Croix; Thomas G. Salomons and his sister María were born in St. Thomas; Guilermo Roebuck was from St. Croix; John Van Rhyn was from St. Martin. See Lee, *Island*, 4–8; and "Padrón de extranjeros, Ponce, 1868," AHMP, bundle 53, box 51.

15. Minvielle to Conroy, March 22, 1872, NA, RG 84, San Juan, vol. 7117.

16. Bishop Jackson's first visit took place on June 4–11, 1872; he arrived with J. C. Du Bois, rector of St. Paul's of St. Croix. Bishop Jackson's second visit was on January 21–26, 1873, when he officiated over the placing of the church's first stone. On March 10 and 11, 1872, C. J. Branch was in Ponce; Du Bois officiated at epiphany services in 1873 at Holy Trinity Church. Branch was also there on September 8, 1873, and returned with the bishop on July 17–26, 1874. See Rivera Torres, *Documentos*, 13; and "Parish of the Holy Trinity, Ponce, Porto Rico," *Spirit of Missions* 38 (February 1873): 126–27.

17. Rivera Torres, *Documentos*, 6–7.

18. Proclamation of the building's consecration, July 23, 1874, copy in APITS; Todd, "Iglesia," 20, 98; Ramón Marín, *Las fiestas populares de Ponce*, 222.

19. Minvielle to Conroy, March 22, 1872, and January 25, 1873, NA, RG 84, San Juan, vol. 7117 and vol. 7118; officer of the bureau to the commissary of the local government, April 19, 1877, AGPR, Obras Públicas, Obras Municipales, box 289, bundle 54-B, file 6; Rivera Torres, *Documentos*, 13.

20. Proclamation of building consecration, July 23, 1874, copy in APIST; Minvielle to Conroy, August 20, 1873, NA, RG 84, San Juan, vol. 7118; Todd, "Iglesia," 20, 98; Colmore, "Beginnings," 399; Vidal Armstrong, *Ponce*, 44; Manuel Ubeda y Delgado, *Isla de Puerto Rico*, 218–21; Minvielle to Conroy, March 22, 1872, NA, RG 84, San Juan, vol. 7117; Burset, "First Fifty Years," 20. For pictorial records of the first church, see J. P. Camy, *Ponce pintoresco* (1881), in Marín, *Fiestas populares*, 146; Todd, "Iglesia," 20, 98; and Dávila Cox, *Este inmenso comercio*, 268. Also see Vidal Armstrong, *Ponce*, 44; Colmore, "Beginnings," 399; Todd, "Iglesia," 20, 98; proclamation of consecration of temple by Bishop Jackson, July 23, 1874, copy in APITS; "Parish of the Holy Trinity," *Spirit of Missions* 38 (February 1873): 126–27; Rivera Torres, *Documentos*, 13; Marín, *Fiestas populares*, 222.

21. Archivo Parroquial de Ponce, Libros de Bautismos (microfilms in CIH).

22. Demographic statistics for Ponce's Catholics in 1883 were 1,252 births, 113 mar-

riages, and 1,406 deaths; see AHDASJ, Disciplina, Padrones, Estadística, 1872–83, bundle P-61; statistics for Ponce's Protestants from APIST, books 1 and 6.

23. Neither Fernández Durand nor Ayot was probably Protestant, but it remains unclear why they remained unmarried as either Catholics or Protestants and what moved them to baptize Ángela with Protestant rites. There is also no indication of why they waited four years to baptize a child born on February 23, 1868. See APIST, book 1.

24. Ibid.

25. Ibid., books 1 and 6.

26. Ibid., book 4, Clergyman's Record, 1876–1900.

27. Ibid., books 1 and 6. It is hard to prove that people with Spanish surnames were not West Indian–born, given the common practice of assuming Spanish names. See various examples in Chinea Serrano, "Racial Politics," 333–35.

28. Ibid., book 1.

29. Ibid.

30. Conroy to the U.S. secretary of state, September 24, 1873, and Minvielle to Conroy, March 22, 1872, NA, RG 84, San Juan, vol. 7230 and vol. 7117.

31. Burset, "First Fifty Years," 22–23; Vidal Armstrong, *Ponce*, 44.

32. Colmore, "Beginnings," 400.

33. Sworn statement by Giolma, June 21, 1874, and the mayor of Ponce to the governor of Puerto Rico, June 21, 1874, in AHN, Ultramar, bundle 2061, file 20; Colomer, "Beginnings," 400; Burset, "First Fifty Years," 23.

34. The twenty-six were Bernardo Eckelman, A. Ganslandt, T. Bronsted, G. H. Lohse, F. Reston, Thomas G. Salomons, Augustus Lion, H. P. Schroeder, John R. Herdons, A. Sinet, James Gilbee, Alejandro Wift, Francis Davidson, Oso Marstrand, F. E. Muller, G. Lohse, Joseph Henna, Henry W. Roebuck, Arthur E. Roebuck, E. Savoide Bright, W. H. Keutsch, Charles Daly, Charles Roebuck, Alexander Westerband, Godfny A. Queely, and Thomas Tindry; see letter to the governor of Puerto Rico, June 21, 1874, AHN, Ultramar, bundle 2061, file 20; Sanz orders in AHN, Ultramar, bundle 2061, file 20.

35. Burset, "First Fifty Years," 23; Colmore, "Beginnings," 399–400; church advertisement in *El Avisador* (October 15, 1874).

36. Lee, *Island*, 14–15; APIST, book 4, Clergyman's Record, 1876–1900, April 23, 1876: Cruz Monclova, *Historia*, vol. 2, part 2, p. 853.

37. Church attendance records show that the number of weekly communicants ranged widely from Sunday to Sunday. Some communion services included as few as five communicants, some as many as thirty-two. See APIST, book 4, Clergyman's Record, 1876–1900; "To the Congregation of Holy Trinity Church Ponce," *El Avisador* (February 11, 1875); and Lee, *Island*, 17–18.

38. Lee, *Island*, 14–15.

39. Pew rental information for 1879 in APIST, book 4, Clergyman's Record, 1876–1900.

40. Ibid.; Lee, *Island*, 17; Alfred Caldecott, *The Church in the West Indies*, 107.

41. Still, why did so many native men and women baptize their children as Protestants when apparently they had little contact with the congregation before or after the

ceremony? Some families may, out of principle, have objected to having their children christened by the priest who had either refused to marry them or charged too much for the ceremony; some natives of the working classes may have perceived Protestant activities as a socially positive association and gravitated to them to improve their standing; or some may have viewed Protestantism as more fulfilling spiritually.

42. Among the fathers of the forty infants baptized during 1877 and 1878 were four clerks, three shoemakers, two merchants, two shopkeepers, two coachmen, two sailors, and one of each in a dozen or so other occupations. See APIST, book 1.

43. Ibid.; also see Eileen J. Findlay, "Domination, Decency, and Desire," 69–70.

44. According to the Anglican Book of Common Prayer, boys must have two male sponsors and one female sponsor, while girls should have two female sponsors and one male sponsor. The sponsors' primary responsibility is to ensure that the baptized children learn the basic tenets of the faith and that in due time they receive episcopal confirmation. See Sidney W. Mintz and Eric R. Wolf, "An Analysis of Ritual Co-Parenthood," 342.

45. Baptism of William Edward Lee, December 30, 1875, APIST, book 1.

46. Ibid.

47. Archivo Parroquial de Ponce, Libros de Bautismos (microfilms in CIH); APIST, book 1. Catholic sample is from May 1869: fifty-five illegitimate births and fifty-one legitimate ones. Protestant sample is from 1876–80: fifty-four illegitimate births and seventy-nine legitimate ones.

48. APIST, books 1 and 4.

49. Ibid.

50. Ibid.

51. Case documents in AHDASJ, Justicia, Procesos Legales, Validación de Matrimonios, Ponce, bundle J-218.

52. Protestant marriage fees are recorded as two to four pesos; see APIST, book 4, Clergyman's Record, 1876–1900.

53. Roura and Hernández to the bishop of Puerto Rico, April 28, 1887, and bishop's determination, May 5, 1887, AHDASJ, Justicia, Procesos Legales, Validación de Matrimonios, Ponce, bundle J-218.

54. APIST, book 1.

55. Certification by Joaquín Calvo dated March 31, 1876, in AHMP, bundle 44, box 42-B, file 12.

56. See copy of royal order of 1871, in AHN, Ultramar, bundle 2061, file 26. In September 1875, Hortensia Mirailh, widow of Carlos Basanta, purchased a plot in the Protestant area next to her husband's grave. See AHMP, "Índice del cementerio antiguo," 1:149. Also see the certification by Joaquín Calvo, March 31, 1876, in AHMP, bundle 44, box 42-B, file 12.

57. Document on meetings of September 18, 1875; document signed by Weichers and Salomons, 1874; and certification by the municipal council of Ponce, October 15, 1875, AHMP, bundle 44, box 42-B, file 12; also see *La Gaceta de Puerto Rico* (July 20, 1876).

58. Bishop to Ponce's parish priest, April 4, 1876, AHMP, bundle 44, box 42-B, file 12.

59. Governor of Puerto Rico to the overseas minister, July 6, 1876; British consul at San Juan to the governor, June 1, 1876, AHN, Ultramar, bundle 5108, file 38, docs. 2 and 3; British consul at San Juan to the governor of Puerto Rico, July 1, 1876; the secretary of governement to the mayor of Ponce, June 7, 1876; and certification by the municipal council of Ponce, June 9, 1876, AHMP, bundle 44, box 42-B, file 12; APIST, Record of Ecclesiastical Duties.

60. The makeshift enclosure around Gavin's tomb measured approximately twenty-two by eleven feet. Letter of protest dated June 17, 1876, by Basanta, Lee, Dodd, Salomons, Henna, and McCormick; the mayor of Ponce to the governor of Puerto Rico, June 17, 1876; the governor of Puerto Rico to the overseas minister, July 6, 1876, AHN, Ultramar, bundle 5108, file 38; see also AHMP, bundle 44, box 42-B, file 12.

61. Mayor of Ponce to the governor, June 24, 1876, AHN, Ultramar, bundle 5108, file 38.

62. Cable of the mayor of Ponce to the governor, June 29, 1876, AHN, Ultramar, bundle 5108, file 38.

63. Governor of Puerto Rico to the overseas minister, July 6, 1876, AHN, Ultramar, bundle 5018, file 38; cable by the mayor of Ponce to the governor of Puerto Rico, July 5, 1876, AHMP, bundle 44, box 42-B, file 12; the bishop quoted in document dated September 4, 1876, AHN, Ultramar, bundle 2061, file 26; the governor to the bishop, July 20, 1875, AHDASJ, Gobierno, Correspondencia Parroquia-Obispo, Ponce, bundle G-26.

64. The Catholic cemetery was valued at almost twenty-five times the value of the Protestant one, at 47,000 pesos. Bertoli had a few years earlier been in charge of the expansions that doubled the Catholic cemetery's size. See Marín, *Fiestas populares*, 218; project description by Juan Bertoli, June 12, 1876, AHMP, bundle 44, box 42-B, file 17. Expansion project information in AGPR, Obras Públicas, Obras Municipales, box 289, bundle 54-B, files 2, 5A, and 6. Also see Ramón López Crespo, "El desarrollo histórico del cementerio," 55. Bertoli also designed the Teatro La Perla; Marín, *Fiestas populares*, 130, 218, 222.

65. AHMP, "Índice del cementerio antiguo," vols. 1 and 2; and certification of project's conclusion, March 26, 1877, bundle 44, box 42-B, file 17. Burial fees collected by the Protestant minister varied according to capacity to pay and ranged between 2.50 and 6.00 pesos. See APIST, book 4, Clergyman's Record, 1876–1900.

66. Archivo Parroquial de Ponce, Libros de Defunciones, (microfilms in CIH); APIST, book 1.

67. APIST, book 1.

68. Sugar production in Ponce fell after the abolition of slavery in 1873; the 1876 harvest was less than half the size of 1871's. Also, Ponce's connections with St. Thomas became increasingly weaker beginning in the 1850s. See Marín, *Fiestas populares*, 264; Dávila Cox, *Este inmenso comercio*, 24, 185; Lee, *Island*, 22; Chinea Serrano, "Racial Politics," 348.

69. As Findlay points out in "Domination," 179, "as the city's population grew, elites felt more and more threatened by the urban poor. A report to the governor of Puerto Rico in 1887 dwelt on the thousands of poverty-stricken vagrants from

neighboring towns and rural areas who swelled Ponce's streets." In the mid-1870s, Governor Sanz warned about the dangers of free black immigration. See Cruz Monclova, *Historia*, vol. 2, part 2, pp. 418–19.

70. APIST, book 4, Clergyman's Record, 1876–1900; Manuel Mayoral Barnes, *Ponce y su historial geopolítico-económico y cultural*, 90.

71. Lee, *Island*, 17–28; Colmore, "Beginnings," 400.

72. APIST, book 4, Clergyman's Record, 1876–1900; Colmore, "Beginnings," 400.

73. Todd, "Iglesia," 20, 98; Rivera Torres, *Documentos*, 13–16.

74. "Asiento de difuntos protestantes habidos en la isla de Vieques desde 1 de septiembre de 1845. Registro del Gobernador de Vieques, 1838–1845," CIH, vol. 4 (copy in AHV).

75. Burset, "First Fifty Years," 25; Cruz Monclova, *Historia*, vol. 2, part 1, pp. 222, 853; order by the overseas minister, October 12, 1870, in *Boletín histórico de Puerto Rico* 2, no. 3: 161–62; Ángel L. Gutiérrez, *Evangélicos en Puerto Rico*, 39, 41–45.

76. Vieques's budget for 1879–80, in AGPR, Vieques, box 5, file 41A; parish priest of Vieques to the bishop, June 22, 1875, AHDASJ, Gobierno, Correspondencia Parroquia-Obispo, Vieques, bundle G-29.

77. Colmore, "Beginnings," 401; Burset, "First Fifty Years," 36; Joseph Bean to Queen Victoria, Advent 1896, in APITS; J. Pastor Ruiz, *Vieques antiguo y moderno*, 41–42.

78. Bean to Queen Victoria, Advent 1896, in APITS.

79. Pastor Ruiz, *Vieques*, 41–42.

80. Colmore, "Beginnings," 401.

81. Notes by Bean, October 19, 1893, and June 19, 1897; and Bean to Queen Victoria, Advent 1896, in APITS; Colmore, "Beginnings," 401–2; Rivera Torres, *Documentos*, 13–14.

82. Significantly, the data on offerings demonstrated the seasonal ups and downs of the population. Monthly collections for 1890 were as follows (in pesos): January, 6.95; February, 7.00; March, 15.15; April, 17.60; May, 7.60; and October, 3.10. See membership list and Bean to Queen Victoria, Advent 1896, APITS; Colmore, "Beginnings," 402; Rivera Torres, *Documentos*, 14; Caldecott, *Church*, 193.

83. Records of baptisms, marriages, and burials for the mid-1890s reveal their relative inexpensiveness. Baptisms cost one peso, marriages between three and four pesos, and burials two pesos. See note by Bean, October 22, 1893, APITS; Rivera Torres, *Documentos*, 15; and Colmore, "Beginnings," 401–2.

84. During an episcopal visit on April 12, 1898, only five members of All Saints were confirmed. At that point Bean had been blinded by cataracts. Rivera Torres, *Documentos*, 15.

85. For a discussion on the social and economic roles of marriage in San Juan, see Félix V. Matos Rodríguez, *Women and Urban Change in San Juan*, 62–63.

CHAPTER 6   *Cuba's First Protestant Congregations*

1. Kenney to Whittingham, November 25, 1873, MDA, Cuba folder 4; Leopoldo J. Alard, "Proceso histórico de la Iglesia Episcopal en Cuba," 7–8; Carlos A.

Tamayo, "Historia de la Iglesia Episcopal de Cuba," 3–4; Harry Beal, "El olvidado precursor," 4; Henry B. Whipple, *Lights and Shadows of a Long Episcopate*, 358–60.

2. Whipple, *Lights*, 359–60; Beal, "Olvidado precursor," 4; Alard, "Proceso," 9–14; Hiram H. Hulse, "The History of the Church in Cuba," 249.

3. Kenney to Whittingham, May 1, 1872, and November 25, 1873, and W. A. Leonard, "Our Missionary in Havana," *Churchman* 5 (June 30, 1877): 703, all in MDA, Cuba folders 4 and 5; Tamayo, "Historia," 28.

4. Kenney to Whittingham, December 10, 1865, and July 8 and 24, 1868; John Vaughan Lewis to Whittingham, August 6, 1868, all in MDA, Cuba, Correspondence, Kenney Letters; Beal, "Olvidado precursor," 4.

5. Kenney to Whittingham, May 1, 1872, and November 25, 1873, MDA, Cuba folder 4.

6. Kenney to Whittingham, November 5, 1873, January 18, 1879, MDA, Cuba folder 5; Kenney's report of 1874, in [Edward Kenney], *Report of Our Mission in Cuba*, 12; Alard, "Proceso," 11; Tamayo, "Historia," 6; Beal, "Olvidado precursor," 4.

7. Kenney to Whittingham, May 1, 1872, MDA, Cuba folder 4; Alard, "Proceso," 12.

8. Kenney to Whittingham, May 1, 1872, and November 25, 1873, MDA, Cuba folders 4 and 5; [Kenney], *Report of Our Mission*, 4–5; Alard, "Proceso," 12.

9. Kenney to Whittingham, November 25, 1873, MDA, Cuba folder 5; Church funds report for 1874, in AEC, RG 65–1.

10. Kenney to Whittingham, February 24, 1874, MDA, Cuba folder 4; report of 1874, in [Kenney], *Report of Our Mission*, 13; Leonard, "Our Missionary," 703; Richard Henry Dana, Jr., *To Cuba and Back*, 80.

11. Kenney to Whittingham, November 25, 1875, and February 14, 1874, MDA, Cuba folder 4; reports of 1874 and 1877, in [Kenney], *Report of Our Mission*, 7, 13; Leonard, "Our Missionary," 703; *Cuba Guild* 1, no. 2 (July 1880): 1.

12. Kenney to Whittingham, May 1, 1872, and October 23, 1878, MDA, Cuba folder 4; reports of 1874 and 1877, in [Kenney], *Report of Our Mission*, 4, 12.

13. Kenney to William Tatlock, August 9, 1879, reproduced in Cuba Church Missionary Guild, *The Mission of the Protestant Episcopal Church in the Island of Cuba*, 7; Kenney to Whittingham, April 1, 1876, MDA, Cuba folder 4.

14. "Kenney to the Children," *Cuba Guild* 1, no. 2 (July 1880): 14–15; Kenney's report of 1879, in Cuba Church Missionary Guild, *Mission*, 3; report of 1877, in [Kenney], *Report of Our Mission*, 4, 8–9.

15. Report of 1877, in [Kenney], *Report of Our Mission*, 4–6; Beal, "Olvidado precursor," 5; "Kenney to the Guild," *Cuba Guild* 1, no. 2 (July 1880): 1.

16. Carlton H. Rogers, *Incidents of Travel in the Southern United States and Cuba*, 161–62; Fredrika Bremer, *The Homes of the New World*, 2:375–76; William Cullen Bryant, *Letters of William Cullen Bryant*, 3:27; [Julia Louisa Matilda Woodruff], *My Winter in Cuba*, 190–91; James William Steele, *Cuban Sketches*, 180–82; diary of Grace Backhouse, April 5, 1855, Backhouse Papers.

17. Cuba Church Missionary Guild, *Mission*, 3; "Kenney to the Guild," and "Kenney to the Children" *Cuba Guild* 1, no. 2 (July 1880): 9, 14; Kenney to friends, Sep-

tember 21, 1876, MDA, Cuba folder 5; [Kenney], *Report of Our Mission*, 5; Beal, "Olvidado precursor," 6.

18. Circular sent to Whittingham (circa 1875); report of the treasurer of the Havana Church Fund (1872); and Kenney to Whittingham, May 1, 1872, MDA, Cuba folders 3 and 5; "Kenney to the Guild," *Cuba Guild* 1, no. 2 (July 1880): 10.

19. [Kenney], *Report of Our Mission*, 9.

20. Ibid., 2; Kenney to Whittingham, October 31, 1874, and November 20, 1878, MDA, Cuba folder 4; "Cuba Church Missionary Society," March 24, 1879, in MDA, Cuba folder 2; Cuba Church Missionary Guild, *Mission*, 2, 14–15.

21. Kenney, report of 1879, in Cuba Church Missionary Guild, *Mission*, 4; "Kenney to the Children," *Cuba Guild* 1, no. 2 (July 1880): 14–15.

22. Kenney, report of 1879, in Cuba Church Missionary Guild, *Mission*, 5; report of 1877, in [Kenney], *Report of Our Mission*, 6; "Cuban Church Missionary Society," March 24, 1879, MDA, Cuba folder 2.

23. Kenney, report of 1879, in Cuba Church Missionary Guild, *Mission*, 3–6; report of 1877, in [Kenney], *Report of Our Mission*, 5; Alard, "Proceso," 9.

24. Kenney to Whittingham, May 1, 1872, MDA, Cuba folder 4; "Objectives," *Cuba Guild* 1, no. 2 (July 1880): 18; Whipple, *Lights*, 360.

25. Kenney to Whittingham, May 1, 1872, MDA, Cuba folder 4; [Kenney], *Report of Our Mission*, 6.

26. [Kenney], *Report of Our Mission*, 5; "Our Mission in Cuba Proceedings of a Committee of Laymen [New York, 1878]," pp. 7–8, MDA, Cuba folder 2.

27. [Kenney], *Report of Our Mission*, 13; Kenney, report of 1879, in Cuba Church Missionary Guild, *Mission*, 4–6; Marcos Antonio Ramos, *Panorama de protestantismo en Cuba*, 99; Kenney to Whittingham, October 19, 1878, MDA, Cuba folder 4; "Kenney to the Guild," *Cuba Guild* 2, no. 1 (July 1880): 11.

28. Kenney to Whittingham, January 18, 1879, MDA, Cuba folder 4; Kenney, report of 1879, in Cuba Church Missionary Guild, *Mission*, 3.

29. "Kenney to Tatlock, August 9, 1879," Cuba Church Missionary Society, *Mission*, 7.

30. [Kenney], *Report of Our Mission*, 14.

31. *The Cuba Commission Report*, 21, 25, 62, 99, 23; Laird W. Bergad, *Cuban Rural Society in the Nineteenth Century*, 249; Juan Pérez de la Riva, "Demografía de los culiés," in *El barracón*, 61, 70.

32. "Kenney to the Guild," *Cuba Guild* 1, no. 2 (July 1880): 9–11; Kenney, report of 1879, in Cuba Church Missionary Guild, *Mission*, 5; Kenney to friends, September 21, 1876, MDA, Cuba folder 5.

33. "Kenney to the Guild," *Cuba Guild* 1, no. 2 (July 1880): 9–11.

34. "Kenney to Tatlock, August 9, 1879," in Cuba Church Missionary Guild, *Mission*, 7.

35. In 1877, Kenney officiated at ten baptisms and one marriage among the plantation slaves. According to Kenney's successor, Reverend Egerton, "the children were all baptized and received Christian names but had no family name, marriage relations not being established among the Negroes." See Kenney to friends, September 21, 1876, MDA, Cuba folder 5; [Kenney], *Report of Our Mission*, 7; Beal "Olvidado

precursor," 5; Egerton to Mrs. James S. Merritt, February 26, 1908, AEC, Cuba Scrapbook; and Bergad, *Cuban Rural Society*, 316.

36. [Kenney], *Report of Our Mission*, 8.
37. Kenney to Whittingham, November 25, 1873, MDA, Cuba folder 4; [Kenney], *Report of Our Mission*, 8; APITS, books 1 and 2.
38. Albion W. Knight, *Lending a Hand in Cuba*, 10; Kenney to Whittingham, November 25, 1873, MDA, Cuba folder 5.
39. [Kenney], *Report of Our Mission*, 8.
40. Ibid.
41. Kenney to Whittingham, November 25, 1873, Kenney to friends, September 21, 1876, and circular sent to Whittingham (circa 1875), in MDA, Cuba folders 4 and 5; [Kenney], *Report of Our Mission*, 4, 13, 6; excerpt from Kenney's letter of July 29, 1879, in Cuba Church Missionary Guild, *Mission*, 9.
42. Kenney, report of 1879, and excerpts from 1879 letters, in Cuba Church Missionary Guild, *Mission*, 5, 9.
43. Kenney to Whittingham, November 25, 1873, and Kenney to friends, September 21, 1876, MDA, Cuba folders 4 and 5; [Kenney], *Report of Our Mission*, 6; excerpts from 1879 letters, in Cuba Church Missionary Society, *Mission*, 9.
44. Kenny, report of 1879, in Cuba Church Missionary Guild, *Mission*, 5; "To the Friends of Our Church Work on the Island of Cuba," MDA, Cuba folder 5.
45. AALH, Cementerio Colón, bundle 8, file 1; and the bishop of Havana to the captain-general, August 27, 1883, ANC, Gobierno General, bundle 369, file 17651.
46. [Kenney], *Report of Our Mission*, 13; circular to Whittingham (circa 1875), MDA, Cuba folder 5; Leonard, "Our Missionary," 703.
47. Kenney, excerpts from 1879 letters, in Cuba Church Missionary Guild, *Mission*, 9.
48. Kenney to Whittingham, October 10, 1876, MDA, Cuba folder 5; Kenney, excerpts from 1879 letters, in Cuba Church Missionary Guild, *Mission*, 9; Alard, "Proceso," 15–16; Beal, "Olvidado precursor," 6; Tamayo, "Historia," 23–27; Egerton to Mrs. James S. Merritt, February 26, 1908, AEC, Cuba Scrapbook; Knight, *Lending a Hand*, 15.

CHAPTER 7   *Revolution, Exile, and Cuban Protestantism*

1. For a fine discussion on how Cuban tobacco workers circulated between Havana and Key West, see Joan Casanovas, *Bread, or Bullets!*, 125 and passim; on their political and racial attitudes, see ibid., 10, 111–12, 63, and 85.
2. "Inventory of the Church Archives in New York City, the Protestant Episcopal Church, Diocese of New York," compiled by the Historical Sources Survey, Work Project Administration, New York City, 1940; *Journal of the Convention of the Protestant Episcopal Church in the Diocese of New York* (hereafter cited as *Journal, New York*) (1869), 119; Carlos A. Tamayo, "Historia de la Iglesia Episcopal de Cuba," 51–52; Palma's letter in the New York press, June 27, 1870, clipping in the Archives of the Diocese of New York of the Protestant Episcopal Church (hereafter cited as ADNYPEC); Kenneth Walter Cameron, *American Episcopal Clergy*, 14.

3. *Journal, New York* (1869), 200; (1874), 141–42; Tamayo, "Historia," 53; "Inventory of the Church Archives"; James Grant Wilson, ed., *The Centennial History of the Protestant Episcopal Church in the Diocese of New York*, 339.

4. Juan Ramón de la Paz y Cerezo, "Síntesis cronológica de la historia de la iglesia episcopal en Cuba" (copy), ACEST; *La Revolución* (May 5 and October 6, 1869); Marcos Antonio Ramos, *Panorama de protestantismo en Cuba*, 92–93; *Libro de Oración Común y Administración de los Santos Sacramentos y otros Ritos y Ceremonias de la Iglesia*; Palma's letter in the New York press, June 27, 1870, in ADNYPEC.

5. *Journal, New York* (1873), 139.

6. Tamayo, "Historia," 53; *Journal, New York* (1870), 149; (1873), 139; (1878), 112; (1879), 120.

7. *Journal, New York* (1879), 120.

8. Ibid. (1878), 112.

9. Ibid. (1883), 148; Palma's letter in the New York press, June 27, 1870, in ADNYPEC.

10. Ramos, *Panorama*, 51.

11. Palma's sermon of October 11, 1874, quoted in Rafael Cepeda, "Joaquín de Palma y Pedro Duarte," 4–5; *La Revolución* (May 5, and October 6, 1869); Almira Lincoln Phelps to Bishop Whittingham, November 22, 1869, MDA, Cuba Correspondence.

12. Palma, quoted in Rafael Cepeda, "Joaquín de Palma," 8–11; and I Peter, 4:12–13: "Beloved, think it not strange concerning the fiery trial, which is to try you, as though some strange thing happened to you. But rejoice, inasmuch as ye are partakers of Christ's sufferings; that, when his glory shall be revealed, ye may be glad also with exceeding joy."

13. *Journal, New York* (1878), 112; (1879), 120; (1880), 117; (1881), 122; (1882), 124; (1883), 148; Wilson, ed., *Centennial History*, 339; John F. Young, "Report of the Bishop of Florida on Work in Cuba," *Spirit of Missions* 49 (November–December 1884): 629; *Journal, New York* (1880), 117; "Inventory of the Church Archives"; Cameron, *American Episcopal Clergy*, 14.

14. J. M. López-Guillén, "Cuba in New York and Brooklyn," *Home Missionary* 72, no. 2 (October 1899): 89.

15. Bishop Young's address of 1876, in *Journal of Proceedings of the Annual Council of the Protestant Episcopal Church in the Diocese of Florida* (hereafter cited as *Journal, Florida*) (1876), 40; Gerardo G. Castellanos García, *Motivos de Cayo Hueso*, 245.

16. Sharon Wells, *Forgotten Legacy*, 17; C. Neale Ronning, *José Martí and the Emigré Colony in Key West*, 20; Jefferson B. Browne, *Key West*, 173.

17. Browne, *Key West*, 117; Terence H. Nolan, William Carl Shiver, and L. Scott Nidy, *Cultural Resources of Key West*, 39; Gerald Eugene Poyo, *With All, and for the Good of All*, 53; Casanovas, *Bread, or Bullets!*, 165, 169.

18. Walter C. Maloney, *A Sketch of the History of Key West, Florida*, 17; Ronning, *José Martí*, 23; Browne, *Key West*, 118–19.

19. Browne, *Key West*, 118–19.

20. Ibid., 29, 44; Paul Harvey, *Redeeming the South*, 34.

21. Michael J. McNally, *Catholicism in South Florida*, 20, 31.
22. Ibid., 33; Gerardo G. Castellanos García, *Misión a Cuba*, 44; Castellanos García, *Motivos*, 246–47; Records of the Cuban Consulate, Key West, Florida, LC, microfilm reel 47; John F. Young, "Cuba," *Spirit of Missions* 49 (October 1884): 484.
23. *El Republicano* 2, no. 39 (February 26, 1870); Manuel Deulofeu, *Héroes del destierro*, 10.
24. Castellanos García, *Misión*, 45.
25. *El Republicano* 2, nos. 39 and 43 (February 26, and March 26, 1870); McNally, *Catholicism*, 33–34.
26. Sterling Augustus Neblett, *Methodism's First Fifty Years in Cuba*, 5–7; Manuel Deulofeu, *Historical and Biographical Notes on the Cuban Mission*, 17–19; report by Charles A. Fulwood on the Cuban mission in Key West, *Thirty-Second Annual Meeting of the Florida Conference of the Methodist Episcopal Church, South*, 28–31; Deulofeu, *Héroes*, 37; Castellanos García, *Motivos*, 248; Ramos, *Panorama*, 97; Jason M. Yaremko, *U.S. Protestant Missions in Cuba*, 4.
27. Joseph D. Cushman, Jr., *A Goodly Heritage*, 108, 145; Henry B. Whipple, *Lights and Shadows*, 360.
28. Young, "Cuba" (October 1884): 484; Castellanos García, *Motivos*, 247–48; Ramos, *Panorama*, 143; *El Republicano* 2, no. 42 (March 19, 1870).
29. Bishop Young's address of 1876, in *Journal, Florida* (1876), 41–42; Young, "Cuba" (October 1884): 484–94; Edgar Legare Pennington, "The Episcopal Church in Florida," 56.
30. Bishop Young's address of 1876, in *Journal, Florida* (1876), 40; Wells, *Forgotten Legacy*, 39; Cushman, *Goodly Heritage*, 98; Pennington, "Episcopal Church," 57–60.
31. Bishop Young's address of 1877, in *Journal, Florida* (1877), 50–53; Young, "Cuba" (October 1884): 484–94; Bishop Young's address of 1878, in *Journal, Florida* (1878), 37–38; Pennington, "Episcopal Church," 57–60.
32. Bishop Young's address of 1878, in *Journal, Florida* (1878), 37; 1878 report of the parish of St. John's, in ibid., 49; 1879 report of the parish of St. John's, in ibid. (1879), 54; Castellanos García, *Misión*, 50.
33. Bishop Young's address of 1880, in *Journal, Florida* (1880), 39; Pennington, "Episcopal Church," 57; Bishop Young's address of 1881, in *Journal, Florida* (1881), 31, 49; Young, "Cuba" (October 1884): 484.
34. 1883 report of the parish of St. John's, *Journal, Florida* (1883), 54; transcribed copy of "Cuba," *Our Home Field* 1, no. 7 (March 1889): 5–6, in the Southern Baptist Historical Library and Archives (hereafter cited as SBHLA), Una Roberts Lawrence Resource Files (hereafter cited as URLRF), box 6, folder 30; Southern Baptist Convention, Home Mission Board minutes, 1875–98, July 12, 1886, in SBCLA; Primitivo Delgado, "The History of the Southern Baptist Missions in Cuba to 1945," 43–45.
35. E. P. Herrick, "Our Cuban Work in Florida," *Home Missionary* 72, no. 2 (October 1899): 85–87.
36. A Cuban Congregationalist mission (Immanuel) was established in Tampa in 1892 under the pastorship of E. P. Herrick. By century's end it had 119 members. See ibid. Also see Alfredo Victorino Díaz to *La Aurora de Yumurí*, June 25, 1884

(copy), in Archivo de la Iglesia Bautista El Calvario, Havana (hereafter cited as AIBC); and Hiram H. Hulse, "The History of the Church in Cuba," 251.

37. O. P. Thackara to Miss Emery, September 10, 1879, in *Spirit of Missions* 45 (February 1880): 51–52. In a letter to the board of missions of the Southern Methodist Church, Reverend Van Duzer wrote about the Key West work: "This is an important mission. It is an entrance-gate through which the island of Cuba, 'so beautiful,' can be entered, and the pure word preached. . . . The gospel must be preached here and carried there in the hearts of converts." See Neblett, *Methodism's First Fifty Years*, 6.

38. Browne, *Key West*, 173; Poyo, *With All*, 53.

39. Deulofeu, *Historical*, 21–23.

40. Young, "Cuba" (October 1884): 484–94.

41. Kerr Boyce Tupper, *Díaz, El Apóstol de Cuba*, 4; copies of meetings' minutes, AIBC; J. W. Jones, "Sketch of Rev. A. J. Díaz, 'The Apostle of Cuba,'" *Seminary Magazine* 9, no. 7 (April 1896): 349–53; Tamayo, "Historia," 65; Young, "Cuba" (October 1884): 489; Una Roberts Lawrence, *Cuba for Christ*, 145; Harold Greer, "Baptists in Western Cuba," 62. For further details on Díaz and his life, see transcribed copy of I. T. Tichenor, "Another Visit to Cuba," *Our Home Field* 1, no. 7 (March 1889), in SBHLA, URLRF, box 6, folder 30; and *The Christian Index* (January 15, 1891): 5.

42. Copies of meetings' minutes (no. 3), and Díaz to *La Aurora de Yumurí*, June 25, 1884 (copy), both in AIBC; *The Christian Index* (January 15, 1891): 5. Established in 1813, the Female Bible Society of Philadelphia aimed at distributing Bibles in Spanish colonial territories. See *A Directory of the Charitable, Social Improvement, Educational and Religious Associations and Churches of Philadelphia*, 498.

43. Tupper, *Díaz*, 5; copies of meetings' minutes, AIBC; Jones, "Sketch," 351–52; Díaz to *La Aurora de Yumurí*, June 25, 1884; *El Triunfo* (November 20, 1884): 2; *El Espectador* (March 1, 1884): 3; transcribed copies of all three in AIBC. Also see Young, "Cuba" (October 1884): 491; George William Lasher, *Anales del evangelio en Cuba*, 37, copy in AIBC; Delgado, "History," 47.

44. Duarte to the governor of Matanzas, November 30, 1888, AHPM, Gobierno Provincial, Orden Público y Policía, bundle 69, file 8165A; Díaz to *La Aurora de Yumurí*, June 25, 1884, copy in AIBC; Francisco J. Ponte Domínguez, *Matanzas*, 233; Tamayo, "Historia," 71.

45. Díaz to *La Aurora de Yumurí*, June 25, 1884, copy in AIBC; souvenir notice of the third anniversary of the founding of Fieles a Jesús, August 5, 1888, AEC, Cuba Scrapbook; "The Beginning of the Cuban Mission: A Letter from the Rev. Pedro Duarte," American Church Missionary Society (1900), AEC, Cuba Scrapbook; "Importante decreto por el que se extendió a Cuba la tolerancia religiosa," *Heraldo Episcopal* (1970): 12; 1886 report by the Ladies' Cuban Guild of Philadelphia, copy in AEC, Cuba Scrapbook.

46. Sixty-eighth and sixty-ninth annual reports of the American Bible Society, May 1885, AEC, Cuba Scrapbook; Young, "Cuba" (October 1884): 484–94; Ramos, *Panorama*, 116.

47. Young, "Cuba" (October 1884): 484–94.

48. Pennington, "Episcopal Church," 69–70; Young, "Cuba" (October 1884): 484–94; Bishop Young, "Cuba," *Spirit of Missions* 50 (July 1885): 381.

49. Pennington, "Episcopal Church," 70; Cushman, *Goodly Heritage*, 152; letter certifying Báez's appointment, dated Trinity Sunday, 1884, AEC, RG 65-1.

50. Bishop Young's address of 1884, in *Journal, Florida* (1884), 44; Young, "Cuba" (October 1884): 484–94; Pennington, "Episcopal Church," 69–70; Díaz to *La Aurora de Yumurí*, June 25, 1884, copy in AIBC.

51. Young's address of 1884, in *Journal, Florida* (1884), 44; Young "Cuba" (October 1884): 484–94; and Young, "Cuba" (July 1885): 382–84.

52. Young, "Cuba," *Spirit of Missions* 50 (July 1884): 353; Young, "Cuba" (October 1884): 488.

53. Báez's report of August 20, 1884, quoted in Young, "Report of the Bishop of Florida on Work in Cuba," 627–29. Also see Young, "Cuba," *Spirit of Missions* 50 (July 1885): 381–89.

54. Bishop Young's address of 1885, in *Journal, Florida* (1885), 48; Young, "Cuba" (July 1885): 381–89; copies of meetings' minutes, AIBC.

55. Louis A. Pérez, Jr., "North American Protestant Missionaries in Cuba," in *Essays on Cuban History*, 60; Lawrence, *Cuba for Christ*, 152; Glenn E. Bryant, "A History of Baptist Mission Work in Cuba," 43; Young, "Cuba" (July 1885): 388; Cuban Guild of Philadelphia, *Cuba, Old and New*, 4.

56. Báez to Joshua Kimber, January 9, 1886, and December 4, 1885, both in AEC, RG 65-1.

57. Báez's report of August 20, 1884, quoted in Young, "Report of the Bishop of Florida on Work in Cuba," 628; Lasher, *Anales*, 37; Báez to Joshua Kimber, January 9, 1886, AEC, RG 65-1.

58. Louis A. Pérez, Jr., *On Becoming Cuban*, 55–57; Pérez, "North American Protestant Missionaries," 56–60.

59. Báez to Joshua Kimber, December 16, 1885, AEC, RG 65-1.

60. Young, "Cuba" (October 1884): 486; Jones "Sketch," 351–52; Tamayo, "Historia," 67, 95–96; Lawrence, *Cuba for Christ*, 146.

61. Báez to William S. Langford, April 12, 1886, AEC, RG 65-1.

62. Account book of the Episcopal mission in Cuba (1884–85), AEC, RG 65-1; report by Báez dated August 20, 1884, quoted in Young, "Report of the Bishop of Florida on Work in Cuba," 627–29.

63. Bishop Young's address of 1885, in *Journal, Florida* (1885), 44; Young, "Cuba" (July 1885): 387.

64. Díaz to *La Aurora de Yumurí*, June 25, 1884, copy in AIBC.

65. Lyne to Kimber, December 30, 1885, Young to Kimber, September 3, 1885, and Báez to William S. Langford, March 2, 1886, all in AEC, RG 65-1.

66. Cushman, *Goodly Heritage*, 169–70; Albion W. Knight, *Lending a Hand in Cuba*, 21; Báez to Langford, March 21, 1886, AEC, RG 65-1.

67. The Cuban Guild was an auxiliary of the American Church Missionary Society and was run by laypersons. See *Directory*, 526–27; and Knight, *Lending a Hand*, 22–23.

68. An advertisement in Havana's *El Espectador* [(March 1, 1884): 3] mentions the "Iglesia Protestante Episcopal de Getsemaní." Copy of document in AIBC.

69. Meetings' minutes in AIBC; Jones, "Sketch," 351; Delgado, "History," 38; de la Cova to Julia E. Emery, November 25, 1885, AEC, RG 65-1; Tamayo, "Historia," 90; Seventy-second Annual Report of the Female Bible Society of Philadelphia, AEC, Cuba Scrapbook.

70. Southern Baptist Convention, Home Mission Board minutes, 1875–98, July 12, 1886, p. 240, in SBCLA; transcribed copy of "Cuba," *Our Home Field* 3, no. 1 (September 1890): 6–7, in SBHLA, URLRF, box 6, folder 30.

71. Báez to William S. Langford, April 12, 1886, and Báez to Kimber, December 19, 1885, both in AEC, RG 65-1; Browne, *Key West*, 44; Lawrence, *Cuba for Christ*, 148–50; Greer "Baptists," 62.

72. Letter to the missionary society, January 13, 1886, AEC, RG 65-1.

73. Báez to Kimber, January 9, 1886, and December 16, 1885, AEC, RG 65-1.

74. Báez to Kimber, January 9, 1886, and Báez to Langford, April 12, 1886, AEC, RG 65-1.

75. Nolan et al., *Cultural Resources*, 40–42; Báez to Langford, March 2 and April 6, 1886, AEC, RG 65-1; Poyo, *With All*, 66; Casanovas, *Bread, or Bullets!*, 169.

76. "Estado general de los actos efectuados por la Misión de la iglesia Católica Apostólica Episcopal en el espacio de dos años de establecida en la Ysla de Cuba," AEC, RG 65-2. An 1860 report from Cienfuegos reported: "The white proletariat treats the colored class on a completely equal footing." Quoted in Casanovas, *Bread, or Bullets!*, 62.

77. "Estado general de los actos efectuados por la Misión de la iglesia Católica Apostólica Episcopal en el espacio de dos años de establecida en la Ysla de Cuba," AEC, RG 65-2.

78. Tamayo, "Historia," 98–103; Duarte to the governor of Matanzas, November 30, 1888, AHPM, Gobierno Provincial, Orden Público y Policía, bundle 69, file 8165A.

79. *Church Work in Cuba under the Auspices of the Ladies' Cuban Guild of Philadelphia, PA,* in AEC, Cuba Scrapbook; Knight, *Lending a Hand*, 22–24.

80. Tamayo, "Historia," 102–5; Knight, *Lending a Hand*, 25–26; occasional leaflets of the American Church Missionary Society (nos. 4 and 5, 1890); and Thirty-fourth Annual Report of the American Church Missionary Society, September 1, 1893, AEC, Cuba Scrapbook. Also see Leopoldo J. Alard, "Proceso histórico de la Iglesia Episcopal en Cuba," 32.

81. Knight, *Lending a Hand*, 25–26; Cuban Guild of Philadelphia, *Cuba, Old and New*, 6; occasional leaflets of the American Church Missionary society (no. 4, 1890) AEC, Cuba Scrapbook; report by Albion W. Knight to Charles E. Magoon, January 23, 1907, NA, RG 199, Records of the Provisional Government of Cuba, Confidential Correspondence, 1906–9; entry 5, box 3, file 56; "Sucesos notables de la Iglesia Episcopal en Cuba," *Heraldo Episcopal* (1971): 8–9.

82. Reports on the Home Mission Board in *Proceedings of the Southern Baptist Convention* (1887–98); transcribed copy of "Mrs. Díaz," *Our Home Field* 1, no. 4 (December 1888): 5, in SBHLA, URLRF, box 6, folder 30; Greer, "Baptists," 62; Meetings' minutes, AIBC; Jones, "Sketch," 352; Browne, *Key West*, 44; Ramos, *Panorama*, 119; Delgado, "History," 56; Harold Edmund Greer, Jr., "History of Southern Baptist Missionary Work in Cuba," 10–12, 49–50.

83. Tupper, *Díaz*, 8–9; Lawrence, *Cuba for Christ*, 154–55. For a description of the church, see *The Church Index* (July 25, 1889): 6, and a transcribed copy of *Our Home Field* 3, no. 9 (May 1891): 6, in SBHLA, URLRF, box 6, folder 30.

84. Meetings' minutes, AIBC; Pérez, *On Becoming Cuban*, 57; George Lester, *In Sunny Isles*, 95; Neblett, *Methodism's First Fifty Years*, 8–9; Greer, "History," 5–7; *Annual Report of Missions of the Methodist Episcopal Church, South* (1884), 20; (1890), 138; (1893), 132–34; Ramos, *Panorama*, 148.

85. Young, "Cuba" (July 1885): 384, 387–88; Pérez, *On Becoming Cuban*, 57; Casanovas, *Bread, or Bullets!*, 209; Greer, "Baptists," 63; Tupper, *Díaz*, 27; transcribed copy of "Imprisonment of Díaz," *Our Home Field* 2, no. 11 (July 1890): 4, in SBHLA, URLRF, box 6, folder 30. Also see transcribed copy of "About Our Work in Cuba," *Our Home Field* 3, no. 4 (December 1890): 6, in SBHLA, URLRF, box 6, folder 30, and transcribed copy of I. T. Tichenor, "A Second Visit to Cuba," *Our Home Field* 1, no. 4 (December 1888): 6, in SBHLA, URLRF, box 6, folder 30.

86. Young, "Cuba" (July 1885): 387; occasional leaflets of the American Church Missionary Society (no. 6), 1891, AEC, Cuba Scrapbook.

87. Transcribed copy of "Our Cuban Cemetery," *Our Home Field* 3, no. 6 (February 1891): 4, in SBHLA, URLRF, box 6, folder 30; Young, "Cuba" (October 1884): 487; correspondence on the Protestant cemetery of Matanzas (1887), AHPM, Gobierno Provincial, Cemeterios, bundle 12, file 9A; letter from the Philadelphia congregation of Matanzas, July 10, 1887, AEC, Cuba Scrapbook; Tamayo, "Historia," 99.

88. Blank burial record card, and meetings' minutes, AIBC; Southern Baptist Convention, Home Mission Board minutes, 1875–98, pp. 444–45, SBHLA; Tupper, *Díaz*, 12; Lasher, *Anales*, 38, 46; transcribed copy of "Cuba," *Our Home Field* 1, no. 1 (August 1888), SBHLA, URLRF, box 6, folder 30; Southern Baptist Convention, minutes (1888), in SBHLA, URLRF, box 6, folder 29; transcribed copy of "Visit to Cuba," *Our Home Field* 1, no. 5 (January 1889): 3–7, in SBHLA, URLRF, box 6, folder 30. On income, see Díaz's report of 1895–96, in Southern Baptist Convention, Home Mission Board minutes, 1875–98, pp. 375, SBHLA; report of the Home Mission Board, *Proceedings of the Southern Baptist Convention* (1891); transcribed copy of "Letter from Díaz," *Our Home Field* 3, no. 2 (August 1891): 7, in SBHLA, URLRF, box 6, folder 30. On Roig's burial, see Casanovas, *Bread, or Bullets!*, 199–200.

89. Lin Liang Yan to Cuba's governor-general, December 11, 1882, and bishop of Havana to the captain-general, August 27, 1883, ANC, Gobierno General, bundle 369, file 17651. Construction of Havana's Chinese cemetery began in May 1893; Oramas, *Cementerios*, 32.

90. Bishop of Havana to the captain-general, August 27, 1883, ANC, Gobierno General, bundle 369, file 17651; Manuel P. Maza Miquel, *El alma del negocio y el negocio del alma*, 71; certificate dated July 3, 1883, ANC, Gobierno General, bundle 457, file 21993.

91. Nuncio Angelo di Pietro to the bishop of Havana, 1887, in Maza Miquel, *Alma*, 73.

92. Ibid., 77–80; transcribed copy of "Cuba," *Our Home Field* 1, no. 1 (August 1888), in SBHLA, URLRF, box 6, folder 30

93. Mayor of Jovellanos to the governor of Matanzas, August 5, 1897, AHPM, Gobierno Provincial, Cementerios, bundle 13, file 18.

94. Bishop of Havana to the overseas minister, in communication of the bishop to Nuncio Angelo di Pietro, June 5, 1888, in Maza Miquel, *Alma*, 78.

95. Bishop of Havana to the captain-general, January 2, February 29, July 7, and September 26, 1888, ANC, Gobierno General, bundle 107, file 5016, 5011, 5003, and 5008; Greer, "Baptists," 63; transcribed copy of "Imprisonment of Díaz," *Our Home Field* 2, no. 11 (July 1890): 4, in SBHLA, URLRF, box 6, folder 30

96. Bishop Santander to the captain-general, September 26, 1888, ANC, Gobierno General, bundle 107, file 5008.

97. Parish priest of El Cerro to the civil governor of Havana, November 25, 1889, ANC, Gobierno Superior Civil, bundle 107, file 5016.

98. Juan Bautista Casas to the captain-general, January 13, 1890, ANC, Gobierno General, bundle 107, file 5016; F. Deschamps to the inspector of cemeteries, February 16, 1888, and bishop to the captain-general, May 2, 1889, ANC, Gobierno General, bundle 107, file 5008.

99. Bishop of Havana to the captain-general, February 29, 1888, ANC, Gobierno General, bundle 107, file 5011.

100. Bishop of Havana to the Madrid nuncio, December 23, 1887, and June 5, 1888, in Maza Miquel, *Alma*, 70–71, 77. According to a 1896 report by Díaz, adult burials cost 5.50 pesos, and children's burials cost 2 pesos; Southern Baptist Convention, Home Mission Board minutes, 1875–98, in SBHLA.

101. Thirty-seventh annual report of the American Church Missionary Society and "The Beginning of the Cuban Mission. A Letter from the Rev. Pedro Duarte," American Church Missionary Society (1900), both in AEC, Cuba Scrapbook; de la Paz Cerezo, "Síntesis cronológica," copy in ACEST; Pérez, *On Becoming Cuban*, 60; Ramos, *Panorama*, 115, 147, 122; transcribed copy of "Cuban Work in Florida," *Our Home Field* 8, no. 10 (May 1898): 1, in SBHLA, URLRF, box 6, folder 30; Tupper, *Díaz*, 24, 27, 35, 37; Southern Baptist Convention, Home Mission Board minutes, 1875–98, pp. 375, 400, 443; I. T. Tichenor, "Díaz in Jail," *Mission Journal* 47, no. 1 (May 1896): 19–21, in SBHLA, URLRF, box 6, folder 30; *El Expedicionario* [Tampa] 2, no. 17 (March 21, 1897), in LC, Arnao Collection; Francisco González del Valle, *El clero cubano*, 171–72; Lester, *In Sunny Isles*, 95; Greer, "Baptists," 64–65; Greer, "History," 7; Delgado, "History," 57.

102. Ramos, *Panorama*, 98; Lester, *In Sunny Isles*; Deulofeu, *Historical*, 30–31; Walter R. Lambuth to Charles Fulwood, January 23, 1898, Archives of the United Methodist Church (hereafter cited as AUMC), Methodist Episcopal Church, South, Missionary Board Correspondence, 1896–99, microfilm reel 183; Knight, *Lending a Hand*, 26–27.

103. Thirty-seventh annual report of the American Missionary Society (1896), AEC, Cuba Scrapbook.

104. Greer, "History," 2–3; Southern Baptist Convention, Home Mission Board minutes, 1875–98, pp. 347, 449–50, in SBCLA; transcribed copy of I. T. Tichenor,

"Our Work in Cuba," *Mission Journal* 46, no. 6 (March 1896): 23–24, in SBHLA, URLRF, box 6, folder 30; "The Mission in Cuba," American Church Missionary Society [1901?], AEC, Cuba Scrapbook. Also see Cuban Guild of Philadelphia, *Cuba, Old and New*, 6.

105. Pérez, "North American Protestant Missionaries," 62. In 1904, the new rector of Fieles a Jesús, Emilio Planas, proposed the creation of a mutualistic society tied to his church. Plans included medical and burial benefits for church members. See documentation in AHPM, Fondo Asociaciones, bundle 101, file 1840B.

Epilogue

1. Robert McLean and Grace Petrie Williams, *Old Spain in New America*, 91.
2. Roberto H. Todd, "La Iglesia Episcopal de Ponce," 98. For an example of attitudes among U.S. missionary leaders, see Walter Lambuth to Someillán, April 13, 1898, AUMC, Methodist Episcopal Church, South, Missionary Board Correspondence, microfilm reel 180. Also see Charles L. Colmer, "The Beginnings of the Church in Puerto Rico," 403; Víctor Burset, "The First Fifty Years of Protestant Episcopal Church in Puerto Rico," 28; and Julian H. Steward, ed., *The People of Puerto Rico*, 60, 275–76.
3. Transcribed copy of *Our Home Field* 8, no. 1 (June 1898): 1, in SBHLA, URLRF, box 6, folder 29; American Church Missionary Society, "The Mission in Cuba: Advent 1900," in AEC, Cuba Scrapbook; Albion W. Knight, *Lending a Hand in Cuba*, 32; Marcos Antonio Ramos, *Panorama de protestantismo en Cuba*, 207–18; transcribed copy of "Bro. O'Halloran at Santiago," *Our Home Field* 9, no. 4 (November 1898): 2, in SBHLA, URLRF, box 6, folder 30; J. M. López-Guillén, "Cuba in New York," *Home Missionary* 72, no. 2 (October 1899): 90; telegram of Charles Fulwood to Bishop Chandler, July 31, 1898, AUMC, Methodist Episcopal Church, South, Missionary Board Correspondence, microfilm reel 182.
4. Louis A. Pérez, Jr., "Protestant Missionaries in Cuba," in *Essays on Cuban History,* 220; Jason M. Yaremko, *U.S. Protestant Missions in Cuba*, xi–xii.
5. Edward J. Berbusse, *The United States in Puerto Rico*, 85–86; Samuel Silva Gotay, "La Iglesia Católica en el proceso político de la americanización en Puerto Rico" 113–14; Peter Steven Gannon, "The Ideology of Americanization in Puerto Rico in 1898–1900," 181.
6. Copy of letter of C. D. Daniel to *Landmark Baptist* (1903); copies of Gertrude Joerg to I. T. Tichenor, September 20 and October 18, 1898, and Díaz to Tichenor, March 3, 1902, all in SBHLA, URLRF, box 6, folders 29 and 31. Also see Yaremko, *U.S. Protestant*, 44.
7. James H. Wilson, *Annual Report of Brigadier General Commanding Department of Matanzas and Santa Clara (August 1, 1899)*, 88–90; Gannon, "Ideology," 111; Berbusse, *United States*, 91–96, 107, 140; Martín Socarrás Matos, *Necrópolis Cristóbal Colón*, 49–50; "Rules and Regulations Respecting Burials, Disinterments, and Transportation of Human Bodies," NA, RG 350, Bureau of Insular Affairs, General Classified Files, entry 5, box 207, file 1604; also see box 124, file 834.

8. Silva Gotay, "Iglesia Católica," 108.
9. Ramos, *Panorama*, 166–67; J. V. Cova's letter, *Christian Index* (August 31, 1899): 5; C. D. Daniel, quoted in *Christian Index* (January 31, 1901).
10. Ramos, *Panorama*, 207–8; Delgado, "History," 57; H. R. Moseley to the Cuban secretary of justice, January 2, 1901, and Mary A. Taylor to Leonard Wood, July 19, 1901, NA, RG 140, Military Government of Cuba, Letters Received, entry 3, box 112, file 5170 and box 144.
11. "Plans for Cuba and Puerto Rico," *Missionary Review of the World* 12 (January 1899): 53; Henry L. Morehouse, *Ten Years in Eastern Cuba*, 5.
12. Fortieth annual report of the American Church Missionary Society (1899), in AEC, Cuba Scrapbook; American Church Missionary Society, *Cuba: The Protege of the United States and the New Charge with Which God Has Given Us* (1905), pamphlet in AEC, Cuba Scrapbook; Knight, *Lending a Hand*, 31; Ramos, *Panorama*, 219.
13. Knight, *Lending a Hand*, 21, 32.
14. Manuel Deulofeu, *Historical and Biographical Notes on the Cuban Mission*, 35; Ramos, *Panorama*, 212.
15. E. P. Herrick, "Our Cuban Work in Florida," *Home Missionary* 72, no. 2 (October 1899): 86; Ramos, *Panorama*, 220.
16. Ramos, *Panorama*, 215; Lambuth to Fulwood, June 7, 1899, AUMC, Methodist Episcopal Church, South, Missionary Board Correspondence, microfilm reel 184. For a list of Cuban missions in place by 1900, see "Christian Missions in Our New Possessions," *Missionary Review of the World* 13 (1900): 205–8.
17. Juan Jorge Rivera Torres, *Documentos históricos de la Iglesia Episcopal Puertorriqueña*, 19, 22–25; Burset, "First Fifty Years," 27–28.
18. *St. John the Baptist Church, San Juan, P.R. Anniversary Booklet 1899–1929*, 3–4, 9; Knight, *Lending a Hand*, 32.
19. Henry K. Carroll, "Puerto Rico as a Mission Field" *Missionary Review of the World* 13 (August 1900): 591; Silva Gotay, *Protestantismo*, 116–17. For a list of Puerto Rican missions in place by 1900, see "Christian Missions in Our New Possessions," 205–8.
20. Silva Gotay, *Protestantismo*, 9, 112–13; Jerry Fenton, *Understanding the Religious Background of the Puerto Rican*, 7; Nélida Agosto Cintrón, *Religión y cambio social en Puerto Rico*, 60–61; Enrique Rodríguez Bravo, "Origen y desarrollo del movimiento Protestante en Puerto Rico," 33; Donald T. Moore, *Puerto Rico para Cristo*, 2.
21. Daniel R. Rodríguez, *La primera evangelización norteamericana en Puerto Rico*, 188–91.
22. P. W. Drury, "The Protestant Church in Porto Rico," 135.
23. Louis A. Pérez, Jr., "North American Protestant Missionaries in Cuba," in *Essays on Cuban History*, 63–64; Louis A. Pérez, Jr., *On Becoming Cuban*, 244–46.
24. D. W. Carter, "Cuba and its Evangelization," *Missionary Review of the World* 15 (April 1902): 259; McLean and Williams, *Old Spain*, 151–54, 159; Pérez, "North American Protestant Missionaries," 63–65; Silva Gotay, *Protestantismo*, 184; Gannon, "Ideology," 278; A. G. Quintero Rivera, *Conflictos de clase y política en Puerto Rico*, 48.

25. Pérez, "Protestant Missionaries," 220.

26. "Cuba," pamphlet dated 1899, by the American Church Missionary Society, copy in AEC, Cuba Scrapbook; Louis A. Pérez, Jr., *Lords of the Mountain*, 60.

27. Knight, *Lending a Hand*, 30; Pérez, *On Becoming*, 246–47; "The Sunday-schools in Santiago and Suburbs, Cuba," *Home Missionary Monthly* 23, no. 15 (October 1901): 281; Agosto Cintrón, *Religión*, 68, 98.

28. De la Cova's letter, *Christian Index* (August 31, 1899): 5; Albion W. Knight, "The Episcopal Church Mission in Cuba," *Missionary Review of the World* 37, no. 3 (March 1914): 199; Manuel P. Maza Miquel, *Entre la ideología y la compasión*, 426–27.

29. Knight, *Lending a Hand*, 33–34; Greer, "Baptists," 65; copy of "Report by the Corresponding Secretary of His Recent Trip to Cuba"; transcribed copy of C. D. Daniel to the *Landmark Baptist* (1903); and copy of Díaz to Tichenor, July 26 and September 28, 1901, all in SBHLA, URLRF, box 6, folders 31 and 29. The most rancorous of the clashes between Cuban pastors and North American missionaries may have been the one that led to Díaz's separation from the Home Mission Board of the Southern Baptist Convention. In 1901, he wrote to I. T. Tichenor, an old supporter: "I see now by many letters received great many people wants to help me on my church affairs, etc., but when I have persecutions, jails, mobs, and yellow fever, I was alone here and nobody dispute this place, now as everything is flowers, I have no admires but competitors."

30. *St. John the Baptist Church*, 20–23, 49, 53; Carroll, "Puerto Rico as a Mission Field," 591.

BIBLIOGRAPHY

Archives

Archives of the Diocese of New York of the Protestant Episcopal Church, New York
City (ADNYPEC)
Archives of the Episcopal Church, Austin Texas (AEC)
 Cuba Records, RG-65
 Puerto Rico Records, RG-77
 Records of the American Church Missionary Society, Cuba Scrapbook
Archives of the United Methodist Church, Madison, N.J. (AUMC)
 Methodist Episcopal Church, South, Missionary Board Correspondence,
1896–99 (microfilm reels 175–85)
Archivo de la Catedral Episcopal Santísima Trinidad, Havana (ACEST)
Archivo de la Iglesia Bautista El Calvario, Havana (AIBC)
Archivo del Arzobispado de La Habana (AALH)
 Asuntos Espirituales
 Cementerio Colón
 Cementerios Rurales
 Exhumaciones
 Expedientes Ultramarinos
 Matrimonios Ultramarinos
Archivo del Servicio Histórico Militar, Madrid (ASHM)
 Ultramar
Archivo General de Puerto Rico, San Juan (AGPR)
 Audiencia Territorial
 Colección Junghams
 Gobernadores Españoles
 Obras Públicas
 Real Audiencia
 Varios
Archivo Histórico de Vieques (AHV)

Archivo Histórico Diocesano de la Archidiócesis de San Juan (AHDASJ)
    Disciplina
    Gobierno
    Justicia
Archivo Histórico Municipal de Ponce (AHMP)
Archivo Histórico Nacional, Madrid (AHN)
    Estado
    Ultramar
Archivo Histórico Provincial de Matanzas (AHPM)
    Miscelánea de Expedientes
    Fondo Asociaciones
    Fondo Gobierno Provincial
Archivo Nacional de Cuba, Havana (ANC)
    Asuntos Políticos
    Gobierno General
    Gobierno Superior Civil
Archivo Parroquial de la Iglesia Salvador del Mundo, El Cerro, Havana (APISM)
    Libros de bautismos, matrimonios y defunciones
Archivo Parroquial de la Iglesia de Todos los Santos, Vieques (APITS)
Archivo Parroquial de la Iglesia Nuestra Señora del Pilar, El Cerro, Havana (APNSP)
    Libros de bautismos, matrimonios y defunciones
Archivo Parroquial de la Iglesia Santísima Trinidad, Ponce (APIST)
    Books 1, 4, 6
    Records of Ecclesiastical Duties
Biblioteca Nacional José Martí, Havana (BNJM)
    Colección Manuscritos Morales
    Colección Manuscritos Pérez
Centro de Investigaciones Históricas de la Universidad de Puerto Rico, Río Piedras
    (CIH)
    Papeles de Vieques
    Libros parroquiales de Ponce (microfilm)
    Libros parroquiales de Vieques (microfilm)
Duke University, Perkins Library, Special Collections Department, Durham, N.C.
    John Backhouse Papers
    Papers of Spain, Ministry of Foreign Affairs, Savannah Consulate
Florence Williams Public Library, Christiansted, St. Croix
    All Saints Church of St. Thomas, baptismal, marriage, and burial registers
    (microfilm)
    Dutch Reformed Church of Christiansted, St. Croix, books of marriages and
    register of members (microfilm)
Library of Congress, Washington, D.C. (LC)
    Arnao Collection
    Del Monte Collection
    Puerto Rican Memorials Collection
    Rare Book Room, Broadside Collection
    Records of the Cuban Consulate, Key West, Florida (microfilm)

Maryland Diocesan Archives [Episcopal Church], Baltimore (MDA)
    Cuba, church correspondence
    Cuba, church history
    Cuba folders
Museo del Cerro, Havana
National Archives, Washington, D.C., and College Park, Maryland (NA)
    Bureau of Insular Affairs, Record Group 350
    General Records of the Department of State, Record Group 59
    Records of Foreign Service Posts, Record Group 84
    Records of the Military Government of Cuba, Record Group 140
    Records of the Provisional Government of Cuba, Record Group 199
New-York Historical Society (NYHS)
    Diary of Elizabeth West Nevins
    Diary of J. B. Dunlop
    Journal Letters of Ledyard Lincklean and Mrs. Lincklean
Public Record Office, Kew, U.K. (PRO)
    Foreign Office
Southern Baptist Historical Library and Archives, Nashville, Tennessee (SBHLA)
    Una Roberts Lawrence Resource Files (URLRF)
    Southern Baptist Convention, Home Mission Board minutes, 1875–98
St. Johns's Anglican Church, Christiansted, St. Croix
    Parish books
St. Paul's Anglican Church, Frederiksted, St. Croix
    Parish books
Virginia Historical Society, Richmond
    Diary of Reverend William Norwood

Newspapers and Periodicals

La Aurora de Yumurí
El Avisador
El Boletín Eclesiástico del Obispado de La Habana
El Boletín Eclesiástico de Puerto Rico
The Christian Index
The Churchman
The Cuba Guild
El Eco del Pueblo
El Espectador
El Expedicionario
La Gaceta de La Habana
La Gaceta de Puerto Rico
The Home Missionary
The Home Missionary Monthly
La Juventud Católica
Missionary Review of the World
Our Home Field

La Propaganda Política
El Republicano
Revista Católica
La Revolución
The Seminary Magazine [by students at the Southern Baptist Theological Seminary]
El Siglo
Spirit of Missions
El Triunfo
La Verdad
La Verdad Católica
La Voz de Cuba

Contemporary Sources

Abbot, Abiel. *Letters Written in the Interior of Cuba*. Boston: Bowles and Dearborn, 1829.

[Aguilera, Francisco Vicente]. *Notes about Cuba*. New York, 1872.

Allen, Lewis Leonidas. *The Island of Cuba; or, Queen of the Antilles*. Cleveland: Harris, Fairbanks, 1852.

American Church Missionary Society. *Cuba: The Protege of the United States and the New Charge with Which God Has Given Us*. 1905.

Annual Reports of the Board of Missions of the Methodist Episcopal Church, South (1874–98).

Armas y Sáenz, Ramón de. *Ley de disenso paterno aplicada a las islas de Cuba y Puerto-Rico por real decreto de 3 de febrero de 1882*. Madrid: Hernández, 1882.

Auchinloss, H. B. "La fabricación del azúcar en Cuba" [1865]. In *La isla de Cuba en el siglo xix vista por los extranjeros*, edited by Juan Pérez de la Riva, 193–228. Havana: Editorial de Ciencias Sociales, 1981.

Bagg, Matthew D. *Journal of Two Months Residence in St. Thomas, Santa Cruz & Porto Rico and the Voyage Thither and Thence [1851–1852]*. New York, n.d.

Ballou, Maturin M. *Due South: Or Cuba Past and Present*. Cambridge, Mass., 1891. Reprint, New York: Negro Universities Press, 1969.

Balmes, Jaime Luciano. *European Civilization: Protestantism and Catholicity, Compared in their Effects on the Civilization of Europe*. Baltimore: Murphy, 1850.

Barras y Prado, Antonio de las. *Memorias, La Habana a mediados del siglo xix*. Madrid: Ciudad Lineal, 1925.

Betancourt Cisneros, Gaspar. *Thoughts upon the Incorporation of Cuba into the American Confederation in Contra-position to those Published by Don José Saco*. New York: La Verdad, 1849.

Betancourt Cisneros, Gaspar, and John S. Thrasher. *Addresses Delivered at the Celebration of the Third Anniversary in Honor of the Martyrs of Cuban Freedom*. New Orleans: Sherman, Wharton, 1854.

Bona, Félix de. *Cuba, Santo Domingo y Puerto Rico*. Madrid: Imprenta M. Galiano, 1861.

Brau, Salvador. *Ecos de la batalla: artículos periodísticos*. San Juan: Imprenta y Librería de José González Font, 1886.

———. *Ensayos: (disquisiciones sociológicas)*. Río Piedras, P.R.: Editorial Edil, 1972.

Bremer, Fredrika. *The Homes of the New World*. 2 vols. New York: Harper and Brothers, 1854.

Browne, Jefferson B. *Key West: The Old and the New*. St. Augustine, Fla., 1912.

Bryant, William Cullen. *Letters of William Cullen Bryant*. Edited by William Cullen Bryant II and Thomas G. Voss. 4 vols. New York: Fordham University Press, 1975–84.

Caldecott, Alfred. *The Church in the West Indies*. 1898. Reprint, London: Cass, 1970.

Carbonell y Padilla, Isidro. "Sobre los matrimonios que van a celebrarse en los Estados-Unidos." *Revista de Jurisprudencia* 3, no. 1 (1858): 432–42.

Carroll, Henry K. "Puerto Rico as a Mission Field." *Missionary Review of the World* 13 (August 1900): 583–91.

———. *Report on the Island of Porto Rico* [1899]. New York: Arno, 1975.

Carter, D. W. "Cuba and Its Evangelization." *Missionary Review of the World* 15 (April 1902): 253–61.

Cattell, Alexander Gilmore. *To Cuba and Back in Twenty-Two Days*. Philadelphia: Times Printing House, 1874.

Censo de población de 31 de diciembre de 1887 a 1ro. de enero de 1888, provincia de Matanzas. Matanzas: Galería Literaria Ricla, 1888.

"Christian Missions in Our New Possessions." *Missionary Review of the World* 13 (1900): 205–8.

Church Work in Cuba Under the Auspices of the Ladies' Cuban Guild of Philadelphia, PA. Philadelphia: Fell, 1890.

Coggeshall, George. *Voyages to Various Parts of the World Made between the Years 1800 and 1831*. New York: Appleton, 1853.

Córdova, Pedro Tomás de. *Memorias geográficas, históricas, económicas y estadísticas de la Isla de Puerto Rico*. 6 vols. 1832. Reprint, San Juan: Instituto de Cultura Puertorriqueña, 1968.

Cova, J. V. "Letter." *Christian Index* (August 31, 1899): 5.

Cowley, Ángel José. *Ensayo estadístico-médico de la mortalidad de la Diócesis de la Habana durante el año 1843*. Havana: Imprenta del Gobierno y de la Capitanía General, 1845.

Cuba, Statistics Commission. *Cuadro estadístico de la siempre fiel isla de Cuba [1846]*. Havana: Imprenta del Gobierno y la Capitanía General, 1847.

Cuba, National Commission of Statistics, Institute of Statistical Research, *Los censos de población y viviendas de Cuba*. Havana: Comité Estatal de Estadísticas, 1988.

The Cuba Commission Report: A Hidden History of the Chinese in Cuba. Introduction by Denise Helly. Baltimore: Johns Hopkins University Press, 1993.

Cuba Church Missionary Guild. *The Mission of the Protestant Episcopal Church in the Island of Cuba*. New York, 1879.

Cuban Guild of Philadelphia. *Cuba, Old and New: A Lesson in Geography for Mission Study Classes*. 1916.

Dana, Richard Henry, Jr. *To Cuba and Back: A Vacation Voyage*. Boston: Ticknor and Fields, 1859. Reprint, edited by C. Harvey Gardiner, Carbondale: Southern Illinois University Press, 1966.

Davis, J. C. [O.D.D.O., pseud.]. *The History of the Late Expedition to Cuba*. New Orleans: Daily Delta Press, 1850.

[Davis, Oliver Wilson]. *Sketch of Frederic Fernández Cavada*. Philadelphia: Chandler, 1871.

Deulofeu, Manuel. *Héroes del destierro: la emigración*. Cienfuegos, Cuba: Imprenta de M. Mestre, 1904.

———. *Historical and Biographical Notes on the Cuban Mission*. Translated by E. Askew. Tampa: Morning Tribune Electric Print, n.d.

D'Hespel D'Harponville, Gustave. *La reine des Antilles*. Paris: Gide et Baudry, 1850.

Dimock, Joseph J. *Impressions of Cuba in the Nineteenth Century: The Travel Diary of Joseph J. Dimock*. Edited by Louis A. Pérez, Jr. Wilmington, Del.: Scholarly Resources, 1998.

A Directory of the Charitable, Social Improvement, Educational and Religious Associations and Churches of Philadelphia. 2d ed. Philadelphia: Civic Club, 1903.

Un emigrado cubano. *Información sobre reformas en Cuba y Puerto Rico*. 2d ed. New York: Hallet and Green, 1877.

Erenchún, Félix. *Anales de la Isla de Cuba (1855)*. Havana: Imprenta del Tiempo–Imprenta La Antilla, 1856–59.

Figuerola-Caneda, Domingo, ed. *Centón epistolario de Domingo del Monte*. 7 vols. Havana: Imprenta El Siglo XX, 1923–57.

Flinter, Jorge D. *Examen del estado actual de los esclavos de la isla de Puerto Rico*. New York: Imprenta Española del Redacto. 1832. Reprint, San Juan: Instituto de Cultura Puertorriqueña, 1976.

Gallenga, Antonio Carlo Napoleone. *The Pearl of the Antilles*. London: Chapman and Hall, 1873. Reprint, New York: Negro Universities Press, 1970.

García de Arboleya, José. *Manual de la Isla de Cuba*. 2d ed. Havana: Imprenta del Tiempo, 1859.

García de Palacios, Juan. *Sínodo de Santiago de 1681*. Madrid: Instituto Francisco Suárez, 1982.

Gibbes, Robert W. *Cuba for Invalids*. New York: Townsend, 1860.

Gómez de Avellaneda y Arteaga, Gertrudis. *Sab and Autobiography* [1841]. Edited and translated by Nina M. Scott. Austin: University of Texas Press, 1993.

González Ponce de Llorante, Antonio. *¿Qué es la anexión?* 2d ed. Havana: Antonio María Dávila, 1852.

Great Britain, Parliament, House of Commons. *British Parliamentary Papers [Slave Trade]*. 95 vols. Shannon: Irish University Press, 1968–71.

Gurney, John Joseph. *A Winter in the West Indies*. London: Murray, 1840.

Un habanero. *Probable y definitivo porvenir de la Isla de Cuba*. 1870.

Hale, John P. *The Acquisition of Cuba. Speech of Hon. John P. Hale, of New Hampshire*. Washington, D.C.: Buell and Blanchard, 1859.

Hazard, Samuel. *Cuba with Pen and Pencil*. Hartford, Conn.: Hartford Publishing, 1871.

Hernández, Francisco Javier. *Colección de bulas, breves, y otros documentos relativos a la iglesia de América y Filipinas*. 2 vols. Brussels: Alfredo Vromant, 1879. Reprint, Vaduz, Liechtenstein: Kraus, 1964.

Hernández Poggio, Ramón. *Aclimatación é higiene de los europeos en Cuba.* Cádiz, Spain: Imprenta de la Revista Médica, 1874.

Howe, Julia Ward. *A Trip to Cuba.* Boston: Ticknor and Fields, 1860. Reprint, New York: Praeger, 1969.

[Hurlbert, William Henry]. *Gan-Eden: Or, Pictures of Cuba.* Boston: Jewett, 1854.

Jameson, Robert Francis. *Letters from the Havana, during the Year 1820.* London: Miller, 1821.

Jones, Alexander. *Cuba in 1851.* New York: Stringer and Townsend, 1851.

Journal of the Convention of the Protestant Episcopal Church in the Diocese of New York. 1869–83.

Journal of Proceedings of the Annual Council of the Protestant Episcopal Church in the Diocese of Florida. 1876–85.

Junta Cubana. *Facts about Cuba Published under the Authority of the N.Y. Cuban Junta.* New York: Sun Job, 1870.

[Kenney, Edward]. *Report of Our Mission in Cuba: October, 1874–October, 1877.* Detroit: Episcopalian Diocese of Detroit, 1878.

[Kimbal, Richard Burleigh]. *Cuba, and the Cubans: Comprising a History of the Island of Cuba, Its Present Social, Political, and Domestic Conditions.* New York: Hueston and Putnam, 1850.

Knight, Albion W. "The Episcopal Church Mission in Cuba." *Missionary Review of the World* 37, no. 3 (March 1914): 193–99.

———. *Lending a Hand in Cuba.* Hartford, Conn.: Church Missions Publishing Company, 1916.

Labra y Cadrana, Rafael María de. *La brutalidad de los negros.* 1875. Reprint, Havana: Universidad de La Habana, 1961.

Lasher, George William. *Anales del evangelio en Cuba. La historia de Díaz.* Translated and expanded by Albertina Díaz Lozano. Havana, 1915–20.

Lee, Albert E. *An Island Grows: Memoirs of Albert E. Lee, Puerto Rico, 1872–1942.* San Juan: Lee, 1963.

Lester, George. *In Sunny Isles.* London: Kelly, 1897.

Le-Roy y Cassá, Jorge. *Estudios sobre la mortalidad de La Habana durante el siglo xix y comienzos del actual.* Havana: Lloredo, 1913.

Levis, Richard J. *Diary of a Spring Holiday in Cuba.* Philadelphia: Porter and Coates, 1872.

Libro de Oración Común y Administración de los Santos Sacramentos y otros Ritos y Ceremonias de la Iglesia. New York, 1865.

López de Haro, Damián. *Constituciones sinodales.* 1646. Reprint, San Juan, 1818.

López de Letona, Antonio. *Isla de Cuba: reflexiones sobre su estado social, político y económico.* Madrid: Ducazal, 1865.

[Madan, Cristóbal F.]. *Contestación a un folleto titulado: Ideas sobre la incorporación de Cuba en los Estados Unidos por don José Antonio Saco.* New York: La Verdad, 1849.

———. [Un hacendado, pseud.]. *Llamamiento de la isla de Cuba a la Nación Española.* New York: Hallet, 1854.

Madden, Richard Robert. *The Island of Cuba: Its Resources, Progress, and Prospects.* London: Partridge and Oakey, 1853.

Maloney, Walter C. *A Sketch of the History of Key West, Florida*. Newark, N.J., 1876.

Marín, Ramón. *Las fiestas populares de Ponce*. Edited and introduction by Socorro Girón. Río Piedras: Editorial de la Universidad de Puerto Rico, 1994.

Martí, José. *Martí y la Iglesia Católica*. Havana: Editorial Páginas, n.d.

Martín de Herrera, José. *Auto del Excmo. é Illmo. Señor arzobispo metropolitano facultando a los párrocos para tramitar expedientes matrimoniales*. Santiago de Cuba: Tipografía Ángela y María, 1887.

[Martínez, Jacinto María]. *Los voluntarios de Cuba y el Obispo de La Habana*. Madrid: Imprenta D. A. Pérez Dubrull, 1871.

McAfee, J. Ernest. "To-day in Porto Rico." *Missionary Review of the World* 38, no. 8 (August 1915): 577–85.

McLean, Robert, and Grace Petrie Williams. *Old Spain in New America*. New York: Association Press, 1916.

Mestre, José Manuel. *Sobre el matrimonio civil*. Havana: Soler Álvarez, 1884.

Moore, Rachel Wilson. *Journal of Rachel Wilson Moore, Kept During a Tour to the West Indies and South America in 1863–64*. Philadelphia: Ellwood, 1867.

Morehouse, Henry L. *Ten Years in Eastern Cuba: An Account of Baptist Missions Therein Under the Auspices of the American Baptist Home Mission Society*. New York: American Baptist Home Mission Society, [1910].

Murray, Amelia Matilda. *Letters from the United States, Cuba and Canada*. 2 vols. London: Parker, 1856.

[Neely, F. Tennyson]. *Greater America: Heroes, Battles, Camps, Dewey Islands, Cuba, Porto Rico*. New York: F. Tennyson Neely, 1898.

Norman, Benjamin Moore. *Rambles by Land and Water, or Notes of Travel in Cuba and Mexico*. New York: Paine and Burgess, 1845.

Pacheco, Juan. *Circular al venerable clero del Arzobispado de Santiago de Cuba*. Havana: Imprenta de la Real Sociedad Económica, 1839.

Pérez Moris, José. *Historia de la insurrección de Lares* [1872]. Río Piedras, P.R.: Editorial Edil, 1975.

Perry, John J. *The Filibuster Policy of the Sham Democracy*. Washington, D.C.: National Republican Committee, 1860.

Philalethes, Demoticus. *Yankee Travels through the Island of Cuba; or the Men and Government, the Laws and Customs of Cuba, as Seen by American Eyes*. New York: Appleton, 1856.

Phillippo, James Mursell. *The United States and Cuba*. London: Pewtress, 1857.

Piñeyro y Barry, Enrique José Nemesio. *Morales Lemus y la revolución de Cuba*. New York: Zazamendi, 1871. Reprint, New York: Unión de Cubanos en el Exilio, 1970.

Proceedings of the Southern Baptist Convention. 1887–98.

Ramos, Francisco. *Apéndice al prontuario de disposiciones oficiales*. San Juan: Imprenta González, 1867.

———. *Prontuario de disposiciones oficiales. Disposiciones más notables del Gobierno Superior desde 1824 a 1865*. San Juan: Imprenta González, 1866.

Rawson, James. *Cuba*. New York: Lane and Tippet, 1847.

Ripley, Eliza McHatton. *From Flag to Flag: A Woman's Adventures and Experiences in the South during the War, in Mexico, and in Cuba*. New York: Appleton, 1889.

Rodríguez, José Ignacio. "Sobre los matrimonios que van a celebrarse en los Estados-Unidos [I and II]." *Revista de Jurisprudencia* 3, vol. 1 (1858): 267–74, 358–62.

Rodríguez García, José A. *De los requisitos previos para contraer matrimonios.* Havana: Tipografía La Lucha, 1892.

Rogers, Carlton H. *Incidents of Travel in the Southern United States and Cuba.* New York: Craighead, 1862.

Rosaín, Domingo. *Necrópolis de La Habana: historia de los cementerios de esta ciudad.* Havana: El Trabajo, 1875.

Ruiz Belvis, Segundo, José Julián Acosta, and Francisco Mariano Quiñones. *Proyecto para la abolición de la esclavitud* [1867]. Río Piedras, P.R.: Editorial Edil, 1978.

Saco, José Antonio. *Contra la anexión.* Edited by Fernando Ortiz Fernández. Havana: Instituto Cubano del Libro, 1974.

Secretaría del Gobierno Superior Civil de la Isla de Puerto Rico. *Registro central de esclavos (6to. Depto.).* San Juan: González Impresor del Gobierno, 1872.

Sedano y Agramonte, José. *Ley Provisional del Matrimonio Civil y su reglamento.* Havana: Soler Álvarez, 1887.

St. John the Baptist Church, San Juan, P.R. Anniversary Booklet 1899–1929, With Historical Notes Regarding St. Luke's Church, Puerta de Tierra, P.R. and Other Matter Concerning the History of the Church's Work in San Juan, Porto Rico. n.d.

Steele, James William. *Cuban Sketches.* New York: Putnam, 1881.

Tacón, Miguel. *Correspondencia reservada del Capitán General don Miguel Tacón con el gobierno de Madrid, 1834–1836.* Edited by Juan Pérez de la Riva. Havana: Biblioteca Nacional José Martí, 1963.

Tanco Armero, Nicolás. "La Isla de Cuba." In *La Isla de Cuba en el siglo xix vista por los extranjeros,* edited by Juan Pérez de la Riva, 107–39. Havana: Editorial de Ciencias Sociales, 1981.

Taylor, John G. *The United States and Cuba: Eight Years of Change and Travel.* London: Bentley, 1851.

Thirty-Second Annual Meeting of the Florida Conference of the Methodist Episcopal Church, South. 1876.

Torrente, Mariano. *Bosquejo económico político de la isla de Cuba.* 2 vols. Madrid: Pita-Barcina, 1852–53.

———. "Memoria del 28 de septiembre de 1852." In *Cuba desde 1850 a 1873.* Compiled by Spain, Overseas Ministry, 168–74.

———. *Política ultramarina que abraza todos los puntos referentes a las relaciones de España con los Estados Unidos, con Inglaterra y las Antillas, y señaladamente con la isla de Santo Domingo.* Madrid: Compañía General de Impresos y Libros del Reino, 1854.

Trollope, Anthony. *The West Indies and the Spanish Main.* New York: Harper, 1860. Reprint, London: Cass, 1968.

Tupper, Kerr Boyce. *Díaz, El Apóstol de Cuba.* 1896.

Turnbull, David. *Travels in the West: Cuba with Notices of Porto Rico and the Slave Trade.* London, 1840. Reprint, New York: Negro Universities Press, 1969.

Ubeda y Delgado, Manuel. *Isla de Puerto Rico: estudio histórico, geográfico y estadístico de la misma.* San Juan: Establecimiento Tipográfico del Boletín Mercantil, 1878.

U.S. Department of State. *Papers Relating to Foreign Affairs*. Washington, D.C.: Government Printing Office, 1875–76.

——, San Juan Consulate. *Despachos de los cónsules norteamericanos en Puerto Rico*. Edited by the Centro de Investigaciones Históricas de la Universidad de Puerto Rico. Río Piedras: Editorial de la Universidad de Puerto Rico, 1982.

U.S. Senate. Senator George E. Pugh of Ohio speaking on the acquisition of Cuba. 35th Cong., 2d sess. *Congressional Globe* 28, no. 1 (February 10, 1859): 934–40.

——. Senator Stephen R. Mallory of Florida speaking on the acquisition of Cuba. 35th Cong., 2d sess. *Congressional Globe* 28, no, 2 (February 25, 1859): 1327–39.

——. Senator Zachariah Chandler of Michigan speaking on the acquisition of Cuba. 35th Cong., 2d sess. *Congressional Globe* 28, no. 2 (February 17, 1859): 1079–86.

Valiente, Porfirio. [Un cubano, pseud.]. *La anexión de Cuba y los peninsulares en ella*. 2d ed. New York: Imprenta de J. Mesa, 1853.

Walker, Charles. "Charles Walker's Letters from Puerto Rico, 1835–1837." Introduction by Kenneth Scott. *Caribbean Studies* 5, no. 1 (April 1965): 37–50.

Whipple, Henry B. *Lights and Shadows of a Long Episcopate*. London: Macmillan, 1899.

Williams, George W. *Sketches of Travel in the Old and New World*. Charleston, S.C.: Walker, Evans, and Cogswell, 1871.

Wilson, James Grant, ed. *The Centennial History of the Protestant Episcopal Church in the Diocese of New York, 1785–1885*. New York: Appleton, 1886.

Wilson, James H. *Annual Report of Brigadier General Commanding Department of Matanzas and Santa Clara (August 1, 1899)*.

Woodruff, Julia Louisa Matilda. [J.L.M. Jay, pseud.]. *My Winter in Cuba*. New York: Dutton, 1871.

[Wurdemann, John George F.]. *Notes on Cuba*. Boston: Munroe, 1844. Reprint, New York: Arno, 1971.

Secondary Sources

Agosto Cintrón, Nélida. *Religión y cambio social en Puerto Rico (1898–1940)*. Río Piedras, P.R.: Ediciones Huracán, 1996.

Agramonte, Roberto D. *Martí y su concepción del mundo*. Río Piedras, P.R.: Editorial Universitaria, 1971.

Arróm, Silvia M. *La mujer mexicana ante el divorcio eclesiástico (1800–1857)*. Mexico City: SepSetentas, 1976.

Baralt, Guillermo A. *Buena Vista: Life and Work on a Puerto Rican Hacienda, 1833–1904*. Chapel Hill: University of North Carolina Press, 1999.

——. *Esclavos rebeldes: conspiraciones y sublevaciones de esclavos en Puerto Rico (1795–1873)*. 3d ed. Río Piedras, P.R.: Ediciones Huracán, 1989.

Barnet, Miguel. *Biografía de un cimarrón*. Buenos Aires: Centro Editor de América Latina, 1977.

Bastian, Jean-Pierre. *Breve historia del protestantismo en América Latina*. Mexico City: Casa Unida de Publicaciones, 1986.

——, ed. *Protestantes, liberales y francmasones: sociedades de ideas y modernidad en América Latina, siglo xix.* Mexico City: Comisión para el Estudio Histórico de la Iglesia en Latinoamérica–Fondo de Cultura Económica, 1990.

Beal, Harry. "El olvidado precursor." *Heraldo Episcopal* (1971): 4–6

Bécker, Jerónimo. *Historia de las relaciones exteriores de España durante el siglo xix.* 3 vols. Madrid: Jaime Ratés-Voluntad, 1924–26.

Berbusse, Edward J. *The United States in Puerto Rico, 1898–1900.* Chapel Hill: University of North Carolina Press, 1966.

Bergad, Laird W. *Cuban Rural Society in the Nineteenth Century: The Social and Economic History of Monoculture in Matanzas.* Princeton, N.J.: Princeton University Press, 1990.

Blankingship, Alexander Hugo. "Un bosquejo de la historia de la iglesia." *Heraldo Episcopal* 4, no. 58 (February 1954): 6–25.

Booth, Karen Marshall. "The Domestic and Foreign Mission Papers: The Puerto Rican Papers, 1870–1952." *Historical Magazine of the Protestant Episcopal Church* 42, no. 3 (1973): 341–44.

Bothwell González, Reece B., ed. *Puerto Rico: cien años de lucha política.* 4 vols. Río Piedras, P.R.: Editorial Universitaria, 1979.

Callahan, William J. *Church, Politics, and Society in Spain, 1750–1874.* Cambridge, Mass.: Harvard University Press, 1984.

Cameron, Kenneth Walter. *American Episcopal Clergy: Registers of Ordinations in the Episcopal Church in the United States from 1785 through 1904.* Hartford, Conn.: Transcendental, 1970.

Carcel Orti, Vicente. *Iglesia y revolución en España (1868–1879).* Pamplona, Spain: Universidad de Navarra, 1979.

Carr, Raymond. *España, 1808–1975.* Barcelona, Spain: Ariel, 1985.

Casanovas, Joan. *Bread, or Bullets!: Urban Labor and Spanish Colonialism in Cuba, 1850–1898.* Pittsburgh: University of Pittsburgh Press, 1998.

Castellanos García, Gerardo G. *Misión a Cuba: Cayo Hueso y Martí.* Havana: Alpha, 1944.

———. *Motivos de Cayo Hueso.* Havana: Ucar, García, 1935.

Centro de Investigaciones Históricas de la Universidad de Puerto Rico [CIH]. *El proceso abolicionista en Puerto Rico: documentos para su estudio.* 2 vols. San Juan: CIH–Instituto de Cultura Puertorriqueña, 1974–78.

Cepeda, Rafael. *La herencia misionera en Cuba.* San José, Costa Rica: Editorial Dei, 1986.

———. "Joaquín de Palma y Pedro Duarte: precursores de la teología de la liberación." *Heraldo Episcopal* (July–September 1982):4–6

———. "Joaquín de Palma: predicador revolucionario." *Juprecu* 15, no. 1 (January 1977): 8–11.

Cepero Bonilla, Raúl. *Azúcar y abolición.* Barcelona, Spain: Editorial Crítica, 1976.

———. *Obras históricas.* Havana: Instituto de Historia, 1963.

Cifre de Loubriel, Estela. *Catálogo de extranjeros residentes en Puerto Rico en el siglo xix.* Río Piedras, P.R.: Editorial Universitaria, 1962.

Coll y Toste, Cayetano, ed. *Boletín Histórico de Puerto Rico.* 14 vols. San Juan: Tipografía Cantero Fernández, 1914–27.

Colmore, Charles L. "The Beginnings of the Church in Puerto Rico." *Historical Magazine of the Protestant Episcopal Church* 11, no. 4 (December 1942): 398–406

Corbitt, D. C. "Immigration in Cuba." *Hispanic American Historical Review* 22, no. 2 (May 1942): 280–308.

Corwin, Arthur F. *Spain and the Abolition of Slavery in Cuba, 1817–1886.* Austin: University of Texas Press, 1967.

Crahan, Margaret E. "Religious Penetration and Nationalism in Cuba: U.S. Methodist Activities, 1898–1958." *Revista/Review Interamericana* 8, no. 2 (Summer 1978): 204–24.

Cruz Monclova, Lidio. *Historia de Puerto Rico (siglo xix).* 3 vols. Río Piedras, P.R.: Editorial Universitaria, 1952–64.

Cuenca Toribio, José Manuel. *Estudios sobre la iglesia española del siglo xix.* Madrid: Rialp, 1973.

Cuesta Mendoza, Antonio. *Historia eclesiástica del Puerto Rico colonial (1508–1700).* Ciudad Trujillo [Santo Domingo], Dominican Republic, 1948.

Cushman, Joseph D., Jr. *A Goodly Heritage: The Episcopal Church in Florida, 1821–1892.* Gainesville: University of Florida Press, 1963.

Dávila Cox, Emma Aurora. *Este inmenso comercio: las relaciones mercantiles entre Puerto Rico y Gran Bretaña, 1844–1898.* San Juan: Editorial de la Universidad de Puerto Rico, 1996.

Deschamps Chapeaux, Pedro. *El negro en la economía habanera del siglo xix.* Havana: Unión de Escritores y Artistas Cubanos, 1971.

Díaz Reyes, Jorge David. "Estudio sobre el clero de Caguas, siglo xix." *Cuadernos de la Facultad de Humanidades* 1 (1978): 67–138.

Díaz Soler, Luis Manuel. *Historia de la esclavitud negra en Puerto Rico.* Río Piedras, P.R.: Editorial Universitaria, 1967.

Dreher, Martín Norberto. "Protestantismo de inmigración en Brasil: su implantación en el contexto del proyecto liberal y modernizador y las consecuencias del mismo." *Cristianismo y Sociedad* 27, no. 99 (1989): 59–74.

Drury, P. W. "The Protestant Church in Porto Rico." In *The Book of Porto Rico,* edited by E. Fernández García, 135–46. San Juan: El Libro Azul, 1923.

Fenton, Jerry. *Understanding the Religious Background of the Puerto Rican.* Cuernavaca, Mexico: Centro Intercultural de Documentación, 1969.

Figueroa y Miranda, Miguel. *Religión y política en la Cuba del siglo xix.* Miami: Ediciones Universal, 1975.

Fitchen, Edward D. "Primary Education in Colonial Cuba: Spanish Tool for Retaining 'la Isla Siempre Leal'?" *Caribbean Studies* 14, no. 1 (April 1974): 104–20.

Foner, Philip S. *A History of Cuba and Its Relations with the United States.* 2 vols. New York: International, 1963.

———. *The Spanish-Cuban-American War and the Birth of American Imperialism, 1895–1902.* 2 vols. New York: Monthly Review Press, 1972.

Garrard Burnett, Virginia. "Protestantism in Rural Guatemala, 1872–1954." *Latin American Research Review* 24, no. 2 (1989): 127–42.

González, Justo L. *The Development of Christianity in the Latin Caribbean.* Grand Rapids, Mich.: Eerdman, 1969.

González-Bohorquez, Valentín. *Origen, desarrollo e impacto social de las Iglesias Evangélicas en Puerto Rico.* [San Juan?]: Ediciones Alternativa, 1992.

González del Valle, Francisco. *El clero cubano y la independencia: las investigaciones de Francisco Gonzalez del Valle (1881–1942).* Edited by Manuel P. Maza Miquel. Santo Domingo: Publicaciones del Centro de Estudios Sociales Padre Juan Montalvo, S.J., 1993.

———. "El clero cubano en la Revolución Cubana." *Cuba Contemporánea* 18, no. 2 (October 2, 1918): 161–79.

———. *La Habana en 1841.* Havana: Oficina del Historiador de La Habana, 1952.

Gordon, Shirley C. *God Almighty Make Me Free: Christianity in Preemancipation Jamaica.* Bloomington: Indiana University Press, 1996.

Greer, Harold. "Baptists in Western Cuba: From the Wars of Independence to Revolution." *Cuban Studies* 19 (1989): 61–77.

Guerra y Sánchez, Ramiro. *Guerra de los Diez Años, 1868–1878.* 2 vols. Havana: Editorial de Ciencias Sociales, 1972.

Gutiérrez, Ángel L. *Evangélicos en Puerto Rico en la época española.* Guaynabo, P.R.: Editorial Chari, 1997.

Harvey, Paul. *Redeeming the South: Religious Cultures and Racial Identities among Southern Baptists, 1865–1925.* Chapel Hill: University of North Carolina Press, 1997.

Helg, Aline. *Our Rightful Share: The Afro-Cuban Struggle for Equality, 1886–1912.* Chapel Hill: University of North Carolina Press, 1995.

Hernández González, Manuel. *La emigración canaria a América.* Tenerife, Canary Islands: Taller de Historia, 1996.

Hernández Ruigómez, Almudena. *La desamortización en Puerto Rico.* Madrid: Ediciones Cultura Hispánica, 1987.

Hernández Suárez, Yoana. "Panorama de los primeros cementerios protestantes cubanos." *Boletín del Archivo Nacional [Cuba]* 12 (2000): 108–35.

Hoetink, H. *The Dominican People, 1850–1900.* Baltimore: Johns Hopkins University Press, 1982.

Howard, Philip A. *Changing History: Afro-Cuban Cabildos and Societies of Color in Nineteenth-Century Cuba.* Baton Rouge: Louisiana State University Press, 1998.

Hulse, Hiram H. "The History of the Church in Cuba." *Historical Magazine of the Protestant Episcopal Church* 6, no. 2 (June 1937): 249–70.

"Importante decreto por el que se extendió a Cuba la tolerancia religiosa." *Heraldo Episcopal* (1970): 12.

"Inventory of the Church Archives in New York City, the Protestant Episcopal Church, Diocese of New York." Compiled by the Work Project Administration, Historical Sources Survey. New York, 1940.

Karras, William J. "Yankee Carpenter in Cuba, 1848." *Americas* 30, nos. 6 and 7 (1978): 17–23.

Kinsbruner, Jay. *Not of Pure Blood: The Free People of Color and Racial Prejudice in Nineteenth-Century Puerto Rico.* Durham, N.C.: Duke University Press, 1996.

Knight, Franklin W. *Slave Society in Cuba during the Nineteenth Century.* Madison: University of Wisconsin Press, 1970.

Lavrin, Asunción, ed. *Sexuality and Marriage in Colonial Latin America.* Lincoln: University of Nebraska Press, 1989.

Lawrence, Una Roberts. *Cuba for Christ*. Richmond, Va.: Home Mission Board of the Southern Baptist Convention, 1926.

Lebroc, Reyneiro G. *Cuba: iglesia y sociedad (1830–1860)*. Madrid, 1976.

Leiseca, Juan Martín. *Apuntes para la historia eclesiástica de Cuba*. Havana: Carasa, 1938.

Lockmiller, David. "The Settlement of the Church Property Question in Cuba." *Hispanic American Historical Review* 17, no. 4 (November 1937): 488–98.

Lockward, Alfonso, ed. *Documentos para la historia de las relaciones dominico americanas*. Santo Domingo: Corripio, 1987.

Lockward, George A. *El protestantismo en Dominicana*. Santo Domingo: Universidad CETEC, 1982.

Marrero, Leví. *Cuba: economía y sociedad*. 15 vols. Madrid: Editorial Playor, 1971–92.

Martínez-Alier, Verena. *Marriage, Class, and Colour in Nineteenth-Century Cuba*. Ann Arbor: University of Michigan Press, 1989.

Martínez-Fernández, Luis. "Crypto-Protestants and Pseudo-Catholics in the Nineteenth-Century Hispanic Caribbean." *Journal of Ecclesiastical History* 51, no. 2 (April 2000): 347–65.

———. "'Don't die here': The Death and Burial of Protestants in the Hispanic Caribbean, 1840–1885." *Americas* 49, no. 1 (July 1992): 23–47.

———. *Fighting Slavery in the Caribbean: The Life and Times of a British Family in Nineteenth-Century Havana*. Armonk, N.Y.: Sharpe, 1998.

———. "Marriage, Protestantism, and Religious Conflict in Nineteenth-Century Puerto Rico." *Journal of Religious History* 24, no. 2 (October 2000): 263–78.

———. *Torn between Empires: Economy, Society, and Patterns of Political Thought in the Hispanic Caribbean, 1840–1878*. Athens: University of Georgia Press, 1994.

Matos Rodríguez, Félix V. *Women and Urban Change in San Juan, Puerto Rico, 1820–1868*. Gainesville: University Press of Florida, 1999.

Mayoral Barnes, Manuel. *Ponce y su historial geopolítico-económico y cultural*. Ponce, 1946.

Maza Miquel, Manuel P. *El alma del negocio y el negocio del alma: testimonios sobre la Iglesia y la sociedad en Cuba, 1878–1894*. Santiago, Dominican Republic: Pontificia Universidad Católica Madre y Maestra, 1990.

———. *Entre la ideología y la compasión: guerra y paz en Cuba, 1895–1903*. Santo Domingo, Dominican Republic: Instituto Pedro Francisco Bonó, 1997.

———. *Esclavos, patriotas y poetas a la sombra de la cruz: cinco ensayos sobre catolicismo e historia cubana*. Santo Domingo, Dominican Republic: Centro de Estudios Sociales Padre Juan Montalvo, S.J., 1999.

McNally, Michael J. *Catholicism in South Florida, 1868–1968*. Gainesville: University Press of Florida, 1982.

Medina Fernández, Antonio. "Historia de la localidad." *El Cerro* 6 (May 1987).

Mintz, Sidney W., and Eric R. Wolf. "An Analysis of Ritual Co-Parenthood (Compadrazgo)." *Southwestern Journal of Anthropology* 6, no. 4 (Winter 1950): 341–65.

Moore, Donald T. *Puerto Rico para Cristo: A History of the Progress of the Evangel-*

ical Missions on the Island of Puerto Rico. Cuernavaca, Mexico: Centro Intercultural de Documentación, 1969.

Morales Carrión, Arturo. *Puerto Rico and the Non-Hispanic Caribbean: A Study in the Decline of Spanish Exclusivism.* Río Piedras, P.R.: Editorial Universitaria, 1974.

Moreno Fraginals, Manuel. "Iglesia e ingenio." *Revista de la Biblioteca Nacional José Martí* 5, nos. 1–4 (January–December 1963): 11–28.

———. *El ingenio: el complejo económico social del azúcar.* 3 vols. Havana: Editorial de Ciencias Sociales, 1978.

Murray, David. *Odious Commerce: Britain, Spain, and the Abolition of the Cuban Slave Trade.* Cambridge, England: Cambridge University Press, 1980.

Neblett, Sterling Augustus. *Methodism's First Fifty Years in Cuba.* Wilmore, Ky.: Ausbury, 1976.

Newmann, Eduardo. *Verdadera y auténtica historia de la ciudad de Ponce desde sus primitivos tiempos hasta la época contemporánea.* San Juan, 1913.

Nolan, Terence H., William Carl Shiver, and L. Scott Nidy. *Cultural Resources of Key West.* Tallahassee, Fla.: Bureau of Historical Sites and Properties, 1979.

Offner, John L. *An Unwanted War: The Diplomacy of the United States and Spain over Cuba, 1895–1898.* Chapel Hill: University of North Carolina Press, 1992.

Oramas, Ángela. *Cementerios de La Habana.* Havana: Editorial José Martí, 1998.

Ortiz Fernández, Fernando. *Contrapunteo cubano del tabaco y el azúcar.* Havana: Jesús Montero, 1940.

———. *Hampa afro-cubana. Los negros brujos (apuntes para un estudio de etnología criminal).* Miami: Ediciones Universal, 1973.

Ortiz Medina, Félix Manuel. "Análisis de los registros de matrimonios de la Parroquia de Yabucoa." *Anales de Investigación Histórica* 1, nos. 1 and 2 (reprint edition): 73–92.

Pantojas García, Emilio. *La Iglesia Protestante y la americanización de Puerto Rico, 1898–1917.* San Juan: PRISA, n.d.

Paquette, Robert L. *Sugar Is Made with Blood: The Conspiracy of La Escalera and the Conflict between Empires over Slavery in Cuba.* Middletown, Conn.: Wesleyan University Press, 1988.

Pastor Ruiz, J. *Vieques antiguo y moderno, 1493–1946.* Yauco, P.R.: Tipografía Rodríguez Lugo, 1947.

Pennington, Edgar Legare. "The Episcopal Church in Florida, 1763–1892." *Historical Magazine of the Protestant Episcopal Church* 17, no. 1 (March 1938): 3–77.

Peralta Brito, Rafael, and José Chez Checo. *Religión, filosofía y política en Fernando A. de Meriño (1857–1906).* Santo Domingo, Dominican Republic: Amigo del Hogar, 1979.

Pérez, Louis A., Jr., ed. *Essays on Cuban History: Historiography and Research.* Gainesville: University Press of Florida, 1994.

———. *Lords of the Mountain: Social Banditry and Peasant Protest in Cuba, 1878–1918.* Pittsburgh: University of Pittsburgh Press, 1989.

———. *On Becoming Cuban: Identity, Nationality, and Culture.* Chapel Hill: University of North Carolina Press, 1999.

Pérez de la Riva, Juan. *El barracón: esclavitud y capitalismo en Cuba.* Barcelona, Spain: Editorial Crítica, 1978.

——, ed. *La Isla de Cuba en el siglo xix vista por los extranjeros.* Havana: Editorial de Ciencias Sociales, 1981.

Pérez Vega, Ivette. *El cielo y la tierra en sus manos: los grandes propietarios de Ponce, 1816–1830.* Río Piedras, P.R.: Ediciones Huracán, 1985.

——. "Las oleadas de inmigración sobre el sur de Puerto Rico: el caso de las sociedades mercantiles creadas en Ponce, 1816–1830." *Revista del Centro de Estudios Avanzados de Puerto Rico y el Caribe* 4 (January–June 1987): 114–23.

Picó, Fernando. *Al filo del poder: subalternos y dominantes en Puerto Rico, 1739–1910.* Río Piedras, P.R.: Editorial de la Universidad de Puerto Rico, 1993.

——. *Libertad y servidumbre en el Puerto Rico del siglo xix (los jornaleros utuadeños en vísperas del auge del café).* 2d ed. Río Piedras, P.R.: Ediciones Huracán, 1987.

Ponte Domínguez, Francisco J. *La masonería en la independencia de Cuba, 1809–1869.* Havana: Masonic World, 1944.

——. *Matanzas (biografía de una provincia).* Havana: Academia de la Historia de Cuba, 1957.

——. *Pensamiento laico de José Martí.* Havana: Modas Magazine, 1956.

Poyo, Gerald Eugene. *With All, and for the Good of All: The Emergence of Popular Nationalism in the Cuban Communities of the United States, 1848–1898.* Durham, N.C.: Duke University Press, 1989.

Pratt, Julius W. "The Ideology of American Expansion." In *Essays in Honor of William Dodd,* edited by Avery Craven, 335–52. Chicago: University of Chicago Press, 1935.

Prien, Hans-Jürgen. *Historia del Cristianismo en América Latina.* Salamanca, Spain: Editorial Sígueme, 1985.

——. "Protestantismo, liberalismo y francmasonería en América Latina durante el siglo xix: problemas de investigación." In *Protestantes, liberales y francmasones: sociedades de ideas y modernidad en América Latina, siglo xix,* edited by Jean-Pierre Bastian, 15–23. Mexico City: Comisión para el Estudio Histórico de la Iglesia en Latinoamérica–Fondo de Cultura Económica, 1990.

Quintero Rivera, A. G. *Conflictos de clase y política en Puerto Rico.* Río Piedras, P.R.: Ediciones Huracán, 1976.

——. *Patricios y plebeyos: burgueses, hacendados, artesanos y obreros.* Río Piedras, P.R.: Ediciones Huracán, 1988.

Ramos, Marcos Antonio. *Panorama de protestantismo en Cuba.* San José, Costa Rica: Editorial Caribe, 1986.

Ramos Mattei, Andrés A. *La hacienda azucarera: su crecimiento y crisis en Puerto Rico (siglo xix).* San Juan: Centro de Estudios de la Realidad Puertorriqueña, 1981.

——. "La importación de trabajadores contratados para la industria azucarera puertorriqueña: 1860–1880." In *Inmigración y clases sociales en el Puerto Rico del siglo xix,* edited by Francisco A. Scarano, 125–42. Río Piedras, P.R.: Ediciones Huracán, 1981.

Rivera Martínez, Antonio. *Así empezó Vieques.* Río Piedras, P.R.: Centro de Investigaciones Históricas de la Universidad de Puerto Rico, 1963.

Rivera Torres, Juan Jorge. *Documentos históricos de la Iglesia Episcopal Puertorriqueña*. Santo Domingo, Dominican Republic: Editora Lozano, 1983.

Rodríguez, Daniel R. *La primera evangelización norteamericana en Puerto Rico, 1898–1930*. Mexico City: Ediciones Borinquen, 1986.

Rodríguez León, Mario A. *Bayamón: notas para su historia*. 2 vols. San Juan: Comité Historia de los Pueblos, 1985.

———. *Los registros parroquiales y la microhistoria demográfica en Puerto Rico*. San Juan: Centro de Estudios Avanzados de Puerto Rico y el Caribe, 1990.

Roig de Leuchsenring, Emilio. *La Habana: apuntes históricos*. Havana: Municipio de La Habana, 1939.

———. *Martí y las religiones*. Havana: Acción, 1941.

———. *Médicos y medicina en Cuba: historia, biografía, costumbrismo*. Havana: Academia de Ciencias de Cuba, 1965.

Roldán de Montaud, Inés. "Origen, evolución y supresión del grupo de negros 'emancipados' en Cuba (1817–1870)." *Revista de Indias* 42 (July–December 1982): 559–641.

Ronning, Neale. *José Martí and the Emigré Colony in Key West*. New York: Praeger, 1990.

Scarano, Francisco A., ed. *Inmigración y clases sociales en el Puerto Rico del siglo xix*. Río Piedras, P.R.: Ediciones Huracán, 1981.

———. *Sugar and Slavery in Puerto Rico: The Plantation Economy of Ponce, 1800–1850*. Madison: University of Wisconsin Press, 1984.

Schmidt-Nowara, Christopher. *Empire and Antislavery: Spain, Cuba, and Puerto Rico, 1839–1874*. Pittsburgh: University of Pittsburgh Press, 1999.

Schroeder, Susan. *Cuba: A Handbook of Historical Statistics*. Boston: Hall, 1982.

Sierra Martínez, José A. *Camuy: notas para su historia*. San Juan: Comité Historia de los Pueblos, 1984.

Silva Gotay, Samuel. "La Iglesia Católica en el proceso político de americanización en Puerto Rico, 1898–1930." *Revista de Historia* 1, no. 1 (January–June 1985): 102–20.

———. *Protestantismo y política en Puerto Rico, 1898–1930*. Río Piedras, P.R.: Editorial Universitaria, 1997.

Smith, Leonard H., Jr., ed. *The Records of the Key West Cemetery, Key West, Florida, 1888–1905*. Clearwater, Fla.: Owl, 1984.

Socarrás Matos, Martín. *La Necrópolis Cristóbal Colón (investigaciones preliminares)*. Havana: Editorial Arte y Literatura, 1975.

Steward, Julian H., ed. *The People of Puerto Rico: A Study in Social Anthropology*. Urbana: University of Illinois Press, 1956.

"Sucesos notables de la Iglesia Episcopal en Cuba." *Heraldo Episcopal* (1971): 8–11.

Tapia y Rivera, Alejandro, ed. *Biblioteca histórica de Puerto Rico*. 2d ed. San Juan: Instituto de Cultura Puertorriqueña, 1945.

Testé, Ismael. *Historia eclesiástica de Cuba*. 5 vols. Burgos, Spain: Tipografía de la Editorial de El Monte, 1969.

Todd, Roberto H. "La Iglesia Episcopal de Ponce." *Puerto Rico Ilustrado* (June 7, 1941): 20, 98.

Tomás y Valiente, Francisco. *El marco político de la desamortización en España.* Barcelona, Spain: Ariel, 1971.

Torres-Cuevas, Eduardo. *Polémica de la esclavitud. José Antonio Saco.* Havana: Editorial de Ciencias Sociales, 1984.

Trejo, Evelia. "La introducción del protestantismo en México: aspectos diplomáticos." *Estudios de Historia Moderna y Contemporánea de México* 11 (1988): 149–81.

Turner, Mary. "Religious Beliefs." In *General History of the Caribbean,* edited by Franklin W. Knight, 3:287–321. London: UNESCO Publishing/Macmillan, 1997.

———. *Slaves and Missionaries: The Disintegration of Jamaican Slave Society, 1787–1834.* Urbana: University of Illinois Press, 1982.

Vidal Armstrong, Mariano. *Ponce: notas para su historia.* San Juan: Comité Historia de los Pueblos, 1983.

Vidler, Alec R. *The Church in an Age of Revolution.* 3d ed. New York: Penguin, 1981.

Vilar, Juan Bautista. *Un siglo de protestantismo en España (Águilas-Murcia, 1893–1979): aportación al estudio del acatolicismo español contemporáneo.* Murcia, Spain: Departamento de Historia de la Universidad de Murcia, 1979.

Wagenheim, Kal, and Olga Jiménez de Wagenheim. *The Puerto Ricans: A Documentary History.* Maplewood, N.J.: Waterfront, 1988.

Wells, Sharon. *Forgotten Legacy: Blacks in Nineteenth-Century Key West.* Key West, Fla.: Historic Key West Preservation Board, 1982.

Yaremko, Jason M. *U.S. Protestant Missions in Cuba: From Independence to Castro.* Gainesville: University Press of Florida, 2000.

Unpublished Materials

Alard, Leopoldo J. "Proceso histórico de la Iglesia Episcopal en Cuba." Seminario Episcopal del Caribe, Carolina, P.R., 1966, copy.

Bryant, Glenn E. "A History of Baptist Mission Work in Cuba." Th.D. diss., Central Baptist Theological Seminary, 1954.

Burset, Víctor. "The First Fifty Years of Protestant Episcopal Church in Puerto Rico." Master's thesis, General Theological Seminary, New York, 1957.

Cabrera Leiva, Guillermo. "El protestantismo norteamericano en las Antillas españolas." Master's thesis, University of Miami, 1951.

Chinea Serrano, Jorge Luis. "Racial Politics and Commercial Agriculture: West Indian Immigration in Nineteenth-Century Puerto Rico, 1800–1850." Ph.D. diss., University of Minnesota, 1994.

Delgado, Primitivo. "The History of Southern Missions in Cuba to 1945." Th.D. diss., Southern Baptist Theological Seminary, 1947.

Findlay, Eileen J. "Domination, Decency, and Desire: The Politics of Sexuality in Ponce, Puerto Rico, 1870–1920." Ph.D. diss., University of Wisconsin, 1995.

Gannon, Peter Steven. "The Ideology of Americanization in Puerto Rico in 1898–1900: Conquest and Disestablishment." Ph.D. diss., New York University, 1978.

García Leduc, José M. "La iglesia y el clero católico de Puerto Rico (1800–1873): su proyección social, económica y política." Ph.D. diss., Catholic University of America, 1990.

Greer, Jr., Harold Edward. "History of Southern Baptist Mission Work in Cuba." Ph.D. diss., University of Alabama, 1965.

López Crespo, Ramón E. "El desarrollo histórico del cementerio de las calles Simón de la Torre y Frontispicio Ponce, Puerto Rico, 1843–1918." Master's thesis, Centro de Estudios Avanzados de Puerto Rico y el Caribe, San Juan, 1987.

Ortiz Díaz, Ángel Luis. "La manifestación anticlerical en Puerto Rico entre 1870–1900." Ph.D. diss., University of Puerto Rico, 1994.

Paz y Cerezo, Juan Ramón de la. "Síntesis cronológica de la historia de la iglesia episcopal en Cuba." Copy in ACEST.

Poyo, Gerald Eugene. "Cuban Emigré Communities in the United States and the Independence of their Homeland, 1852–1895." Ph.D. diss., University of Florida, 1983.

Rabin Siegal, Robert. "Los tortoleños: obreros de Barlovento en Vieques 1864–1874." Monograph. Copy in AHV.

Rivera Martínez, Antonio. "La primera iglesia evangélica en Puerto Rico." Mimeographed. Copy in CIH.

Rodríguez-Bravo, Enrique. "Origen y desarrollo del movimiento protestante en Puerto Rico, 1898–1940." Ph.D. diss., George Washington University, 1972.

Scarano, Francisco A. "Sugar and Slavery in Puerto Rico: The Municipality of Ponce, 1815–1849." Ph.D. diss., Columbia University, 1978.

Tamayo, Carlos A. "Historia de la Iglesia Episcopal de Cuba desde 1871 hasta 1898." Seminary of the Southwest, Austin, Tex., 1994, copy.

INDEX

Page numbers in italics indicate illustrations.

About the Author

Luis Martínez-Fernández has a Ph.D. in history from Duke University and is currently an associate professor of history and chair of the Department of Puerto Rican and Hispanic Caribbean Studies at Rutgers University. His previous books include *Torn between Empires: Economy, Society, and Patterns of Political Thought in the Hispanic Caribbean, 1840–1878* (1994) and *Fighting Slavery in the Caribbean: The Life and Times of a British Family in Nineteenth-Century Havana* (1998). He received a Pew Evangelical Scholars Program Fellowship, which helped support the research and writing of this book, and in 2000 was awarded the Lydia Cabrera Prize by the Conference on Latin American History. With his family he attends the Princeton Alliance Church in Plainsboro, New Jersey.